War and Peace

War and Peace

Essays on Religion and Violence

Edited by
Bryan S. Turner

Anthem Press
An imprint of Wimbledon Publishing Company
www.anthempress.com

This edition first published in UK and USA 2014
by ANTHEM PRESS
75–76 Blackfriars Road, London SE1 8HA, UK
or PO Box 9779, London SW19 7ZG, UK
and
244 Madison Ave. #116, New York, NY 10016, USA

First published in hardback by Anthem Press in 2013

© 2014 Bryan S. Turner editorial matter and selection;
individual chapters © individual contributors

The moral right of the authors has been asserted.

All rights reserved. Without limiting the rights under copyright reserved above,
no part of this publication may be reproduced, stored or introduced into
a retrieval system, or transmitted, in any form or by any means
(electronic, mechanical, photocopying, recording or otherwise),
without the prior written permission of both the copyright
owner and the above publisher of this book.

British Library Cataloguing-in-Publication Data
A catalogue record for this book is available from the British Library.

Library of Congress Cataloging-in-Publication Data
A catalog record for this book has been requested.

ISBN-13: 978 1 78308 330 5 (Pbk)
ISBN-10: 1 78308 330 1 (Pbk)

This title is also available as an ebook.

CONTENTS

Acknowledgments   vii

Contributors   ix

Introduction by Bryan S. Turner   1

War

Chapter 1	Sacred Memory and the Secular World: The Poland Narratives *Alisse Waterston*	19
Chapter 2	A Messianic Multiple: West Papua, July 1998 *Eben Kirksey*	37
Chapter 3	Lincoln, the Ministers of Religion and the American Jeremiad *Jonathan Keller*	63
Chapter 4	Spiritual Violence: Max Weber and Norbert Elias on Religion and Civilization *Bryan S. Turner*	79

Peace

Chapter 5	Quakers, the Origins of the Peace Testimony and Resistance to War Taxes *Ana M. Acosta*	101
Chapter 6	A Sacred Ground for Peace: Violence, Tourism and Sanctification in Hiroshima 1960–1970 *Ran Zwigenberg*	121
Chapter 7	The Sectarian as a Category of Secular Power: Sectarian Tensions and Judicial Authority in Lebanon *Raja Abillama*	145

Chapter 8	The Commodification of Love: Gandhi, King and 1960s Counterculture *Alexander Bacha and Manu Bhagavan*	163
Chapter 9	The Religion of Brotherly Love: Leo Tolstoy and Max Weber *Bryan S. Turner*	185
Chapter 10	Conclusion: War and Peace *Bryan S. Turner*	205

ACKNOWLEDGMENTS

These chapters were originally presented to the weekly seminar of the Religion Committee at the Graduate Center of the City University of New York in 2010 and 2011. The Religion Committee is supported by a Mellon Foundation grant through which the seminar is funded. I am grateful to the Provost Professor Chase Robinson for his continuing support for the development of research on religion at the Graduate Center.

Elena Knox, research assistant in the Centre for Religion and Society at the University of Western Sydney, Australia, proofread the entire manuscript.

Chapter 4 was originally published as Bryan S. Turner, "Weber and Elias on Religion and Violence: Warrior Charisma and the Civilizing Process" in Steven Loyal and Stephen Quilley (eds), *The Sociology of Norbert Elias* (Cambridge: Cambridge University Press, 2004), 245–64. I am grateful to Cambridge University Press for permission to reprint this chapter.

CONTRIBUTORS

Raja Abillama is a doctoral candidate at the City University of New York's Graduate Center. He is currently finishing his dissertation on personal status laws, religion and secularism in Lebanon.

Ana M. Acosta teaches in the Department of English at Brooklyn College, City University of New York. She has published articles on religion, science and the Enlightenment. Her book, *Reading Genesis in the Long Eighteenth Century: From Milton to Mary Shelley*, was published by Ashgate in 2006. In 2010 she co-authored *Literature: A World of Writing*, a writing handbook and genre anthology published by Pearson/Longman. Currently, she is at work on a book-length project entitled *Stages of Enlightenment*, which examines the intersection of the religious epistemologies of Roman Catholicism and the different Protestant sects in Britain in the long eighteenth century.

Alex Bacha is a graduate student in American history at Hunter College. He graduated from New York University in 2006. His interests include cultural and environmental history, as well as culinary history and the history of tourism.

Manu Bhagavan is an associate professor in the Department of History at Hunter College and the Graduate Center at the City University of New York. He has previously taught at Carleton College, the University of Texas at Austin and Yale University, and is a recipient of a 2006 Fellowship from the American Council of Learned Societies. He is the author of *Sovereign Spheres: Princes, Education and Empire in Colonial India* (Oxford University Press, 2003), and *The Peacemakers: India's Gamble for One World* (HarperCollins India, 2012).

Jonathan Keller is a doctoral candidate in political science at the Graduate Center, City University of New York, specializing in political theory, American political thought, and religion and American politics. He received his MA in political science from the University of Massachusetts at Amherst. Before returning to academia, Keller conducted research on right-wing political movements for non-profit organizations in New York City, and was a speechwriter for former New York State governor Mario M. Cuomo. Currently, he teaches in the Political Science Department at Hunter College, and is writing his dissertation on Old Testament narratives in American political thought.

Eben Kirksey was a cultural anthropologist in the Graduate Center City University of New York who studies the political dimensions of imagination as well as the interplay of natural and cultural history. He is now a lecturer at the University of New South Wales, Sydney, Australia. His first book, *Freedom in Entangled Worlds* (Duke University Press, 2012) is about an indigenous political movement in West Papua, the half of New Guinea under Indonesian control. As a guest co-editor of *Cultural Anthropology*, Kirksey assembled a collection of original research articles from the emerging field of multispecies ethnography.

Bryan S. Turner is presidential professor of sociology and director of the Committee on Religion in the Graduate Center, City University of New York, and the director of the Centre for Religion and Society at the University of Western Sydney. His most recent publication is *Religion and Modern Society* (Cambridge University Press, 2011). He is the series editor of *Key Issues in Modern Sociology* and *Tracts for Our Times* for Anthem Press. With Simon Susen he edited *The Legacy of Pierre Bourdieu: Critical Essays* (Anthem Press, 2011) and with Jack Barbalet and Adam Possamai he edited *Religion and the State: A Comparative Sociology* (Anthem Press, 2011).

Alisse Waterston is professor of anthropology at John Jay College of Criminal Justice, City University of New York, and editor of *Open Anthropology*. Her work focuses on the human consequences of systemic violence and inequality, including the socio-cultural, political-economic and psychological aspects of displacement, diaspora, structural violence and war. Her forthcoming book is titled *My Father's Wars: Myth, Memory and the Violence of a Century, an intimate ethnography*. Recent publications include *Anthropology off the Shelf: Anthropologists on Writing* (co-edited with Maria D. Vesperi); *An Anthropology of War: Views from War Zones*; "Teaching Genocide in an Age of Genocides" (*American Anthropologist*); and "The Story of My Story: An Anthropology of Violence, Dispossession and Diaspora" (*Anthropological Quarterly*). Waterston has also written extensively on urban poverty, homelessness and substance abuse in the US, including the acclaimed ethnographies *Love, Sorrow and Rage: Destitute Women in a Manhattan Residence* and *Street Addicts in the Political Economy*. Professor Waterston serves on the Executive Board of the American Anthropological Association, and chairs the Board's committee on scholarly publications.

Ran Zwigenberg is a native of Israel. He graduated in history from Hunter College, after which he went to work for the United Nations. He recently completed his PhD in history at the Graduate Center of the City University of New York. His research focuses on modern Japanese and European history, with a specialization in memory and intellectual history. His dissertation deals comparatively with the commemoration of and the reaction to the Holocaust in Israel and Europe, and the Atomic bombing of Hiroshima in Japan. He recently finished a year as a research fellow of the Japan Foundation and Hiroshima City University, working on the commemoration and experiences of survivors of the A-bomb, after which he worked as a Social Science Research Council's IDRF Fellow on the Israel and European portions of his research. Zwigenberg has won the prestigious ACLS dissertation completion award, and presented his work in Europe, the US and Japan.

INTRODUCTION

Bryan S. Turner

Introduction: The Westphalian System

Although religion and politics may appear to belong to different orders of social reality, they are in fact intimately connected. For example, the church and the state make significant, often contradictory, claims upon believers and citizens, and often they are exclusive. Citizens may not be permitted to have dual citizenship in two separate states and few citizens have the luxury of possessing several passports. Religions often claim to possess a universal Truth that rules out adherence to other faiths. Apostasy may be regarded as a serious crime and conversion to another faith may, in some societies, be illegal. While the tension between religion and politics has a long history, with contemporary globalization conflicts between religions and between religion and politics are set to become more, rather than less, problematic. To take one recent well-known example, in 2012, a network of anti-Muslim conservatives in California produced an amateurish film on YouTube which presented offensive images of the Prophet. When this product was eventually translated into Arabic in the days leading up to September 11, it caused a global conflict spreading across the Muslim world. This event, though tragic, is now a common problem of international relations. Religious identities and beliefs are now deeply embedded in political culture and the basis of secularism, such as the division of church and state, can no longer be secured. The result is that states are, albeit reluctantly, involved in the management of religion in the interests of public stability (Barbalet, Possamai and Turner 2011).

Conflicts involving religions typically hinge on the relationship between space, sovereignty and identity, and all three are involved in the construction of modern citizenship. Legality and sovereignty are tied to possession of the land in which the state claims authority over the actual bodies of its citizens. Those bodies that find themselves stranded in "no-man's land" are bodies without rights, and can be easily disposed of because they are without legal protection (Agamben 1998). Full citizenship belongs to those individuals who have a legitimate claim on membership of a polity, which gives them a secure right of residence and entitlement to resources. Perhaps the main oddity of the universalistic nature of secular citizenship is that, generally speaking, we become citizens by the accident of birth (Shachar and Hirschl 2007). As a result, citizenship identity is tied to a particular political space by possession of key documents, such as a birth certificate, a social security card, or a passport, which create the juridical framework of society as an imagined community that is held together by a shared language, religion and culture (Anderson 1990). In the modern world, these imagined communities are legal fictions, because, as a result of migration and multiculturalism, civil society is in reality divided by diverse religious and cultural traditions. Some societies, as a consequence of the growth of legal pluralism, may have different and occasionally competing legal systems. The conflict between the Shari'a and Western legal traditions such as Anglo-Saxon common law in Africa, for example in Nigeria, would be one further instance of social complexity. Because there is rarely any neat relationship in such complex multicultural societies between space, sovereignty and identity, religious differences often give rise to frictions that can evolve into more open and violent conflicts.

Unsurprisingly the social sciences and humanities have been significantly influenced by the idea of the "spatial turn." To some extent, this development – a critical awareness of the spatial dimensions of all social relations – has been brought about by the transformation of the discipline of geography, where the Marxist theory of space, as conceived by David Harvey (2006), has been especially influential. This reconceptualization of space cannot be divorced from the processes of globalization in reshaping the territory of the state and refashioning the global city as a nexus of power. Global spatial reconfigurations have brought into question the sovereignty of the state (whose porous boundaries are now recognized) and have reshaped our understanding of society as no longer conceived simply as a nation-state. Sociologists such as John Urry (2000) have drawn attention to the idea that "society" is now an assembly of flows and networks. The impact of these spatial transformations on both citizenship and religion is profound, since neither secular citizenship nor religious communities sit comfortably within the bounded territory of the nation-state, and these political developments have given rise to new ways of describing political membership such as flexible citizenship, quasi-citizenship and semi-citizenship. This new vocabulary attempts to describe the complex and uneven bundles of rights that can accrue to migrants, both legal and illegal. With the need for greater security and control of borders, documentation has become increasingly important in verifying identity and, given the absence of adequate documentation in many developing societies, citizenship comes to hinge literally on paper, giving rise to the important notion of "paper citizenship" (Sadiq 2009). Correspondingly, we have a new vocabulary of religion, with terms such as "post-secular religion" and "hybrid religions" to describe the globalization of spirituality and the emergence of post-institutional, post-orthodox religions. Modern societies are characterized by shifting political and religious boundaries, where diversity is an obvious, but not inevitable, source of social conflict (Turner 2008). Of course, many American sociologists will argue that the cultural melting pot in the United States has been successful and that many of the divisions that once separated Protestant, Catholic and Jew have melted with both social and geographical mobility (Putnam and Campbell 2010). However, these optimistic assessments appear to underestimate the social tensions that cluster around conservative Christian opposition to Islam on the one hand and to liberal values (such as the lobby for same-sex marriage) on the other. These divisions became more obvious in the political competition in 2011–12 between the right wing of Republicanism and the Democratic Party, which was clearly illustrated by the rise of the Tea Party.

From the ancient time of the Greek *polis*, diversity (in gender, ethnicity or religion) was seen to be the origin of social conflict and the condition that produced the necessity for politics (Saxonhouse 1992). In the modern period, the German sociologist Max Weber came to define the state as a political institution claiming a monopoly of violence within a given territory. Modern sovereignty required a uniform system of law, a unified system of taxation, a national military force and the presumption of cultural (including religious) uniformity. Following after Weber, the legal theorist Carl Schmitt (1996), working within the crisis that came to face the Weimar Republic, argued that politics was the struggle between friend and foe, and that sovereignty was the power to declare a state of emergency. Contemporary writing on the state and citizenship has, by contrast, emphasized the importance of globalization in eroding this autonomy of the nation-state, claiming in particular that state borders are often more porous than they used to be. Thus, by the late twentieth century, globalization, especially the globalization of the labor market and the demand for migrant labor, has rendered Weber's and Schmitt's assumptions about the state increasingly problematic. A variety of changes – the rise of legal pluralism, labor migration, the emergence of mega-cities, the spread of diasporic communities and the resulting complexity of modern identities – have brought the sovereignty of the state into question, and one source of social conflict is that there is no simple equation between civil and religious identity in the public domain. National citizenship is now seen by many political observers to be too rigid, narrow and exclusive to cope with the growing number of migrants and refugees in the modern world. In Europe, the growth of the European Union has also required drastic changes to citizenship rights in a context of what sociologists call post-national membership (Soysal 1994). More generally, there is the recognition that multicultural societies such as Canada and Australia will require multicultural citizenship, including notions of "group rights" to cope with their growing diversity and avoid social conflict (Kymlicka 1995).

The rise of the nation-state and the progress of citizenship rights extended over some three centuries from 1600 onwards. These political developments can also be said to chart the growth of Western secularization. The Reformation settlement gave rise to an individualistic culture and a religious framework in which the authority of priests and the centrality of the rituals of the church were weakened. The Bible became the principal basis of religious authority and it was assumed that laypeople should have access to biblical truth through the vernacular languages of Europe. In England, the King James Bible and the *Book of Common Prayer* became the national vehicle of religious belief and identity. By the end of the seventeenth century, the religious conflicts of the Civil War had been settled by the Glorious Revolution, by the union of Scotland and England, and by new ideas about tolerance, as illustrated by John Locke's *Letter Concerning Toleration*. The assumption of liberal secularism was that religion is a matter of private conscience and should not impinge on the public domain. Of course, Locke was mainly concerned to bring an end to intolerance between Catholics and Protestants, and between the Puritan sects. His ideas were not challenged by a multi-faith environment that is now characteristic of modern Britain, where it is now necessary to find a basis for the social inclusion of the full range of world religions alongside a plethora of sects and "cults." The liberal framework of tolerance has now been challenged by the rise of public religions and religious nationalism – such as Liberation Theology in Latin America, the Iranian Revolution, the Moral Majority in the United States and Solidarity in Poland – which no longer fall comfortably under the umbrella of the liberal version of tolerance (Casanova 1994). With the growth of modern fundamentalism, urban piety movements and revivalism, many forms of religion intrude on politics and public debate. Whereas sociologists of religion in the 1960s predicted the inevitable growth of secularization, the contemporary world appears to be alive with both religious growth and religious controversy.

Despite social and political changes, the organization of religion and politics in the West remains a legacy of the Treaty of Westphalia (1648), which was designed to end the religious wars that had their origins in the previous century. The Westphalian system laid down the juridical foundations of citizenship within the sovereignty of the nation-state, established a new pattern of international diplomacy and set the scene for the great land rush of 1600–1900, leaving behind a legacy of unsolved aboriginal rights. National citizenship assumed an homogenous identity for members of the state (especially in terms of religion), and religion was to be established by the prince. What we call the modern system of international relations was an outcome of Westphalia. However, the diplomatic arrangements of 1648 were an attempt to resolve problems left over by the Peace of Ausburg in 1555, which was a settlement between the Holy Roman Emperor Charles V and an alliance of Lutheran princes. Augsburg sought to establish a peace by recognizing the legal division of the German-speaking states of the Holy Roman Empire between Roman Catholicism and Lutheranism. It created an early form of secularism in the principle of *Cuius regio, eius religio* (Whose realm, his religion) by which the prince of a particular state would select which religion (Catholicism or Lutheranism) would be officially recognized in the public domain. The other key provision for religious harmony was the principle of *reservatum ecclesiasticum* by which, in the event of a Catholic prince converting to Lutheranism, *Cuius regio, eius religio* would not apply. This measure involved a provision to prevent any further erosion of Catholic influence in Europe.

The result of the treaty was that the nation-states of Europe became confessional states and hence, while Westphalia is often seen to involve the separation of church and state as a step towards institutional secularization, it in fact involved the reverse. It ensured that there was a necessary legal linkage between religion and politics. The outcome of the Reformation was to ensure the centrality of the state to the exercise of religion. One example is England, which is often regarded as the epitome of a liberal tolerance in which an individual's beliefs are protected from the intervention of the state. Elizabeth I famously said that she sought no windows into men's souls. Nevertheless, the monarch was the head of the state and the established church in an arrangement that is best described as caesarism rather than secularism. The creation of the United Kingdom required the suppression of ethno-religious differences at the periphery (Hechter 1975), the supremacy of Protestantism and the development of a state apparatus that could exert control over the archipelago of the British Isles.

The treaties of Augsburg and Westphalia were primarily peace treaties that attempted some settlement of the violence that had troubled the German states. The Reformation had set the stage for complicated and divisive diplomatic relations stretching across Europe. These treaty documents sought to create a range of social arrangements to overcome or at least mitigate the cycle of human violence that had troubled Europe for decades. They involved a conceptualization of peace which, according to article I of the Treaty of Westphalia, "must be so honest and seriously guarded and nourished that each part furthers the advantage, honour and benefit of the other." Article I went on to urge princes to forget the conflicts of the past and work towards a "faithful neighbourliness." The Treaty of Westphalia is often regarded as a political document, but it was equally important in seeking to restore the economies of the region that had been destroyed by decades of warfare. Much of the inspiration for economic reform came from the efforts of Cardinal Jules de Mazarin, who wanted to undo the cycle of religious conflict by improving the economic basis of the German states. In 1642, he had been involved in peace plans that were directed towards establishing fair trade in which the Rhine River would become the basis of economic development, but this commercial growth required an end to the system of tariffs that had hindered trade between northern and southern Germany. Religious peace required neighborliness, but also a sound economic basis if the cities along the Rhine-Main-Danube complex were to recover from war and flourish in peace time.

Religion and the City

The city has played a central role in the "religious imaginary" of the Abrahamic religions. Whereas the countryside was the abode of pagans, Judaism, Christianity and Islam saw their cities as places of divine inspiration: Jerusalem, Rome and Mecca. Indeed much of the language of religion and politics comes from St Augustine's account of the Holy City. Following the barbarian attack by Alaric on Rome in 410, Augustine set about writing a defense of Christianity which had been criticized as the cause of Rome's decay. He sought to show that the *civitas dei* was characterized by the love of God, whereas the secular city rested ultimately on force. Augustinian theology established a basic idea in Western Christianity that life on Earth is merely a journey towards an eternal city based on love. Nevertheless, while they reside in this world, Christians must obey the secular laws of the land. They must, in fact, be better citizens than their secular peers. Augustine (1998) wanted to establish the fact that Christians were not the cause of Roman decline, but were, on the contrary, citizens of outstanding virtue.

With globalization and the rise of the mega-city, urban life has become precarious and cities are often sites of terrorism. In the West, the mass transit systems of cities like New York, London, Madrid and Tokyo are especially vulnerable to attack. Cities have also become sites of religious conflict. Jerusalem, which plays a major role in the theology of all three Abrahamic religions, has been the focus of bitter conflict not only between but within major religious traditions. Because pilgrimage is an important religious rite, access to the sacred city gives rise to historic tensions over divine space.

Europe has had a long history of genocidal violence especially against Jews, who were predominantly an urban, rather than rural, community. Although St Paul proclaimed the start of a new dawn in which there was neither Jew nor Christian, tensions between these religions became a basic pattern of Western history. In Augustine's theology of salvation, the Jews at the Day of Judgment could enter into paradise, but in this world Jews were outside the human community. In medieval Spain, Jews often held high office at the court, but they were also periodically forced to convert to Christianity or suffer exile (Kruger 2011). The Holocaust has become not just a symbol of violence towards European Jews but a symbol of basic inhumanity. This European genocide was tragically illustrated by the killing of Jews in the village of Jedwabne in Poland (see Chapter 1 by Alisse Waterston on the violence of Christians towards their Jewish neighbors).

In the West, there is a nexus that spreads out from the city to include civility, civil society and citizenship. Once again, it was Max Weber (1978) who identified the city as the cradle of rights. He contrasted the military city of Eastern empires with the cities of northern Italy. These cities developed various internal organizations, such as the militia, that were important in the emergence of civil society, and they often enjoyed an autonomy, such as immunity from taxation by the local prince. Within their walls, there emerged what Weber called "the city-commune," comprising a network of associations and organizations that began to create a civil society. Such a social environment was conducive to the emergence of a merchant class who enjoyed expanding trade relations within their hinterland and other towns and cities. In the "patrician city," the burgher assembly or *parlementum* came to constitute the principal sovereign organ of the commune. Weber laid the claim that out of this burgher culture began to emerge the ethos of modern citizenship in which there was local representation and the culture of public debate. Modern citizenship appeared to Weber to be tied to the history of the city. Although this characterization of the Occidental city has often been criticized as an example of Orientalism, on the grounds that cities in the Islamic world often had urban associations that clustered around the mosque and the public baths, these criticisms often miss an important aspect of Weber's argument. In *Economy and Society*, he claimed that Christianity had contributed to the breakdown of family and kinship as the principal form of urban solidarity. Because of the early Christian view that membership of the church was based on a common faith and not on kinship, Christianity offered a revolutionary picture of social bonds. In the Christian commune, there was, according to the theology of St Paul, neither Christian nor Jew, neither slave nor free man, and neither man nor woman. Membership of the primitive church required a spiritual circumcision of the heart. This observation connects Weber's account with Augustine's view that the Christian community was spiritual.

Following Weber's sociology of the city and citizenship, political philosophers and political sociologists have often seen the survival of ethnic, tribal or kinship connections as blocking the evolution of civil society, which requires universalistic arrangements for political parties, religions and secular associations to flourish. Critics of the Weberian legacy argue that universalistic notions of citizenship obscure the actual diversity of societies and that, in particular, they have neglected the important connections between citizenship and gender. In many Middle Eastern societies, the continuity of tribe and kinship networks often means that religious identities and kinship identities cannot be distinguished from one another. What is equally clear is that religion has played a major role in defining citizenship in the Middle East, and in defining its gendered nature (Joseph 2000). Religion supports and is a necessary component of the patriarchal systems that underpin the power of men within the family, tribe and state. More importantly, citizenship as a legal entity has, in the Middle East, often been constituted through membership of a religious community and hence the distribution of rights and resources is organized on the basis of membership of religious sects. What follows is that the nation is imagined as an assembly of subcommunities that are in turn defined by religion. Political conflicts between and within the nation-state assume the form of religious conflicts, and establishing peaceful relations between different religious communities is a difficult, protracted and unpromising process (Sennott 2001).

One further consequence is that civil society is not understood as an arena of secular negotiation and compromise, but rather as a sphere in which absolute religious claims to truth cannot be subject to debate and compromise. Sami Zubaida (1988) argues that where Islam is the dominant religion, the only contractual relations are with God and hence the conventional political processes of debate, contest and opposition are regarded as inadmissible. Similar arguments could be made with respect to ultra-Orthodox groups in Israel who reject the claims of secular Zionism, define citizenship in terms of Jewish identity, reject secular marriages and refuse to serve as combat troops within the army (Ben-Porat and Turner 2011). In practice, we have seen in recent years a flourishing opposition to patriarchy by Muslim women through the agency of voluntary associations, and the Arab Spring of 2011 has created opportunities for Islamic organizations such as the Muslim Brotherhood in Egypt to enter into democratic politics.

In the modern world, therefore, many observers believe that the social ties of community, nation and citizenship are breaking down. There has been, it is argued, a significant secularization of the West in which the religious foundations of a common city life are more or less extinct. We no longer possess the liturgical framework that created a set of common experiences of membership. Furthermore, the growth of mega-cities means that the associational organization of citizens is no longer practical. In a global world of mass migration, expanding diasporas, international marriages and global networks, the traditional forms of citizenship are now too restrictive and brittle to contain and express the complexities of modern identities. The idea of citizenship as a national, rather than city, identity is also being transformed by globalization. The contemporary literature on citizenship talks about its flexibility, its partial, fragmented and temporary character (Ong 1999, 2008). But we do not possess strong notions of secular global identity and, with the crisis of security that followed the attack on the Twin Towers in New York, there is now growing control and regulation of the flow of individuals between and within societies. Against the idea of the increasingly porous nature of national boundaries, many sociologists have claimed that with securitization there has been a "return of the state" (Calhoun 2007), and that, within societies, there is evidence of growing privatization of security through gated communities resulting in an "enclave society" (Turner 2007). Safe borders are an important and basic requirement of security, but also remain an inevitable source of conflict in a global political environment where differentiated religious identities rarely correspond to the political borders of secular citizenship (Shamir 2005; Rumsford 2006).

The Clash of Civilizations

Any discussion of religion in relation to war and peace will inevitably confront Samuel Huntington's clash of civilizations thesis that first appeared in *Foreign Affairs* in 1993, and then in an expanded version as *The Clash of Civilizations and the Remaking of World Order* in 1996; it was subsequently reaffirmed as an article in 2003 in *The Hedgehog Review*. Huntington argued that, after the Cold War, international conflict would take place, not in terms of politics and economics, but through culture and religion. He divided the world into large civilizational blocs, and claimed that conflict would either occur between core states or along micro-fault lines. The most significant set of conflicts would be between Muslim and non-Muslim communities.

The main criticisms of the Huntington thesis have not rejected the proposition that modern conflicts are cultural and religious; they have argued rather that "civilizations" are not coherent, self-contained and timeless categories, but shifting, overlapping and internally complex systems (Sen 1999). Islam is a good example of this configuration because it is, like Christianity, internally divided into many forms and traditions. Conflicts between Sunni and Shi'ite adherents are as important and devastating as conflicts between Catholics and Protestants. The work of Marshall Hodgson (1974) on the diversity of Islamic civilizations in "Islamicate history" from the perspective of an integrated Mediterranean system might be taken as a salutary warning against any oversimplified notions of *one* Islamic world. Hodgson developed a post-national epistemology and theory of the world in *Rethinking World History*, demonstrating the limitations of any bi-polar notion of Islam versus Christianity. Many modernizing societies – such as Japan and South Korea – have embraced aspects of Westernization while retaining many of their traditional values and institutions. Huntington's thesis, which has been influential in American foreign policy, has also been criticized as an ideological justification of aggressive military interventions in Iraq and Afghanistan (Berman 2003). For its critics, Huntington's work does not have any convincing predictive power and remains unfulfilled (Fox 2005). Huntington also implicitly raises a question about whether human beings have become more or less violent over the long history of human societies – an issue that is discussed with respect to the work of Norbert Elias in Chapter 4.

Despite powerful criticisms of Huntington, many of the major conflicts in the twenty-first century are, at one level, conflicts between communities operating in or defined in terms of some version of Islam and Christianity. Examples of such binary definitions of identity in religious conflicts are numerous: Muslims and Christians in northern and southern Nigeria; Muslims and Catholics in Iraq; Copts and Muslims in Egypt; Muslims and evangelical Christians in Java; Russian Orthodox and Muslims in Chechnya; Catholics and Protestants in Northern Ireland. Beyond the Christian-Muslim conflict, there is the violent encounter between Buddhists and Muslims in southern Thailand. Critics of Huntington emphasize the fact that these religious identities are merely constructed labels, and that we must guard against the "essentialization" of these categories. Many sociologists of immigration have pointed out that, in the past, migrants from Turkey to Germany were simply regarded as "Turks" but are now seen as "Muslims." Others point out that, while the conflict in Chechnya was an ethnic and nationalist struggle, it too has acquired the mantel of a religious conflict. The problem appears to be that, while academics can recognize that identities such as "Jew" or "Christian" or "Muslim" are socially constructed and are therefore variable and unstable, social actors involved in conflict may have little choice but to recognize their opponents in terms of a simplified classificatory system: us and them. Thus religious tensions appear to be an invariable feature of modern politics. The case of Lebanon, with its complex mixture of religious and ethnic identities, has attracted much attention from social scientists. Raja Abillama, in his study of sectarianism as a category of secular authority in Chapter 7 of this book, provides an instructive inquiry into how the categories of Christian, Muslim and Druze in Lebanon are constructed by the law, and how the notion of sectarian conflict is managed by state authorities. I have regarded his chapter as a contribution to peace studies, because it helps us to understand the management of religion by the state.

Conclusion

The rise of so-called "public religions" in the latter half of the twentieth century has complicated the conventional views about secularization, the diminishing influence of religion in civil society and the neat, if artificial, separation of church and state. The academic vocabulary of religious studies has, given the political conflicts in the "real world," become deeply political. To take one notorious example, there is now very little academic agreement about the meaning of *jihad* in the Islamic tradition. Chase Robinson (2009), complaining that the interpretation of early Islamic history is now all too frequently used for political purposes, tried to establish a minimal level of understanding. In early Islam, religion and politics were never separated, and Islam spread through much of the Middle East and North Africa through "tribally organized militias giving way to professionally recruited and salaried armies" (Robinson 2009, 206). Early Islam was thus organized in terms of religio-political parties that agreed upon the religious character of the state. These historical facts lay the foundation for controversies over jihad. Did early Islam spread because it was a militarized religion with the motivation to destroy all of those who did not accept the authority of the Prophet? Or does jihad really mean the internal moral and religious struggle of human beings to become genuinely pious? Trying to make a judgment about such matters is, for Robinson, complicated by the fact that the Qur'an does not provide a secure guide to orthodoxy, because the Qur'anic text was "fluid" and, furthermore, "much of the early law was generated without reference to what the text says [...] *The authority of the Qur'an, in other words, is a matter of history*" (Robinson 2009, 214). History involves interpretation and judgment, both of which are or can be influenced by contemporary debates that are often political rather than academic. In short, it is very difficult to come to some decisive conclusion about what jihad actually means, but this fact does not stop journalists and others confidently referring to the threatening activities of jihadists.

Many of these interpretive problems have arisen in this collection of essays that attempt to explore the complexities by which war has been both condemned and condoned by religious and secular ideologies that loudly proclaim peace. Several contributions to this collection have directly addressed the legacy of pacifism, from the Quakers to Leo Tolstoy. The pacifist tradition of the Quakers has been especially influential in the West, despite the relatively modest numbers of the Friends (see Chapter 5 by Ana M. Acosta on the origins of the Quaker Peace Testimony). Modern social and political movements have also been deeply influenced by charismatic figures such as Mahatma Gandhi, Martin Luther King and Nelson Mandela (see Chapter 8 by Alexander Bacha and Manu Bhagavan). Gandhi was influenced by both Tolstoy's radical pacifism and the teachings of the Quakers. Religion is pre-eminently about hope and the possibility of reconstructing human societies in both space and time; human history is punctuated by countless millenarian and messianic movements. Eben Kirksey, reflecting on Jacques Derrida's discussion of messianic hope in Chapter 2, coins the expression "messianic multiple" to describe the messianic hopes of West Papuans, which is not fixed on one person or on a single event, and as such can better survive the disappointments and catastrophes that rain down upon the people of this region. Messianic hopes that continue to emerge out of the many violent conflicts of modern history are indeed the heart of a heartless world. However, what we might call the "religious imaginary" contains both the hope for peace and the justification for violence. The Abrahamic religions (Judaism, Christianity and Islam) all share a theology of brotherly love and compassion, and the Sermon on the Mount may be justifiably regarded as a serene statement of the Christian ethic of care. Nevertheless, as an organized religion, Christianity has at various times accepted a doctrine of the just war. St Augustine, in seeking to maintain a united universal church, came to accept the fact that punishment was necessary to control such deviations as Donatism and Pelagianism. Indeed, corrective punishment was a necessary part of discipline. In the twentieth century, in response to colonialism in Egypt, Muslim teachers embraced the necessity of jihad not simply as an internal moral struggle but, where necessary, a violent opposition to British rule.

Are there any conclusions to be drawn from these specific examples? One constant in these comparisons is the institutionalization of religious orthodoxies that divide the inside world of members and the outside world of non-believers. Wilfred Cantwell Smith (1972) made a valuable distinction between faith and religion, where the latter is regarded as the inflexible and congealed form of a living faith. When institutional religion formulates an orthodoxy in which religious Truth divides the world into believers and infidels, the conditions for conflict are already present, and when orthodoxies come to claim monopolies, not only over belief but over territory, sacred spaces and symbolic resources, the potential for violence is further institutionalized. Entry into and exit from social groups with definite boundaries become more costly, and in religious groups, rules relating to exit can become punitive. In his famous account of *Exit, Voice and Loyalty*, Albert O. Hirschman (1970, 17), comparing the differences between markets, firms and social groups, observed that "exit has often been branded as *criminal* for it has been labeled desertion, defection, and treason."

Among religious groups, apostasy rules can demand the death of a deserter. In short, when faith – Jesus's gospel of brotherly love or Siddhartha Gautama's message of suffering and compassion – is translated into a universal church or into a galactic Buddhist polity thereby combining space, identity, written scriptural orthodoxy and material resources, the possibilities for competition and conflict between religious groups are enhanced and consolidated.

One central theme running through this collection is the inevitable tensions between religious notions of love and peace, and the inevitability of politics that requires legitimate use of force to ensure its sovereignty over territory. This tension was powerfully explored by Max Weber, especially in two lectures late in his life, namely "science as a vocation" and "politics as a vocation." This theme, while a general aspect of these chapters, is fully explored in Chapter 9 with reference to Weber and Tolstoy. Another theme is the inescapable impact of history on contemporary conflicts. For example, Oliver Cromwell invaded Ireland in 1649 at the head of his New Model Army to re-establish authority over the ongoing Catholic rebellion. Thousands were killed when his troops stormed the towns of Drogheda and Wexford. Cromwell's actions were justified in his own mind by the need to protect Protestant England from Roman Catholic resistance and the threat of a successful royalist uprising. Cromwell has shaped the writing of the history of Ireland ever since, and his legacy survives in the politics of Northern Ireland where marching Ulstermen celebrate the continuity of the Protestant faith (McElligott 2001). A similar historical legacy hangs on the Battle of Culloden on 16 April 1746, when the Jacobite rising against the House of Hanover was finally defeated. The subsequent suppression of Jacobitism by the Earl of Cumberland (the "Butcher") was brutal. The Jacobite Wars came to be seen as a critical turning point in the English hegemony over Scotland, the triumph of Protestantism over Catholicism, the destruction of the clans and the end of the Highlands (Roberts 2002). The writing of history consequently turns into the writing of nationalist history.

In conclusion, the West is littered with a history of crusades, religious wars, *pogroms*, and religious intolerance. In the East, Buddhism, which is pre-eminently concerned with human suffering, evolved in Japan into military sects in which personal discipline turned into martial art techniques, and in modern Thailand Buddhist *sanghas* are involved in conflict with Muslim communities in the southern regions. The establishment of tolerance between religions has proved to be an elusive goal despite the good intentions of religious leaders. War and peace, which are, in this world, constant companions, have both found their inspiration in religious belief and practice. The essays in this volume explore the achievements of peace and the failures of civility, in which faith has inspired men to love their neighbors, and where religion has often been the occasion of violence.

References

Agamben, Giorgio. 1998. *Homo Sacer: Sovereign Power and Bare Life*. Stanford: Stanford University Press.

Anderson, Benedict. 1990. *Imagined Communities: Reflections on the Origins and Spread of Nationalism*. London: Verso.

Augustine. 1998. *The City of God against the Pagans*. Cambridge: Cambridge University Press.

Barbalet, Jack, Adam Possamai and Bryan S. Turner, eds. 2011. *Religion and the State: A Comparative Sociology*. London: Anthem Press.

Ben-Porat, Guy, and Bryan S. Turner, eds. 2011. *The Contradictions of Israeli Citizenship: Land, Religion and State*. London: Routledge.

Berman, Paul. 2003. *Terror and Liberalism*. New York: W. W. Norton.

Calhoun, Craig. 2007. *Nations Matter: Culture, History and the Cosmopolitan Dream*. London and New York: Routledge.

Casanova, José. 1994. *Public Religions in the Modern World*. Chicago: Chicago University Press.

Finley, Moses I. 1983. *Politics in the Ancient World*. Cambridge: Cambridge University Press.

Fox, J. 2005. "Paradigm Lost: Huntington's Unfulfilled Clash of Civilizations Prediction into the 21st Century." *International Politics* 39(2): 193–213.

Harvey, David. 2006. *Spaces of Global Capitalism: Towards a Theory of Uneven Geographical Development*. London: Verso.

Hechter, Michael.1975. *Internal Colonialism: The Celtic Fringe in British National Development, 1536–1966*. London: Routledge.

Hirschman, Albert O. 1970. *Exit, Voice, and Loyalty*. Cambridge, MA: Harvard University Press.

Hodgson, Marshall G. S.1974. *The Venture of Islam: Conscience and History in a World Civilization*. Chicago: University of Chicago Press.

Huntington, Samuel P. 1993. "The Clash of Civilizations." *Foreign Affairs* 72(3): 22–48.

———. 1996. *The Clash of Civilizations and the Remaking of World Order*. New York: Simon & Schuster.

———. 2003. "America in the World." *The Hedgehog Review* 5(1): 7–18.

Joseph, Suad, ed. 2000. *Gender and Citizenship in the Middle East*. New York: Syracuse University Press.

Kymlicka, Will. 1995. *Multicultural Citizenship: A Liberal Theory of Minority Rights*. Oxford: Clarendon Press.

Kruger, Steven. 2011. *The Spectral Jew: Conversion and Embodiment in Medieval Europe*. Minneapolis: University of Minnesota Press.

Locke, John. 2009. *A Letter Concerning Toleration*. New York: Classic Books America.

McElligott, Jason. 2001. "Cromwell, Drogheda, and the Abuse of Irish History." *Bullán: An Irish Studies Review* 6(1): 109–32.

Ong, Aihwa.1999. *Flexible Citizenship: The Cultural Logics of Transnationality*. Durham, NC: Duke University Press.

———. 2008. "Please Stay: Pied-a-Terre Subjects in the Megacity." In *Citizenship between Past and Future*, edited by Engin Isin, Peter Nyers and Bryan S. Turner, 81–91. London: Routledge.

Putnam, Robert D. and David E. Campbell. 2010. *American Grace: How Religion Divides and Unites Us*. New York: Simon & Schuster.

Roberts, John Leonard. 2002. *The Jacobite Wars: Scotland and the Military Campaigns of 1715 and 1745*. Edinburgh: Edinburgh University Press.

Robinson, Chase. 2009. "The Ideological Uses of Early Islam." Review of *The First Muslims: History and Memory*, by Asma Afsaruddin. *Past and Present* 203(1): 205–28.

Rumsford, Chris. 2006. "Theorizing Borders." *European Journal of Social Theory* 9(2): 155–69.

Sadiq, Kamal. 2009. *Paper Citizens: How Illegal Immigrants Acquire Citizenship in Developing Countries*. Oxford: Oxford University Press.

Saxonhouse, Arlene W. 1992. *Fear of Diversity: The Birth of Political Science in Ancient Greek Thought*. Chicago: University of Chicago Press.

Schmitt, Carl. 1996. *The Concept of the Political*. Chicago: University of Chicago Press.

Sen, Amartya.1999. "Democracy as Universal." *Journal of Democracy* 10(3):3–17.

Sennott, Charles M. 2001. *The Body and the Blood: The Middle East's Vanishing Christians and the Possibility of Peace*. New York: Public Affairs.

Shachar, Ayelet and Ran Hirschl. 2007. "Citizenship as Inherited Property." *Political Theory* 35(3): 253–87.

Shamir, Ronen. 2005. "Without Borders? Notes on Globalization as a Mobility Regime." *Sociological Theory* 23(2): 197–217.

Smith, Winifred Cantwell. 1972. *The Faith of Other Men*. New York: Harper & Row.

Soysal, Yasemin. N. 1994. *The Limits of Citizenship: Migrants and Postnational Membership in Europe*. Chicago: University of Chicago.

Turner, Bryan S. 2007. "The Enclave Society: Towards a Sociology of Immobility." *European Journal of Social Theory* 10(2): 287–303.

Turner, Bryan S., ed. 2008. *Religious Diversity and Civil Society: A Comparative Analysis*. Oxford: The Bardwell Press.

Urry, John. 2000. *Sociology beyond Societies: Mobilities for the Twenty-First Century*. London: Routledge.

Weber, Max. 1978. *Economy and Society*. Berkeley: University of California Press.

Zubaida, Sami.1988. *Islam, the People and the State*. London: Routledge.

WAR

Chapter 1

SACRED MEMORY AND THE SECULAR WORLD: THE POLAND NARRATIVES

Alisse Waterston

Jewish Narratives of Poland: An Intimate Ethnography

"What?! You slept with the enemy?" my nice Jewish doctor snapped back, hearing I'd stayed with a Polish Christian family in my dead father's old *shtetl*. Just a few years earlier, the same thought might have entered my own mind had I entertained such an idea. For me, as for my physician, Poland had been "fixed in my Jewish imagination as the land of unreconstructed anti-Semitism," to use Eva Hoffman's words (Hoffman 2004, 137). To think differently about Poland and Polish Christians would signify disloyalty of the worst kind: betrayal of the sacred memory of the persecution and suffering of the Jews, a suffering, we have been taught, that extends into thousands of years of the Jewish plight.

Indeed, a few years earlier, on my first pilgrimage to Poland, I felt a terrible unease. On that occasion, I walked the streets of my father's hometown, recoiling from the townsfolk, and reaching out to no one. I recall looking suspiciously at a huddle of old women chatting on a stoop. I took special notice of the old men, some walking on the street, others grouped on a corner, who peered back at me with equal suspicion. Wasn't it anti-Semitism I saw in their glower?

That first trip in the summer of 2001 coincided with a series of critical events in Poland around the release of Jan Gross's book, *Neighbors: The Destruction of the Jewish Community in Jedwabne, Poland*. One month before my arrival in Jedwabne, a commemorative ceremony was held on what became a sacred and contested site: the spot on which the Jewish townsfolk were set afire in a barn exactly 60 years earlier.

Gross's slim volume packed a huge charge. In Jedwabne, it was not the Germans who annihilated the Jews but the Polish Christians who had slaughtered their Jewish neighbors. There were draggings, knifings and pummelings, and then the major event: Jews burnt alive in the barn.

By the time I arrived in August, the ceremonies were over, and a new, controversial tomb-like monument was in place. But my trip was not triggered by Gross's book or the intense debate and discussion in Poland that resulted. I was there as part of my long-term, anthropological study of my father's life, an intimate ethnography of a charming, difficult man whose life was torn apart by the upheavals of the twentieth century, including the political and structural violence of his homeland (Waterston 2005; Waterston and Rylko-Bauer 2006). In 1913, my father was born Menachim Mendel, or Mendeleh in the Yiddish diminutive, the youngest of Priwa and Itsak Isak Waserstein's seven children. World War I left the Wasersteins "helpless, the poorest of the poor," according to my father's account.

My father raised me on stories of Polish anti-Semitism, imbued as a natural, fundamental and timeless feature of the Polish spirit. "The Polish were very anti-Semitic and they had to relieve themselves to get rid of the Jews," my father said, not just as recollection but also as warning to a Jewish daughter about to visit Poland for the first time. Mendel backed his statements with anecdotes, his kind of proof: the songs ridiculing and demonizing the Jews, derogatory comments by Christian teachers and schoolboys, all the nasty rumors; even the bells of the church, he claims, rang out hatred for the Jews.

Though Gross's book was published in 2001, the story of the Jedwabne massacre was not new to me.[1] I grew up on it, hearing from an early age what happened that sweltering day in July 1941. My father and his immediate family escaped the burning, having left for Cuba starting in the 1920s, the last of them arriving in Havana in 1939. Among the Wasersteins who remained in Jedwabne was Szmul Wasersztajn, my father's cousin, known to the family as "Shmulke," whose postwar testimony provided the basis for *Neighbors*: "Local hooligans armed themselves with axes, special clubs studded with nails, and other instruments of torture and destruction," Shmulke offered in chilling testimony. "(They) chased all the Jews into the street […] people were beaten murderously and forced to sing and dance. In the end they proceeded to the main action – the burning. Jews were ordered to line up in a column, four in a row […] and all were chased into the barn. Then the barn was doused with kerosene and lit."[2] Gross's main argument brought shockwaves to Poland. "In July 1941," Gross concludes, "half of the population of a small East European town murdered the other half – some 1,600 men, women and children" (2002, 7).

Shmulke Wasersztajn was saved by a Christian neighbor, who hid him in a barn, although his mother, Chajcia, was killed in the massacre. Eventually, Shmulke would join the Waserstein clan in Havana, after the extended family set down roots on the island. There, Shmulke's testimony would become family legend, passed from one generation to the next.³ For me, my father recounts the massacre:

> When the stable wasn't big enough for all the Jews to be burned there, they took out the younger people – you know, 13, 14, 15, 18 years old, and they took them to the Jewish cemetery. They made them dig a ditch. The boys had to dig a ditch, and they put them in a row and they put them with hammers: "Next!" and "Next!" and each one of them [...] each and every one of them [...] screamed out, "*Shema Yisroel Adonai Elohenu, Adonai Echad!*" ["Hear O Israel, The Lord our God, The Lord is One"].

In an article Barbara Rylko-Bauer and I wrote about our projects and the challenges of intimate ethnography, we discussed the kinds of emotions each of us knew we must confront in our respective projects: "The emotions," we wrote, "are like a mound on a field that indicates something important lies beneath, needing to be excavated" (2006, 402). I would try to confront my conflicting emotions of loyalty and betrayal to my father and to my sense of collective identity first by exploring my father's reflexive attachment to the experience of Jewish suffering (even as he reinvented himself in new circumstances). In listening carefully to my father's rendition of the massacre, I hear that his narrative is only partially an accounting of events – the "happenings"; the tension between myth and fact is evident in this recitation. In my father's telling, the story becomes a legend, even as it "speaks truth" to the violence and horror. In this storyteller's hands, Jedwabne is a parable of heroism and suffering, with young boy-heroes shouting the main statement of their Jewish belief (the *Shema*) at the moment of their deaths. The narrator invokes the sacred, not as protection from the violence of the world but to move the now-dead boys to another, more exalted place, immune from, detached from the wounds of the flesh. This maneuver shifts the secular dynamic to sacred ground, thereby leaving the whole history behind the event untouched by critique, analysis or insight. And yet, throughout his life my father remained burdened by the defining events of the century, including the massacre in Jedwabne, and his earliest experiences of war on Polish soil. Relentlessly pursued by annihilationists, my father embodied the diasporic Jew whose *habitus* drove his desire to repeatedly tell the story that kept him faithful to the suffering he really did endure.

I would also attempt to confront my conflicting emotions and sense of collective identity by expanding the focus of my inquiry beyond my father's life history: I would sleep with the enemy.

Return to Poland: Journey beyond Myth

Serendipity played a part in the next stage of my project. On a cool autumn day in 2005, I began sharing "my father's story in history and anthropology" with a group of undergraduate students in my 59th Street City University of New York classroom. In the middle of the lecture, one student shot up his arm. "What?" I asked, slightly annoyed at the interruption at a key moment in my narrative. "I'm from Jedwabne," Stasio Danielski said.[4] I was shocked. Though I had already been to Poland, been to Jedwabne, it still struck me as a mythic place. How could there be a real-life, flesh-and-blood, Polish Christian *person* from Jedwabne – my student, someone in my care, in my trust?

Thus began "the Poland Narratives," my effort to gather voices of Polish Christians. This part of my project has taken me to Greenpoint, Brooklyn, home to a large population of working-class Polish Americans and Polish Christian immigrants, and back to Jedwabne in 2008 with my student Stasio.

Stasio and I stayed with his uncle Nelek and aunt Elka in Lomza about 15 kilometers from Jedwabne. Nelek and Elka were generous hosts, insisting I use their bedroom while they moved into the living room, sharing that space with their nephew. Things moved very slowly in the Danielski household. The food, vodka and conversation flowed but it seemed forever before they would take me to Jedwabne.

Finally the day did arrive. We pulled into Jedwabne. Nelek drove to the monument, though I hadn't asked him to do so. Elka dug into a grocery bag, pulling out a glass memorial candle and placing it gently at the foot of the stone.

A short distance away is the old Jewish cemetery. Seeing it for the first time seven years earlier was for me a stark emblem of Jewish extermination on Polish soil: the graves untended; broken stones the only remnants. This time even those relics were unseen. I could not find them buried beneath the overgrown grasses that I slogged through while Stasio filmed me from the sidelines.

We walked to the well-tended Christian cemetery to visit the graves of Stasio's family and those of aunt Elka's relatives. Stasio's grandma and grandpa, Nelek's sister, Elka's parents. Elka wiped the headstones, swept dirt off each grave and laid her candles on them. The grocery bag was now empty. Together, we lit each candle.

Afterward, we wandered through the cemetery and came upon a startling find. There, in a condition much more ragged than the Polish Christian graves yet in much less a state of decay than in the Jewish cemetery, were the graves of German soldiers killed in Jedwabne during World War I. Rustic wooden crosses, bouquets of plastic flowers strewn about and the remains of memorial candles marked this cemetery.

Though the Jewish cemetery looked different from the time of my first visit, the Jedwabne massacre monument looked the same as it had seven years earlier. Joanna Michlic has written about the sequence of events from the time Gross's book was published in Poland in May 2000 to the commemoration ceremony on 10 July 2001. She notes that Gross's volume ignited an intense, difficult, disturbing and ongoing debate in postcommunist Poland about Polish Christian and Jewish relations and the Holocaust, particularly the role of ethnic Poles in colluding with or resisting the annihilationist project (Michlic 2002, 9; Brand 2001; Polonsky and Michlic 2004; Chodakiewicz 2005). Participants in this "battle over the memory of Polish-Jewish relations and the Polish collective self-image" (2002, 7) include representatives from secular and religious segments of Polish society – priests, presidents, scholars and intellectuals, politicians and journalists. It has also involved interested observers outside of Poland, including rabbis and politicians as well as scholars and members of the postgeneration like myself.

Michlic posits two approaches to the "rewriting" of the history of Polish-Jewish relations: a self-critical stance (2002, 10) in which Polish Christians face their "dark past" in relation to Jews and they come to terms with the distortions in their "collective self-portrait [...] solely as victims (of the Nazis) and (as) heroes" (2002, 3); and a self-defensive stance that effectively silences any questions about the past, collective memory and Polish national identity. Among those in the self-defensive camp, Michlic explains, are right-wing nationalists many who are virulent anti-Semites, and who have a large presence in the right-wing media in Poland.

In the midst of this politically and emotionally charged discussion came a decision from the Polish state authorities: "*an appropriate commemoration* of the Jewish victims of the Jedwabne massacre" would be installed (2002, 12; emphasis mine) and marked with the words, "To the memory of Jews from Jedwabne and the surrounding area, men, women and children, inhabitants of this land, who were murdered and burned alive on this spot on July 10, 1941." More than that, the new monument would replace an old plaque in place since 1963. That plaque, its message now refuted by Jan Gross's revelations, had been inscribed with these words: "The place of destruction of the Jewish population. Here Gestapo and Nazi gendarmes burnt alive 1600 people on 10 July 1941" (2002, 21–2; see also Gross 2002, 114).

Mourning in Jedwabne: Sites of Memory and Memorialization

John Matteson's essay on "Grave Discussions" describes how public memory is shaped and enshrined by monuments that look like graves, and how commemorative ceremonies sanctify a particular reading of the past (2001). Examining how and why monuments to the American Revolution were developed in nineteenth-century New England, Matteson writes, "commemoration [is] a word that means 'to be mindful together' [...] 'together' is key, for commemorative objects [...] establish common cultural ground [...] the monument tries to place [...] limits so that we truly may be mindful together" (2001, 419).

But that was in *New* England, the British enemy by then far away, and the "we" referred to the making of an American citizenry in context of the making of a particularly "American" national narrative. In Jedwabne, the Jews came back to haunt; the monument the product of a dynamic interaction between memory and politics, narrative and history, and the sacred and the secular. The result was that sacred memory in Poland was forced to shift, implemented by secular authority. For Jews, the sacred – that which must be protected from criticism – is upheld in the "appropriate" commemoration in Jedwabne: memories of the Holocaust, its victims and perpetrators, and is consistent with a larger Jewish motif: the root of the problem – the root of the massacre lies in anti-Semitism. At the same time, Poles were called upon to confront "their dark past" now inscribed with a new narrative. For some among them, the sacred memories of Polish identity and faith were defiled, and the monument a sacrilege. It is difficult to get beyond the impasse.

We may never know the full extent of what "happened" in Jedwabne in July 1941; discussion seems to have stalled around a relatively narrow set of issues and partial bits of evidence. The number of dead, for example, returns as a significant point of contention. Did the dead number 200, 400, 1,600? In the wake of Gross's book, Poland's Institute of National Remembrance (IPN) launched an exhumation at the site of the mass burning in May 2001 (2003 Institute of National Remembrance).[5] One month later, the IPN called it off in response to objections by some Jewish religious leaders who considered the exhumation a "desecration of the dead" (CNN 2001; Gross 2002, 122). At that point, 200 remains had been found; for some, proof that the number of dead is significantly fewer than 1,600. There was also the matter of bullets of German make pulled from the site, evidence, some argued, that the Nazis had committed the deed, not the Polish neighbors, although later the bullets were revealed to be of a type used by Germans in World War I. Were these parts of the weaponry, I can't help but wonder, that played in the deaths of soldiers buried in Jedwabne's cemetery for the German war dead from World War I?

Can there ever be a "being mindful together" in Jedwabne? It strikes me, listening to the words as well as the silences of my new friends in Jedwabne, that the monument and how it evolved ruptures as much as it might heal, creates new silences as much as it opens up dialogue. For those who live in

Jedwabne, the monument stands as an unbearable accusation even if for the rest of Poland it opened up a space to dialogue about "Poland's dark past." Jedwabne and its current residents – one, two, even three generations after the event – seem to be bearing the brunt of that dark past. "Jedwabne is cursed," Poland's chief rabbi Michael Schudrich told me, as if to quarantine the problem and locate it in the township.[6] The public dialogue offers folks from Jedwabne little consolation; only the right-wing nationalists seem to lift the burden of guilt off their shoulders, entrapping them further into hostile relations (imagined or concrete) with Jews.[7]

Despite the strengths of Gross's book and despite that it opened the possibility for critical self-reflection in Poland, it also helped reinscribe Polish anti-Semitism as a monolith and as an explanation. Blinded by "the burden of (my own) instilled memory" (Sand 2009, 1–22; see especially 14), I also accepted that image and that argument by uncritically accepting Gross's assertion that "half the town murdered the other half" (Gross 2002, 7; Waterston 2005, 48). But sleeping with the enemy has made me see things differently, revealing that easy explanations and blanket accusations seep in easily but are off the mark. That does not mean I pretend anti-Semitism doesn't exist. It does not mean I ignore the reality of the massacre in Jedwabne – a slaughter that took members of my own family.

The Polish Christians and Jews were torn apart, and the Polish Christians and Jews tore each other apart. Some might consider the destruction an inevitable instance of ethnic conflict, causal in its own right, a reflection of timeless, tribal hatred and enmity that seethes (Lewis 1990; Huntington 1993; Kaplan 1993; cf. Bowen 1996). This is the primordialist view, an explanation that carries great weight in our times, though sophistry, not evidence, supports it. Others might be stymied by the neighbor-on-neighbor violence that erupted in Jedwabne in 1941 (and in other towns during the same period). Varshney (2001, 2002), for example, might not have expected it, considering these neighbors intermingled in everyday life at work, in school and in the marketplace. Polish Christians and Jews in Jedwabne had a long history of "interethnic interaction" of a kind that would make this spectacular form of "ethnic conflict" unlikely.[8]

But ethnicity does not by itself structure hostile (or peaceful) social relations nor does it by itself produce the violent polarization that left the Jews of Jedwabne dead. For that we need to look at a longer and larger history – the social relations of land and labor in Poland; Poland's relations with its neighbors over centuries of European war; the Partitions of Poland as the spoils of war and the effects of these historical processes on the polity, the Polish national identity, collective anxiety, and the making of "Poland's threatening Other" – the Jew (Michlic 2006). We also need to examine the workings of Jewish collective memory steeped in a Jewish people "consciousness" and for some, "a set of sacred and inviolable truths" – collective memory that was (and is) itself situated in nationalism and nation-building projects (Rushkoff 2004, 53; Sand 2009). This is a deeper, more nuanced understanding of violent history that may help reveal what made Jedwabne possible even as it requires confronting the sacred.

Return to Poland: Journey into History

Norman Davies begins his famous history of Poland with a now ancient description of a place depicted by a traveler from the south. It was the tenth century, the traveler a merchant from the Umayyad Caliphate that had expanded its dominion to Al-Andalus. The place he described was a province that would soon become known as Poland. Only fragments remain of the travelogue written by Ibrahim ibn Ya'qub, who some say was a Jew but who we know traversed thousands of kilometers to arrive in "the land of the Slavs [...] (a place that) produces an abundance of food, meat, honey, and fish" (1982, 3; Tighe 2001, 189).[9]

On the eve of the second millennium, the world was in great motion as human collectivities defined by culture, language, religion, occupation, networks and power met and moved across lands and settled in new places. Global migration is not a uniquely contemporary phenomenon; the migrations of medieval times were also of the "global" type. Across seven civilizations, medieval migrations "encompassed the then-known world [...] (when) merchants, intellectuals, and religious thinkers interacted, as did the little people along the trade routes spanning the globe and in the vast cultural borderlands in which civilizations overlapped" (Hoerder 2002, 8, 23). As people interacted, they also intermixed, making for ever-changing cultural forms in the context of historical events, shifting circumstances, socio-political and economic conditions, and circuits of people, goods and beliefs.

Ibn Ya'qub was part of that migratory process, a visitor with the Khalif of Cordoba. Ya'qub's dispassionate observations of that northern land include mention of "Mesko [*sic*], King of the North," a successor to the legendary Piast the peasant, father of the first "Polish" dynasty (Davies 1982, 3–4). King Mieszko I, a converted Christian, ruled the Polanie, "the people of the open fields." There they dwelt, cradled between the Odra and Vistula rivers, where the food and meat and honey and fish were abundant.

In the century following ibn Ya'qub's visit, Jews found permanent settlement in parts of Polanie, where they were traders, could own land and served in the royal mint. The specific trajectory of the Jewish migration to Polanie is uncertain. By the twelfth century, Jewish settlement in general extended from Byzantium to the Iberian Peninsula, from southern Slavic territories to Western Europe. Historians believe the Crusades led Jews from the west to Poland; others suggest Jews arrived upon the fall of the Khazar Empire in the east (Michlic 2006, 28, 289n11; Ta-Shma 1997, 291–3; Sand 2009, 210–49).

Jewish settlements in cities, towns and villages across Poland flourished during the Piast and Jagiellonian kingdoms over the next several centuries. Jews were made use of by the ruling class as merchants, bankers, intermediaries in exchange relationships and long-distance traders with connections "over the whole of Europe all the way to the Mediterranean," networks Christian traders did not possess (Meijers 1991, 136). In turn, Jews were granted legal protections, given relative political autonomy, and provided freedom of religion and commerce, codified in the Statute of Kalisz in 1264.

In Poland's feudal system, the ruling elite shared power with regional overlords to exact tribute from peasant producers. The tributary mode of production prevailed between the fourteenth and eighteenth centuries when the landed nobility (*szlachta*), some with their own armies, controlled surplus-producing peasants and used Jewish go-betweens to gather tribute (Wolf 1996, 1997). "Jews were actual figures in peasants' lives," Hoffman notes, "often standing in a complicated relationship with them [...] We know that Jewish estate stewards, who acted as collectors of taxes and rents, met with particular resentment, since they were seen by the peasants as their direct exploiters, rather than the intermediaries they really were" (Hoffman 1997, 43). The roots of the resentment were structural and political-economic, even if antipathy was articulated or understood in cultural or religious terms.

The burgher class was particularly hostile to the Jews, their sentiments enlarging as competition between the two merchant estates increased, the Catholic Church grew in influence over the Polish domain starting in the fifteenth century, the Polish kingdom joined forces with the Grand Duchy of Lithuania to form a commonwealth in the sixteenth century, and the political and economic crises of multiple wars took its toll, especially during the seventeenth century. Still, during these three centuries the Jewish population saw steady growth in number, wealth and well-being. They institutionalized a system of localized self-government called the *kahal* (the Jewish Commune) and developed a Poland-wide political-juridical body, Va`ad Arba Aratzot (the Council of Four Lands). These rights could only be granted by royal decree and patronage; in turn, the Jewish Commune assessed and collected royal taxes.

By the seventeenth century, when the Polish monarchical state was at the height of power, wealth and prestige in Eastern Europe, it was also situated on a series of fracture zones – "lines of instability that radiate out from specific and discernible crises" – instabilities that are political and economic (Nordstrom 2009, 72).

The Chmielnicki revolt in mid-century reflects one such fracture zone, a series of violent uprisings against Polish imperial expansion of the Ukraine and against exploitation of peasants by Polish nobles and their intermediaries, the Jews. Conflicts within the ruling elite, between king and nobility, signal another fracture zone (Davies 1982, 340–41) while the Kingdom of Poland was situated on the fracture zone of competing, expansionist and warring empires – Swedish, Ottoman, Russian, Austrian, British, French and Danish. In addition to the Chmielnicki revolt, seventeenth-century Poland was at war with Russia, Sweden and the Ottoman Empire. By the end of the century, Poland was in shambles, its population decimated, its political infrastructure shaken, the kingdom made ripe to be "swallowed up" by three empires in the century to follow (Hoffman 1997, 61; Frost 2004).

Still another fracture zone, not disconnected from those already mentioned, was economic, involving trade networks, mercantile wealth and peasant labor in the tributary mode. The Vistula River provided the main artery for international trade goods, especially grain and lumber. While the grain trade flourished, peasant life remained difficult. Expansion of the grain trade put enormous pressure on rural labor: "In order to meet the demand," Davies argues, "the noble landowners exacted more work and harsher conditions from their peasants," pointing to the social dynamics that would also play into domestic tensions (1982, 280). In their capacity as traders, merchants and middlemen, Jews stood on the fracture zones, their social, political and economic fates tied to the larger quakes of the times.

It cannot be said that anti-Jewish sentiment was uniform across these centuries or among the social groups (estates) that comprised the Polish social order. The church, one among the powerful Polish estates, was rooted in Roman Catholicism, its liturgy, teachings and propaganda, including anti-Jewish belief and rhetoric that resonated or held sway only at particular moments. For example, the church lent its ideological support to the burghers, supporting their interests against Jewish competitors. Michlic captures the flavor of religiously-imbued rhetoric in her list of titles by Roman Catholic burghers in the sixteenth and seventeenth centuries: "Jewish Cruelties, Murders, and Superstitions"; "Jewish Cruelty over the Holy Host and Christian Folk"; and "The Heavy Injuries and Great Worries Inflicted by the Jews on the Mirror of the Polish Crown" (2006, 32). With the crises of the seventeenth century, not least of which were war and economic contraction, the volume of anti-Jewish rhetoric got louder and the persecution of Protestants increased. Hoffman notes Poland became xenophobic, "less hospitable to differences of all kinds" (1997, 60), and the number of Jews accused of and executed for ritual murder rose. For example, in the mid-to-late 1600s, "'blood libel' accusations were made against Jews – namely that they had used the blood of Christian infants slaughtered in secret, mixed with flour to make special Passover bread [...] (one) Jew who had converted to Christianity, but who had lapsed back into Judaism, was burned at the stake for heresy and possible witchcraft [...] eight Jews were killed in a blood-libel riot [...] a Jewish pharmacist was burned for blasphemy" (Tighe 2001, 192).

Bigotry always has a history and a context, and is intimately tied to power interests. In periods of political and economic crisis, scapegoating – a maneuver of deflection – will rear its ugly head. In their analysis of original source materials on ritual murder, including ritual murder trials in Poland over three centuries, Guldon and Wijaczka document a dramatic increase in accusations during times of crisis. Conflicts between Christians and Jews, they argue, were exacerbated in the mid-seventeenth to early eighteenth centuries, "during periods of war and epidemics" (1997, 140).

This was the troubled and troubling state of affairs in Poland at the dawn of the eighteenth century when upheaval cast upon upheaval. The world was in transition, entering a new mode of production whereby monetary wealth could buy labor power, shifting social relations of production from the tributary mode. Western Europe would enter this mode sooner than Eastern Europe (Prak 2001, 161) but the early significance to the east was in the competitive relationships with the expanding empires in its midst. In particular, the Russian Empire, its eye on the Ottomans, would exert great influence on changing the course of Polish history. By the end of the eighteenth century, the Jewish parliament would be dismantled, and Hasidism, a new Jewish movement, would emerge, in part as response to the destruction of Jewish religious and political infrastructures. By century's end, Poland would be partitioned: Russia, Austria and Prussia (1772); Russia and Prussia (1793); Russia, Prussia and Austria (1795), a political "vivisection" that would inspire passions in the coming age of nationalist ideology and movement.

Nationalism and the Making of Fixed Imaginaries: Ethnic Poland and the Jews

From the standpoint of our own time, certain social facts and truths seem eternal – as if they have always been and always will be, even in the face of evidence that refutes such a view. The so-called "spirit" that "lives" behind the modern nation-state gives particular ones a quality of timelessness. The nation-state may be new (its "founding" celebrated with annual festivities, etc.) but the "nation" as a people with ancient collective roots, a common origin and fate, and that has permanence, is often accepted as truth, though it seems a great leap of faith to believe it. The plain fact that the nation-state emerged at the end of the eighteenth century with nationalist ideology flourishing thereafter does not deflect members' belief in the solidity of their own, homogenous "nation" with a purported traceable lineage and common, territorial root. This idea of the nation may prove to be, as Hobsbawm and others suggest, a historically contingent political and ideological form, not a timeless, natural essence. "We now know," Hobsbawm writes, "[nations] are not 'as old as history,'" and quotes Gellner: "Nations as a natural, God-given way of classifying men, as an inherent though long-delayed political destiny, are a myth; nationalism, which sometimes takes pre-existing cultures and turns them into nations, sometimes invents them, and often obliterates pre-existing cultures: *that* is a reality" (2006, 47; Hobsbawm 2004, 3, 10). Even as the nation is "constructed from above," it finds resonance with "ordinary people [whose] assumptions, hopes, needs, longings and interests" get framed in nationalist terms. Their imaginations thus stirred, ordinary people can find comfort in the idea of *their* community in a world marked by violent upheaval, displacement and disruption (Hobsbawm 2004, 10; see also Anderson 1991; Smith 2010). The process of nation building involves a choice – to pull from a finite set of cultural understandings and symbols and make them potent. It is in this way that "a people," and memories of their "tradition" is an invention, negotiated by leaders (Anderson 1991; Sand 2009). Ultimately, ideas about the group can become sacred belief, and the nation of which they are a part can become a fetish. For Christians in Poland, the Jew became a potent symbol of what Poland would not be.[10] For Jews in Poland (and elsewhere), diaspora became the sacred symbol of the Zionist cause.[11] In each case, sentiments of national separateness and unity are nurtured and nourished. There is no state of exception in this process or in the outcome; ironically, the symbolic power of uniqueness obscures that all "peoples" and their "nations" have been constructed by means of the same basic principles.[12]

The Polish nationalist narrative did not simply march along in a smooth, linear path to become a cohesive story of a homogeneous ethnic, racial and religious entity with deep roots in the land of open fields. Like many of its counterparts in the European states that surrounded it, Poland in the nineteenth century was engaged in revolt against foreign (dynastic) rule, and in developing and applying ideas about the nation that saw stirrings in the prior century. Michlic's rich reconstruction of that period reveals the process to be as complex as the set of alliances and antagonisms that characterized the political, economic and social relations of the period. The place of Jews in Polish society and ultimately in the Polish conception of itself as a nation was a subject of debate and disagreement that included Jewish representatives: at certain points and among certain political sectors, Jews were considered "an intrinsic part of the Polish social landscape" while at other points and among other political and intellectual leaders, they were considered a "nation within a nation" (Michlic 2006, 41–2).

The flame of ethnic nationalism in Poland grew ever more intense with each defeat against the forces of partition.[13] With the last of these defeats in 1864, nationalist rhetoric increasingly took on an anti-Semitic tone until it was part and parcel of the formal political sphere. "Anti-Jewish tropes became a powerful emotive tool for nation building," Michlic explains. Her description of this relatively recent process is summarized here:

> The concept of the Jew as the harmful alien other constituted one of the major aspects of the thinking among significant segments of conservative and Catholic elites [...] (they) made it a focal point of their ideology. They transferred it to the level of modern national politics, and in this new form they took it back to society. Without that transfer the concept of the Jew as a national threat could not have become so powerful, potent, and long-lived [...] They used it as a tool in raising national cohesiveness among ethnic Poles of different social classes with conflicting social and economic interests. (2006, 60–61)

Why Remember?

Those "conflicting social and economic interests" were shaped by the new world order in which declining and nascent imperial forces would contract or expand on the battlefields of modern warfare, and in which states would become configured on geo-political maps and with their own romantic ideas of the nation. "Capitalist imperialism is ultimately about the creation, maintenance, or enlargement of the capital accumulation of an imperial state's enterprises," war scholar Stephen Reyna explains, a condition no less true at the turn of the last century as now (2009, 54). Political violence and war did not decline with modernity, but escalated in scale of technological capacity and in scale of the unfathomable numbers of dead people and ruined infrastructures (Hinton 2002; Baumann 2005). "Empires are especially gory structures," Reyna explains the phenomenon. "Violence is used to create (modern) systems, keep them going, or make them bigger."

World War I was billed as the "war to end all wars," seductive rhetoric we now know was empty. Poland would become an independent republic in 1918, once its autonomy got the support of the Western powers.[14] Independence was followed by seven years of border wars and military skirmishes. At the time of the 1941 massacre in Jedwabne, Poland was again at war. Or rather, Poland was still at war with itself and with the imperial powers that once again came to occupy, then divide up, the country.[15]

Two years before the massacre, German forces invaded Poland from the west and the Soviets entered from the east, having come to their own agreement on Poland with the Ribbentrop (German)–Molotov (Soviet) Pact in 1939. After some wrangling, the two powers determined that Jedwabne would fall under Soviet dominion. With the agreement signed, Poland underwent a ruthless, intense process of ghettoization of the Jews and Germanization of non-Jews in the west, and a ruthless, intense process of Sovietization in the east that included most if not the entire Podlaskie province where Jedwabne is situated. Gross describes the process of Sovietization in places like Jedwabne: "[It] took a heavy total on the local people [affecting] all nationalities and social classes, but the brunt of propaganda and Soviet repressions was directed against the Polish state. Local elites were arrested or deported. Private property was gradually taken over […] a vigorous campaign of secularization targeted all religious institutions and personnel" (2002, 30–31). These conditions of scarcity, competition, destruction and divisiveness exacerbated existing tensions between the two main social groups.

Two years later, Nazi forces marched eastward, violating the German–Soviet agreement, occupying cities and towns, including Jedwabne. Hostilities between neighbors were now beyond feverish, torn in the twentieth century by the combined projects of ethnic nationalism, two enormous imperial powers, and war – an interwoven set of systemic and structural forces. The dark and powerful forces of modernity created the conditions and cultivated the kinds of passions that made the spectacular violence of July 1941 in Jedwabne *probable*, not just possible. Considering the circumstances, it is surprising there were not many more such events.

Amidst the maelstrom, my father was born in 1913. Fear and sorrow pervade his accounts of the first war and postwar period when he suffered hunger, despair and estrangement. As he talked about this time, he would sometimes cry or punctuate the story with a faint sob. As he talked about the massacre in Jedwabne, there were no tears, just fear, defensiveness and grief. In these ways, my father transmitted what he knew and saw, what he felt and heard, and so the texture of his memory and the sense of his experience became palpable to me.

Eva Hoffman asks, "why remember, to what end, and in what way?" and then she instructs: "The task is not only to remember but to remember strenuously – to explode, decode, and deepen the terrain of memory. What is at stake is not only the past but the present" (1997, 13–14).

I take Hoffman's injunction to heart in this essay. My father was an exile in the sense that Edward Said has described: a state of being, in a jealous state, with resentment, always out of place, he *felt* his difference (Said 2001, 173–86). It would be too easy to lay the blame for his wounds singularly on his old neighbors, on anti-Semitism (historically specific, not timeless), or my father's sacred belief in Jewish victimization, all of which were in dynamic interaction.

It would be misguided to ascribe the crimes (my father's exile; the massacre in Jedwabne) solely to the passions of the perpetrators and the victims.

There is bigger culpability, and it lies in the structures of power and the ideological systems it elaborates, including racialized ethnic hatred, xenophobia and jingoism – forces at strong play in the contemporary world. To point to this larger culpability as I have tried to do in this essay is not to offer excuses or exonerate individual perpetrators of violence from being held accountable. I offer it as an instance of my own attempt in these Poland narratives to remember strenuously, an effort that has led me to ask and seek answers to painful, difficult questions about violence – for my father's time and for my own.

Acknowledgment

I am grateful for the support of Bryan S. Turner and members of the Committee for the Study of Religion at the Graduate Center of the City University of New York (CUNY). I would like to thank Barbara Rylko-Bauer, Sebastian Chrostowski, Ric Curtis, Gelya Frank, Samuel Heilman, Jack Jacobs, Joanna Michlic, Carolyn Nordstrom, Robert Riggs and Maria D. Vesperi for their useful insights, encouragement and assistance. I extend my deepest appreciation to Howard Horowitz and to the extended "Danielski" household in the US and Poland. The research on which this chapter is based was supported in part by a Mellon Foundation fellowship sponsored by the City University of New York Graduate Center, Committee for the Study of Religion; a research assistance grant from John Jay College, CUNY; and a PSC-CUNY Research Award.

Notes

1 *Neighbors* was first published in Poland in 2000.
2 Gross dedicated *Neighbors* to Shmulke, the witness, whose testimony serves as a main source for the author's reconstruction of that history.
3 Shmulke documented the events in Jedwabne in his book *La Denuncia: 10 de Julio de 1941*, coauthored with Yehudi Monestel Arce and published in Costa Rica in 2001.
4 Names of Polish Christian informants in this study are pseudonyms.
5 The IPN is a state commission for the prosecution of crimes against the Polish Nation http://www.ipn.gov.pl/portal/en/1/2/Institute_of_National_Remembrance__Commission_for_the_Prosecution_of_Crimes_agai.html (accessed 15 August 2010).
6 This quotation is from an interview I conducted with Rabbi Schudrich in 2008.
7 See Kurkowska (2008) on the construction of monuments and memory in Jedwabne, and Tokarska-Bakir (2008) on "the experience of Jedwabne" since the publication of *Neighbors*.
8 Varshney argues that "associational forms of interethnic engagement" are more solid than the everyday forms in terms of protecting against ethnic violence and keeping the peace (2001, 363).

9 I follow Tighe (2001) for the spelling of Ibrahim ibn Ya'qub.
10 This is not to suggest that "the Jew as other" was the only cultural symbol to inform Polish identity as a nation. Other tropes were invoked, including those developed by nineteenth-century Romantic writers and composers. For example, Adam Mickiewicz, author of *Pan Tadeusz*, the Polish national epic, developed a character that would become the iconic Polish folk hero. The mazurkas and polonaises by Chopin, himself a national icon, became quintessentially Polish.
11 The image of the Wandering Jew, ever "unsettled," cast out and exiled from an "original" homeland, is a key motif of the Jewish national movement, even as the legend itself is polysemic (see Anderson 1965; Konner 2003).
12 Sand offers a cogent description of the process: "Since the fundamentals of nation building almost always included some cultural components, linguistic or religious, that survived from earlier historical phases, clever engineering contrived to make them into hooks on which the history of nations could be skillfully hung. The people became a bridge between past and present, thrown across the deep mental chasm created by modernity, a bridge on which the professional historians of all new nation-states could comfortably parade" (2009, 27); see also Tokarska-Bakir on the significant role of historians in crafting national narratives in Poland (2007).
13 The two main Polish uprisings occurred in 1830–31 and 1863–64.
14 Number 13 of President Woodrow Wilson's Fourteen Points, a political speech made to the Senate, indicated US support of Polish independence: "An independent Polish state should be erected which should include the territories inhabited by indisputably Polish populations, which should be assured a free and secure access to the sea, and whose political and economic independence and territorial integrity should be guaranteed by international covenant." See http://avalon.law.yale.edu/20th_century/wilson14.asp (accessed 29 July 2011).
15 See Michlic (2006, 109–30) on anti-Jewish rhetoric and violence as it relates to the formation of the new Polish nation-state and the growing sway of ethno-nationalism in Poland in the period from 1919 to 1939 when the Third Reich and the Soviet Union invaded it.

References

Anderson, Benedict. 1991 [1983]. *Imagined Communities*. London and New York: Verso.
Anderson, George K. 1965. *The Legend of the Wandering Jew*. Lebanon, NH: Brown University Press.
Baumann, Zygmunt. 2005 [1989]. *Modernity and the Holocaust*. Cambridge: Polity Press.
Brand, William, ed. 2001. *Thou Shalt Not Kill: Poles on Jedwabne*. Warsaw: Towarzystwo "Wiez."
Blobaum, Robert, ed. 2005. *Anti-Semitism and its Opponents in Modern Poland*. Ithaca, NY: Cornell University Press.
Bowen, John. 1996. "The Myth of Global Ethnic Conflict." *Journal of Democracy* 7(4) (October): 3–14.
Chodakiewicz, Marek Jan. 2005. *The Massacre in Jedwabne, July 10, 1941: Before, During, After*. New York: East European Monographs, 655.
CNN. 2001. "Polish Mass Grave Dig Ends." Online: http://articles.cnn.com/2001-06-04/world/poland.grave_1_witold-kulesza-search-for-more-graves-exhumation?_s=PM:WORLD (accessed 16 August 2010).
Davies, Norman. 1982. *God's Playground: A History of Poland, Volume 1: The Origins to 1795*. New York: Columbia University Press.

Frost, Robert I. 2004. *After the Deluge: Poland-Lithuania and the Second Northern War, 1655–1660.* Cambridge Studies in Early Modern History. Cambridge: Cambridge University Press.
Gellner, Ernst. 2006 [1983]. *Nations and Nationalism.* Malden, MA: Blackwell Publishing.
Glowacka, Dorota and Joanna Zylinska. 2007. *Imaginary Neighbors: Mediating Polish-Jewish Relations after the Holocaust.* Lincoln: University of Nebraska Press.
Gulden, Zenon and Jacek Wijaczka. 1997. "The Accusation of Ritual Murder in Poland, 1500–1800." In *Polin, Volume 10: Jews in Early Modern Poland,* edited by Gershon David Hundert, 99–140. London: The Littman Library of Jewish Civilization.
Gross, Jan T. 2002 [2001]. *Neighbors: The Destruction of the Jewish Community in Jedwabne, Poland.* Princeton: Princeton University Press.
Hinton, Alexander Laban, ed. 2002. *Annihilating Difference: The Anthropology of Genocide.* Berkeley: University of California Press.
Hobsbawm, Eric J. 2004 [1990]. *Nations and Nationalism since 1780: Programme, Myth, Reality.* New York: Cambridge University Press.
Hobsbawm, Eric and Terence Ranger, eds. 1989 [1983]. *The Invention of Tradition.* New York: Cambridge University Press.
Hoerder, Dirk. 2002. *Cultures in Contact: World Migrations in the Second Millennium.* Durham, NC and London: Duke University Press.
Hoffman, Eva. 1997. *Shtetl: The Life and Death of a Small Town and the World of Polish Jews.* Boston: Mariner Books/Houghton Mifflin Company.
Huntington, Samuel P. 2011 [1996]. *The Clash of Civilizations and the Remaking of the World Order.* New York: Simon & Schuster.
Institute for National Remembrance. 2003. "Beginning of the Search in the Jedwabne Site." 18 November. Online: http://www.ipn.gov.pl/portal/en/19/192/Beginning_of_the_Search_in_the_Jedwabne_Site.html (accessed 15 August 2010).
Kaplan, Robert D. 1996 [1993]. *Balkan Ghosts: A Journey Through History.* New York: Vintage Books.
Konner, Melvin. 2003. *Unsettled: An Anthropology of the Jews.* New York: Viking Compass, Penguin.
Kurkowska, Marta. 2008. "Jedwabne and Wizna: Monuments and Memory in the Lomza Region." In *Polin, Volume 20: Making Holocaust Memory,* edited by Gabriel N. Finder, Natlaia Aleksiun, Antony Polonsky and Jan Schwarz, 244–70. London: The Littman Library of Jewish Civilization.
Lewis, Bernard. 1990. "The Roots of Muslim Rage." *Atlantic Magazine.* September. Online: http://www.theatlantic.com/magazine/archive/1990/09/the-roots-of-muslim-rage/4643/ (accessed 10 June 2011).
Matteson, John T. 2001. "Grave Discussions: The Image of the Sepulchre in Webster, Emerson and Melville." *The New England Quarterly* 74(3): 419–46.
Meijers, Daniel. 1991. "The Sociogenesis of the Hasidic Movement: An Orthodox-Jewish Regime and State Formation in Eighteenth Century Poland." In *Religious Regimes and State Formation: Perspectives from European Ethnology,* edited by Eric R. Wolf, Adrianus Koster and Daniel Meijers. Albany: State University of New York Press.
Michlic, Joanna Beata. 2002. "Coming to Terms with the 'Dark Past': The Polish Debate about the Jedwabne Massacre." *ACTA* 21. Jerusalem: Hebrew University of Jerusalem. Online: http://sicsa.huji.ac.il/actatxt1.html (accessed 11 September 2010).
———. 2006. *Poland's Threatening Other: The Image of the Jew from 1880 to the Present.* Lincoln: University of Nebraska Press.
Nordstrom, Carolyn. 2009. "Global Fractures." In *An Anthropology of War: Views from the Frontline,* edited by Alisse Waterston. New York: Berghahn Books.

Polonsky, Antony and Joanna B. Michlic, eds. 2004. *The Neighbors Respond: The Controversy over the Jedwabne Massacre in Poland*. Princeton: Princeton University Press.
Prak, Maartin Roy. 2001. *Early Modern Capitalism: Economic and Social Change in Europe, 1400–1800*. London: Psychology Press, Taylor & Francis Group.
Reyna, Stephen. 2009. "Global Warring Today: 'Maybe Somebody Needs to Explain'". In *An Anthropology of War: Views from the Frontline*, edited by Alisse Waterston. New York: Berghahn Books.
Rushkoff, Douglas. 2004. *Nothing Sacred: The Truth About Judaism*. New York: Three Rivers Press.
Said, Edward. 2001. *Reflections on Exile and Other Essays*. Cambridge, MA: Harvard University Press.
Sand, Shlomo. 2009. *The Invention of the Jewish People*. Translated by Yael Lotan. London and New York: Verso.
Smith, Anthony D. 2010 [2001]. *Nationalism: Theory, Ideology, History*. Cambridge: Polity Press.
Ta-Shma, Israel. 1997. "On the History of the Jews in Twelfth- and Thirteenth-Century Poland." In *Polin, Volume 10: Jews in Early Modern Poland*, edited by Gershon David Hundert, 287–317. London: The Littman Library of Jewish Civilization.
Tighe, Carl. 2001. "*Kazimuh* – Jewish Kraków." *Journal of European Studies* 31: 187–215.
Tokarska-Bakir, Joanna. 2007. "Jedwabne: History as Fetish." In *Imaginary Neighbors: Mediating Polish-Jewish Relations after the Holocaust*, edited by Dorota Glowacka and Joanna Zylinska. Lincoln: University of Nebraska Press.
———. 2008. "You from Jedwabne." In *Polin, Volume 20: Making Holocaust Memory*, edited by Gabriel N. Finder, Natlaia Aleksiun, Antony Polonsky and Jan Schwarz. London: The Littman Library of Jewish Civilization: 413–28.
Varshney, Ashutosh. 2001. "Ethnic Conflict and Civil Society: India and Beyond." *World Politics* 53 (April): 362–98.
———. 2002. *Ethnic Conflict and Civic Life: Hindus and Muslims in India*. New Haven: Yale University Press.
Waterston, Alisse. 2005. "The Story of My Story: An Anthropology of Violence, Dispossession, and Diaspora." *Anthropological Quarterly* 78(1): 43–61.
Waterston, Alisse and Barbara Rylko-Bauer. 2006. "Out of the Shadows of History and Memory: Personal Family Narratives in Ethnographies of Rediscovery." *American Ethnologist* 33(3): 397–412.
Waserstein Kahn, Samuel and Yehudi Monestel Arce. 2001. *La Denuncia. 10 de Julio de 1941*. San José, Costa Rica: Editorial Guayacán Centroamericana, S. A.
Wilson, Woodrow. 1918. *President Woodrow Wilson's Fourteen Points*. New Haven: Lillian Goldman Law Library, Yale University. Online: http://avalon.law.yale.edu/20th_century/wilson14.asp (accessed 29 July 2011).
Wolf, Eric. R. 1966. *Peasants*. Englewood Cliffs: Prentice Hall.
———. 1997 [1982]. *Europe and the People Without History*. Berkeley: University of California Press.

Chapter 2

A MESSIANIC MULTIPLE: WEST PAPUA, JULY 1998

Eben Kirksey

Introduction: Signs of Hope

Hopes connected to the arrival of a messiah contain "the attraction, invincible élan or affirmation of an unpredictable future-to-come (or even of a past-to-come-again)," in the words of Jacques Derrida (2002, 253). "Not only must one not renounce the emancipatory desire," writes Derrida, "it is necessary to insist on it more than ever" (2002, 74). Describing a universal structure of feeling that works independent of any specific historical moment or cultural location, Derrida describes what he calls *messianicity without messianism*, a quasi-transcendental notion that "is not bound up with any particular moment of (political or general) history or culture" (2002, 253). Derrida's sense of expectation is thus not oriented towards a specific program, event, project or messiah (Derrida 1994, 24–5; 2002, 167). His idea of messianicity is that it is "without content," in contrast to messianism which contains specific objects of desire (Derrida 1994, 28).[1]

Rather than Derrida's messianicity without messianism, or fixation on the arrival of any single messiah, I discovered a different sort of messianic logic at work in West Papua, the half of New Guinea under Indonesian rule. West Papuans harbor hopes for a *messianic multiple*; they have pinned their freedom dreams on multiple specific figures, political events and future possibilities.[2] The messianic multiple is a structure of feeling that moves around like liquid mercury – dancing about in different directions, coalescing around multiple figures of desire.[3] Operating in the imagination of a single person, the messianic multiple animates a cautious form of hope that flits around from object to object, probing the field of historical possibility. When it catches hold of a crowd, a multitude of creative agents, the impossible comes within reach (Hardt and Negri 2004, 56–7).[4]

My first research in West Papua took place in 1998, amidst acute environmental, political and social crises that were rocking Indonesia and Southeast Asia. An El Niño drought hit the previous year, coinciding with the start of the Asian financial crisis that left millions of people holding devalued currency (Hill 1996, 93–103). The drought led to massive forest fires, smog clouds and widespread crop failures. A "poison fog blanket" covered the region, in the lurid words of one journalist (Vidal 1997, 3). The island of New Guinea was hit by an erratic snowfall as well as by outbreaks of diseases such as malaria, tuberculosis, diarrhea and cholera (Kompas 1997; Walters 1997, 6–7). Over seven hundred people reportedly died from illness and famine in West Papua alone (Bird 1998, 172–5). In the first three weeks of 1998 there were more than thirty outbreaks of violence in Indonesia, which is more than the whole previous year (Lioe 1998). In Java, Indonesia's center of political power, social unrest spread like wildfire.

For many Indonesians these crises were oddly signs of hope – they fueled speculation about revolutionary transitions on the horizon.[5] The corrupt regime of Major-General Suharto, who had been president for over thirty years, was beginning to fail. The homogeneous, empty time of the Suharto regime was quickly giving way to a new era in which the Indonesian people began to focus their collective energy on particular figures and anticipate coming horizons of transformation (cf. Benjamin 1968, 261). The collective excitement of the Indonesian people – an expectation of sweeping changes that could come at any moment – was driven by a messianic spirit.[6]

Messiahs, like many other figures, embody hope in their flesh and blood. Seeing "every second of time [as] the strait gate through which the Messiah might march" produces a revolutionary consciousness, in the words of Walter Benjamin, the celebrated German philosopher from the Frankfurt School (1968, 264).[7] Desires for sudden transformations in Indonesia were not pinned on a specific messiah. Instead of anticipating a messiah marching through the gate, this movement imagined the moment when Suharto would be forced to march out through the gates of the presidential palace – never again to return. Suharto became a figure who embodied all of the ills facing the nation – a doppelgänger of the messiah, embodying evil rather than hope.

Arriving in West Papua on the heels of Suharto's departure in July 1998, I found a messianic spirit on the loose. After the resignation of Suharto, dreams were being refigured around multiple objects emerging on imagined horizons. Stumbling onto the scene amid powerful countervailing forces, I found that West Papuan activists were bringing a seemingly impossible collective dream, plans for establishing an independent nation, into contact with the field of historical possibility. In startling encounters with indigenous activists, I learned about improbable conspiracies among world leaders. Wrangling with

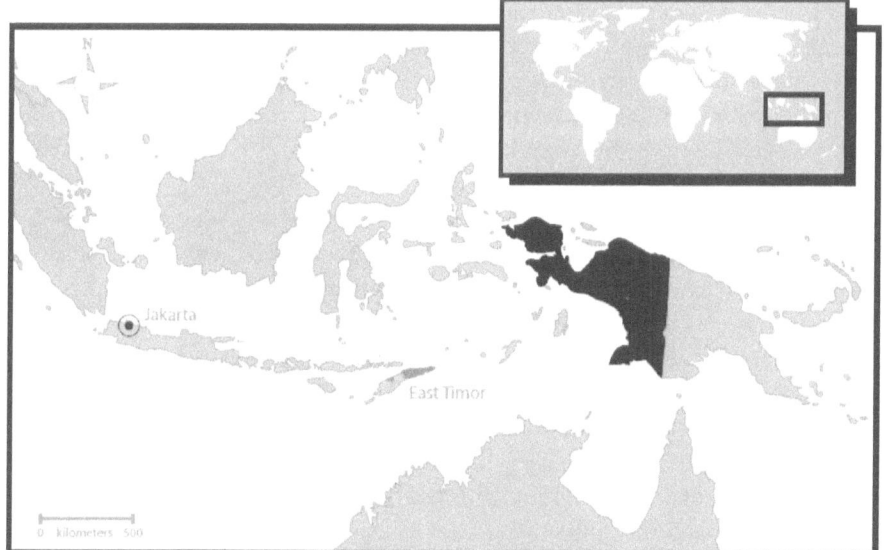

Figure 1. West Papua

intractable bureaucracies and meeting people who refracted global history through a strange lens, I found that messianic dreams were capturing my imagination. Admittedly, I was fascinated by, deeply fearful of, and inextricably implicated in, the messianic promises of the third millennium, the fabled era that began to unfold as my fieldwork was taking place.[8] Like many people my age in the United States – members of what some commentators have dubbed the "millennial generation" – I felt a growing sense of anticipation as the Y2K approached (Haraway 1999, 41). I had lost faith in the predictable march of progress and the bureaucratic institutions governing the modern world. Personally I was never a believer in organized religion. Still, I found secular elements of the messianic idea beginning to move within me.

The United Nations, He Has Sins

Amidst sensational reports of major transformations on future horizons, I settled into a mundane routine in Abepura, a suburb of Jayapura, the capital city of West Papua. I rented a small room in a maze of cinderblock walls, tin roofs and gravel alleyways. Nine West Papuan and Indonesian students became my flatmates in a ramshackle boarding house that had been cobbled together out of plywood and tin roofing. Our shared cooking facilities consisted of a counter, a garden hose and a portable kerosene stove. As I tried to go about a narrowly defined program of anthropological research, as I attempted to study the El Niño drought that had hit the region in 1997, West Papuans began to make and commemorate history in the streets. Enrolling in anthropology classes at the local university, trying to steer clear of political activity, I became a regular patron at the university library, where I read through a treasure trove of theses written by West Papuan students and a haphazard collection of books in Indonesian and English.

One afternoon, outside the library, I was waylaid by Agus, a short, older man with a deeply creased face who wore a soul patch – a small beard on the lower lip that was once equally popular in rural parts of West Papua and metropolitan centers of style in the global north. He asked me to return the next day, around the same time, with a tape recorder. When I showed up, as promised, he launched into a monologue in thickly accented Logat Papua. "On this little tape I want to record a statement. If you go to the Global World Body's place of gathering, please pass on this language," he said. We were standing outside the library, with passers by looking at us askance. "This language is named the rough language, villager language, that I am talking. You can translate it into refined English if you want, to pass it along."

Agus was the first of many West Papuan activists who tried to gain my ear. I was perhaps expecting to encounter a representative of an indigenous culture who would teach me about the opposite of what I already knew: telling me myths in contrast to history, revealing ideas about cyclical time instead of a linear model, describing immanent gods instead of a transcendent God.[9] Instead of these predictable differences, I discovered startling and disquieting tales when I tried to listen carefully to indigenous voices (Tsing 2007, 39). Seemingly familiar stories were related to me in unfamiliar ways. As Agus told me about his freedom dreams – trying to translate his lived experience into the language of history, law and human rights – I found myself struggling to keep up.

Agus talked about the US officials who betrayed his nation, allegations that I was unable to understand at the time. "Kennedy, and his secretaries, have sins," Agus told me. "He already saw, but he pretended not to know. He already saw, but he plays dumb. It doesn't matter, just kill them." I tried hard to follow his wandering narrative, without dates, where the identities of different historical actors and institutions bled together. Agus knew that his people had been betrayed by global power brokers. But he was only able to partially translate his knowledge into a historical narrative I could readily understand. "My message is that the United Nations, he has sins," Agus said. "Above the UN is God, below him are governments. Is that the Global World Body? Is that the UN? Does the UN rule the kingdom of heaven? No, he is just a regular human."

I left this encounter feeling uneasy and confused. Already socialized into the political culture of Indonesia, I knew that Agus was telling me about things that the government deemed sensitive. We would both get in serious trouble, even in the post-Suharto era, if the authorities caught us talking politics. Was there truth to this story about the Kennedy family and the United Nations? Or was Agus just rambling, perhaps delusional? Only years later, after long hours spent reading archival documents and piecing together different events in other interviews, did I begin to appreciate the complexity of the historical events that Agus was trying to tell me about that afternoon outside the library.

In 1962, after a protracted military conflict between the Dutch and the Indonesians over the future of West Papua, the Kennedy administration intervened. One cynical US official, Robert Komer, a balding and bespectacled former CIA analyst who was a key architect of Kennedy's policy on Southeast Asia, argued in an internal White House memo: "A pro-Bloc (if not Communist) Indonesia is [an] infinitely greater threat [...] than Indo possession of a few thousand square miles of cannibal land" (Pemberton 1987, 86). The words of Agus echoed in my head when I later came across these historical sources: "Kennedy may be dead, and his secretaries may be on pensions, but their sins must not be covered up. It must be transparent, it must be open, to save those of us who remain, the dregs of a race that is being killed."

West Papuans, who have long been viewed in Eurocentric circles as peoples without history, are clearly aware of the historical agreements, events and actors that enabled Indonesia to take over their land. Translating West Papuan historical consciousness into no-nonsense historical narrative is no easy task. Robert F. Kennedy, the president's brother and then attorney general, traveled to Indonesia and Holland in February 1962 to begin talks about this disputed territory. US officials helped broker the New York Agreement, a ceasefire between Holland and the Republic of Indonesia that was signed on 15 August 1962. This accord effectively transferred West Papua from Dutch to Indonesian control via a temporary UN protectorate. The treaty guaranteed West Papuans the right to participate in an "act of self-determination" that would give them the opportunity to decide "(a) whether they wish to remain with Indonesia; or (b) whether they wish to sever their ties with Indonesia" (Subandrio, van Rouen and Schurmann 1962). A referendum that clearly presented this choice never took place.[10] In 1969, Indonesia staged the so-called Act of Free Choice, where 1,022 handpicked Papuan delegates, representing a population of around one million, unanimously declared their desire to join Indonesia.

"In the opinion of the Western observers and the Papuans who have spoken out about this, the Act of Free Choice ended up as a sham," concludes Pieter Drooglever, who wrote an 854-page historical monograph on the subject. After extensive research in Dutch government archives, as well as a careful study of UN, US and Australian records, Drooglever wrote: "A press-ganged electorate acting under a great deal of pressure appeared to have unanimously declared itself in favor of Indonesia" (Drooglever 2009, 758). Cold War politics and the interests of "big power," concludes historian John Saltford, meant that independence for West Papua was never considered to be a serious option once the New York Agreement of 1962 was signed (Saltford 2003, 180).

The promise of an act of self-determination contained in the New York Agreement took on heightened significance amid broader political crises that were sweeping Indonesia in 1998. In June of that year, at the moment when Agus spoke to me outside the library, people throughout West Papua saw new horizons of possibility opening up. Unbeknownst to me at the time, a letter from US congressional representatives was circulating in West Papua, spreading like wildfire as activists made hundreds of photocopies and handed them out to trusted kin and friends. The letter was addressed to Indonesia's new president, B. J. Habibie, and called for dialogue on the political status of East Timor and West Papua. The leading signatories were representative Christopher Smith, a Republican from New Jersey, and representative Patrick Kennedy, the son of senator Ted Kennedy and a Democrat from Rhode Island. With the Kennedy family name on this letter, many West Papuans believed that global power brokers were ready to right historical wrongs (Rutherford 2012, 56).

Amid an audible political buzz on the streets, I struggled to find certainty about my immigration status. I had been granted a visa from the Indonesian embassy in Washington that was only good for two months and I wanted to extend it another six months. Again, I found myself waiting for minor bureaucratic miracles. On 1 July 1998, I began the day by waiting in line at the Immigration Office. Years later, when I started researching West Papua's movement for freedom (*merdeka*) in earnest, I learned that this day was the 27th anniversary of the transmission of an independence manifesto over a single-sideband (SSB) radio. My journal entries over the next few days chronicled my struggle to navigate Indonesian officialdom and my initial attempts to understand the political developments taking place all around me:

Wednesday, 1 July 1998

Early this morning I went to the Immigration Office in downtown Jayapura. After I quietly waited for over two hours, the officials told me that I needed an additional letter of support from Bird of Paradise University before they could process my visa extension. I passed by a small demonstration outside the Regional People's Provincial Assembly (DPRD) after I left Immigration. Beyond a core group – a tight knot of people who were passionately chanting and dancing – people were casual and friendly. An hour later the group of protesters had swelled to about 100 people. Police in riot gear surrounded the protesters, while several thousand quiet onlookers stood by. Later in the day I heard that the Morning Star flag, the banner of West Papua's independence movement, had been waved at this event. In the afternoon I traveled an hour and a half by a series of public buses to meet with a high-level university official. I asked for a letter required by the Immigration Office. He promised to produce it by tomorrow morning.[11]

Thursday, 2 July 1998

This morning there was a massive show of force by the police and army in downtown Jayapura. Hundreds of troops lined the streets. As I walked to the post office to check my email at the cybercafé, the streets were strangely silent. No demonstrators were in sight. From there I went directly to campus, picked up the letter, and then delivered it to Immigration. After I waited for several hours, the immigration officials changed what they told me the day before. They asked me to return in late August, so that I could extend my visa just as the new semester is about to begin at the university.

Friday, 3 July 1998

Today I introduced myself to the head of the anthropology department at the university. I presented him with all my documents, and then we walked together to the other side of campus. Along the road we bumped into Michael Howard, a visiting professor from Simon Fraser University. A small group of protesters gathered nearby, in front of the main university buildings at the side of the road. A truck full of Indonesian troops, Mobile Brigade (Brimob) police in riot gear, drove by on the road. I could see many of the troops turn their heads in apparent surprise to look at the demonstration. But the truck did not stop. Professor Howard left, and then some other staff from the anthropology department joined our conversation. One of the staff members had just returned from a Discovery Channel filming expedition to the remote Mamberamo River. He laughed with us about the field methods of the British film crew and the American anthropologist who accompanied them. When a question was asked during filmed interviews, the people would ask for money before answering.

Our conversation was suddenly interrupted by people running from the direction of the demo. Immediately everyone around me began to run. Most kept an amused air. I managed to get into a nearby canteen, along with most of the people who had been talking with me. The proprietor quickly locked the door and pulled the curtains over the windows.

We continued our conversation as people flashed by the windows. Several minutes later intense bursts of popping explosions began. Firecrackers? Soon we all realized that this was gunfire. It must be rubber bullets and blanks, we agreed. The shooting continued in drawn-out clouds for several minutes. Then a pause. Suddenly the explosions began again – this time much closer. We all scrambled to find limited protection under tables and against the wall. After several minutes of silence we all returned to our seats and sheepishly ordered sugary lime drinks. We chatted nervously. When we could see other students and professors calmly walking outside, we left the canteen by the back door. After slipping out a back gate of the campus, which was being guarded by students, we heard the first news of students being shot. One law student was shot in the head – the bullet entered near his eye and exited out the back of his head along with most of his brains. A young middle-school girl, an uninvolved bystander, had also just been shot in the leg.[12]

One of the anthropology lecturers who had been in the canteen with me was so scared that he could hardly talk. He was Indonesian, a recent arrival from Java. He feared retribution from the West Papuan students. "Does reform always have to be like this?" he asked.

Walking along one of the side streets near campus, we ran into some professors from the English language department. "Why did the shooting start?" we asked. There were rumors that the students had been throwing stones. Someone else said that the students had roughed up an Indonesian intelligence agent who was spying on the demonstration. "We are seeing the beginning of a revolution," they joked.

Over the course of a few days, I made abrupt transitions from the dead halls of Indonesian bureaucracy into lively spaces where the pulse of revolutionary momentum was accelerating. For a brief moment, when I ran with my newfound friends from the anthropology department into the canteen ahead of the Indonesian police, we were swept up in the crowd "all happy and excited over this bit of fun" (Orwell 1936).[13] Then, in the space of a few minutes, we collectively experienced a rapid succession of affective responses from nervous anxiety, to raw fear, to humor. With this sudden rush of emotions, we did not know what to expect. It seemed like anything could happen at any time.

Wild rumors started to circulate about my presence on the margins of the demonstration at Bird of Paradise University. The students were telling each other that Amnesty International had sent me to campus on a fact-finding mission. When some of my new West Papuan friends intimated that they knew about my human rights work, I protested. I tried to convince them that

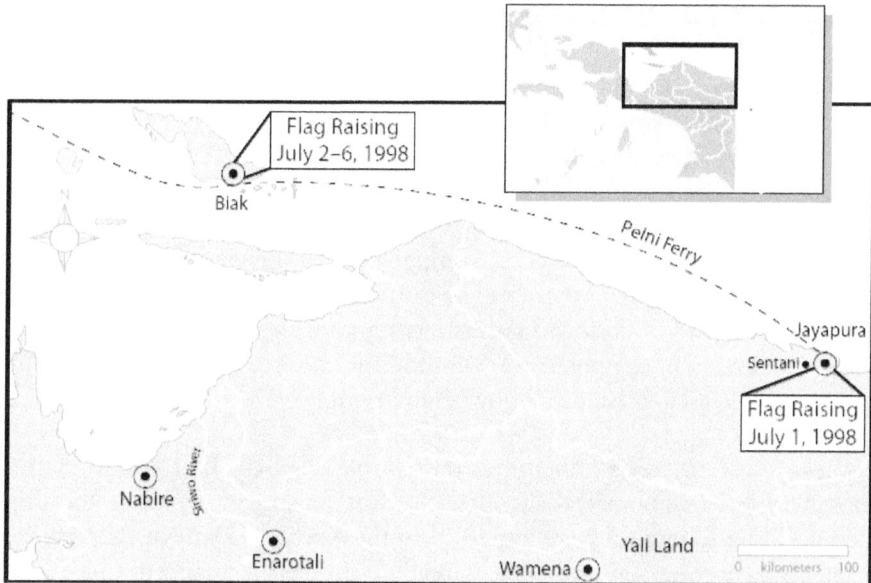

Figure 2. North coast of West Papua

I really was just an anthropology student, working on independent research. Some seemed to believe me. Others, with a wink and a nod, promised not to blow my cover. "Be careful," one West Papuan student cautioned as we relaxed together on the front porch of my boarding house on the night after the demonstration. "Indonesian spies are starting to follow you." Shaken by the violence at Bird of Paradise University and worried about getting in trouble with the cops, I spontaneously decided to leave Jayapura the following day. I had befriended a Belgian entomologist who promised to introduce me to a Mee community, a group of hunter-gatherers living in the Siriwo River Valley. Hoping to leave the trouble behind in Jayapura, I set out to conduct what I then saw as real anthropological research in the hinterlands.

Skirting a police blockade in downtown Jayapura the next afternoon – Saturday, 4 July 1998 – I jostled along with other sweaty bodies toward the harbor. Along with several thousand West Papuan and Indonesian passengers, I boarded an ocean liner, a passenger ferry in the Indonesian government Pelni fleet that plies fixed routes with predictable regularity. Undoubtedly many of my fellow travelers were, like me, fleeing recent unrest. The ship was destined for Biak, an island off the north coast of West Papua. In Biak I planned to get on another boat, a ferry to Nabire, a coastal city with logging roads leading to Mee lands in the Siriwo River Valley. Instead of being a predictable journey, however, the passenger ship delivered me straight into another protest.

Sunday, 5 July 1998, 7:00 AM

Our ship has just docked in the Biak harbor, and outside a crowd is chanting "*Papua merdeka!*" [Free Papua!]. The Morning Star flag is flying on a nearby water tower. As soon as the ship docked, several young men boarded and ran around the ship waving banners and shouting. Other passengers are saying that these men are now asking for money. My newfound friend and traveling companion, the Belgian entomologist, appears to be the only other foreigner on the passenger ship. The harbor is devoid of any Indonesian government authorities. These youths have reportedly been occupying the harbor for the last several days. My connecting ferry to Nabire is nowhere in sight.

Unbeknownst to me at the time, the people of Biak had endowed this passenger ferry with special significance. Rumors spread ahead of the ship that powerful foreigners were aboard.[14] In the words of Danilyn Rutherford, a cultural anthropologist who has already published a nuanced analysis of the dynamics that unfolded in the Biak harbor, "evidence of foreign attention brought to mind not only the gaze of outsiders, but also their impending presence." Several weeks later, Rutherford arrived in Biak to interview her trusted long-term friends about recent events. One of her friends talked about going to meet the ship that I happened to be on. As he was leaving home, his neighbor asked him with great excitement, "has the foreigners' ship arrived?" (Rutherford 2012, 56).

Years later I interviewed an elder Biak cultural leader who helped me understand the excitement that had been building in the crowd: "There was something that was awaited with much anticipation by the West Papuans. In three days the UN was to arrive. This anticipation gathered the masses, pulled in the masses from the villages" (Anonymous 2002a). On 4 July 1998, the day before the ship's scheduled arrival, when the Morning Star flag was already aloft in the Biak harbor, it was announced that Jamsheed Marker, special envoy of UN secretary general Kofi Annan, would be passing through Jakarta. Marker had been sent by Annan after pressure from Portugal, the former colonial power in East Timor. At the same time as the flag raising in Biak, there were four days of clashes between pro- and anti-Indonesian groups in East Timor that left at least two people dead. The mandate of this UN envoy was limited to reviving the stalled dialogue between Indonesia and Portugal about East Timor's future (Anonymous 1998). Members of the crowd in the Biak harbor were nonetheless waiting to see if a UN envoy was on board the passenger ferry as it docked. More rumors began to circulate. CNN journalists were reportedly on board. As passengers tried to disembark, people thronged aboard, caught up in the excitement of the moment. Members of the waiting crowd were carefully scrutinizing the passengers, searching for messianic figures who might be traveling in disguise.

Local Messianic Visions

Months earlier a small prayer group had formed in Biak. The prayer group was named after two biblical figures, the prophet Deborah and the warrior Barak, who together led an army of ten thousand.[15] Members of this group began to think of themselves as biblical Israelites. Instead of living in Egypt under oppression of the Pharaoh, they were living in Indonesia, the largest Islamic nation in the world. Hoping to follow in the footsteps of mid-twentieth-century Israelites, the members of the Deborah and Barak prayer group quietly began laying the spiritual groundwork for creating their own nation. The prophesied coming of a particular messiah, the Second Coming of Christ, was inspiring messianic visions as the year 2000 approached. In Christian communities around the world, including parishes in Biak, possibility of the imminent return of Jesus to Earth seemed to become very real (Anonymous 2002b; Giay 2007; Timmer 2000, 30).

Shortly after the fall of Suharto, exhilarating news began arriving in Biak. Members of the Deborah and Barak prayer group heard about the demonstration outside the provincial assembly – the peaceful protest I had glimpsed after one of my visits to the immigration department. They heard that the Morning Star flag had been raised in Jayapura. Rumors began to spread that a powerful outsider was about to arrive in Biak. On the evening of 1 July 1998, the same day as the Jayapura protest, Tanjung Karma, a member of a prominent Biak family, conferred with the leaders of the Deborah and Barak prayer group. They decided to mobilize immediately for a flag raising. There was a person from the outside, said Tanjung, who would speak to the Biak crowd during the event. Filep Karma, Tanjung's brother, who happened to be passing through Biak, was this "person from the outside." Karma was a civil servant in the governor's office in Jayapura, who had become savvy about foreign worlds during earlier studies in the Philippines. In the Biak tongue, Filep Karma was regarded as *amber beba*, 'a big foreigner' (Rutherford 2003).

Filep Karma had already been caught by the revolutionary spirit. Reading the letter from US congressmen Patrick Kennedy and Christopher Smith that was circulating through underground activist networks had spurred him to action. Years later, Karma, as a civil servant in the provincial administration of the Indonesian government, told me: "When I read that letter from the members of the US Congress, it lit my passion for the struggle on fire." Karma became determined to lead local Biak groups in raising the Morning

Star flag. "It happened spontaneously," Karma recalled. "We didn't have a planning meeting. I didn't really know the people in Biak, and they didn't really know me."

After getting inspired to do something, Filep Karma was at loose ends. He did not have a Morning Star flag. "I had seen the flag before, but I didn't remember what it looked like. We looked all over Biak but couldn't find one." Teaming up with an elderly Biak matron who has since passed away, Karma set out to make a flag. "Sewing would have taken too long; the police would have caught us by the time we were done. So we bought some white cloth along with blue and red spray paint."

Before dawn the next day, 2 July, the freshly painted Morning Star flag was raised atop the water tower in Biak's harbor. With the flag overhead, Filep Karma gave a public speech that linked Christian rhetoric to desires for national freedom: "The struggle in West Papua, and my own struggle, is based on the primary law of the Bible. This law was lovingly given to us by the Lord, your God" (Elsham 1999, 11). Karma urged the people gathered – at that point just members of the Deborah and Barak prayer group and a few others – to use peaceful tactics of resistance.

Revolutions are unexpected for everyone, even their organizers (Jameson 2009, 62). At first just a few people gathered in the streets of Biak. The flag began to draw larger and larger crowds. By noon more than a thousand people had joined them. Filep Karma urged the crowd to "defend the flag only using the Bible and hymns as weapons." He told the assembled masses: "Indonesian law states that security personnel or police can let bullets fly if their life is at risk. If we are only armed with the Bible and hymns, then the police will not shoot us" (Elsham 1999, 10–11). At 2:30 that afternoon, a joint police and military operation attempted to disperse the crowd at the base of the water tower. They launched canisters of tear gas into the crowd with no apparent effect. When a low-ranking police officer, a second-class sergeant, beat an elderly demonstrator named Thonci Wabiser, the crowd spontaneously retaliated, demolishing a truck belonging to Indonesian security forces. During this confrontation, 13 members of the security forces sustained injuries. Two of these men, reportedly in critical condition, were evacuated to Java for medical treatment. The security forces eventually retreated and, for the time being, left the demonstrators at the base of the water tower in peace (Elsham 1999, 13–14).

Looking to the future rather than to violent ends, Derrida draws a helpful distinction between the apocalyptic and the messianic.[16] Departing from the work of Marx, who perhaps imprudently writes about the end of history (in the name of the beginning of a different one), Derrida describes a "desert-like messianism." His messianicity without messianism is like an "abyssal and chaotic desert, if chaos describes first of all the immensity, excessiveness, disproportion in the gaping hole of the open mouth" (Derrida 1994, 28). Perhaps a few West Papuans were quietly holding on to the spirit of contentless messianicity, waiting for the unexpected to appear out of an empty abyss, while they were gathered under the water tower. But the public speeches and accounts from survivors suggest otherwise – that the crowd harbored freedom dreams teeming with heterogeneous content.

There was not a clear consensus about a single object of desire as the crowd rallied under the flag. In other words, the people who took part in this event were not fixated on any one thing.[17] Instead the crowd anticipated many different things, a messianic multiple.[18] The growing excitement was animated by both secular and religious hopes. Will UN special envoy Jamsheed Marker come to witness the demonstration? Perhaps Kofi Annan himself? Will CNN journalists arrive? Jesus? Or maybe the messianic spirit was already working in Filep Karma, prompting his bold actions. Imagination met collaborative action in this moment. As the crowd defiantly gathered under the water tower, a single future event came into view against the broader background of historical possibility. The protesters imagined the moment when West Papua would be granted independence. In a speech under the Morning Star flag, Filep Karma declared:

> We, the people of West Papua, pledge to struggle to uphold the ideal of the independence of West Papua.
>
> We, the people of West Papua, declare that the Republic of Indonesia cannot interfere in the affairs of West Papua.
>
> We, the people of West Papua, ask that our security be guaranteed by the United Nations and by no one else. (Human Rights Watch 1998)

With this statement Karma was trying to welcome "distant audiences, earthly and divine," in the words of Danilyn Rutherford (2012, 97). But Karma's speech ultimately failed to find a proper reception among heavenly hosts or abroad. His words were heard only by his local followers and the security forces stationed nearby. Still, for the assembled crowd, his speech helped bring a seemingly impossible desire, national independence, within reach. Some revolutionary movements anticipate changes that will occur solely as a result of outside intervention, while others see that concrete action in the world is necessary.[19] The Biak protesters took bold steps by assembling on the streets. By staging the demonstration in the harbor and raising the Morning Star flag, they amped up the momentum of the revolution. Yet after this initial action, the group lacked direction. They waited in vain for outside help. At the time, no one knew if the demonstration would end in bloody defeat or in recognition of the demands for independence articulated by Karma. Everyone held their breath to see if their collective hopes would be actualized.[20] Everyone was waiting, searching future horizons for signs of what might come next.

Sunday, 5 July 1998, 3:00 PM

We waited for the excitement to die down before getting off the ship. Many offices in the harbor had been ransacked and covered with graffiti proclaiming freedom for West Papua. Papers were strewn all over the lawn. No police or military troops were to be seen, and all the shops in the nearby market were boarded up. The entomologist and I stopped to chat with protesters who were guarding the gate to the harbor. They told us that a crowd had turned over a police truck and injured a number of officers a few days ago. Surprisingly no West Papuans have yet been killed in retaliation. A Hercules troop carrier flew in yesterday, they said, carrying about five hundred soldiers. The men whom I talked with at the gate were afraid that there could be a major retaliation any time. They were afraid to leave the dock area. If they leave the safe space of the harbor, the men said, the military would single them out and kill them.

The men standing watch at the gate to the harbor were visibly disappointed when they realized that they were talking to the only two foreigners who had arrived on the ship. We were disoriented from our overnight journey and sweaty from the midmorning sun. Everyone quickly surmised that we were not emissaries from the United Nations. Looks of dread began to spread over the faces of the young men. They were anticipating violent retribution by Indonesian troops at any moment. Christian messianic hopes are often accompanied by ambivalent fears. Pessimism about the course of current history is often wedded to desires for ultimate salvation (Harding 1994, 14–44). The Great Tribulation, which has perhaps already begun, will end horrifically for unbelievers and gloriously for the faithful. Some people gathered under the Morning Star flag in the Biak harbor began to wonder if their own faith was strong enough for them to endure the coming trials. The day after the arrival of the passenger ship, Indonesian security forces launched an all-out assault on protesters who were still camped out under the water tower. In the early morning hours of 6 July 1998, Indonesian soldiers and police officers surrounded the sleeping masses. They opened fire just before dawn (Elsham 1999, 19–20).

Monday, 6 July 1998

The entomologist was sure that an Indonesian spy watched us yesterday when we were talking with the West Papuan men guarding the gate to the harbor. He suggested that we stay at a relatively upscale hotel to reduce our chances of being interrogated. After checking in to Hotel Irian, a colonial-era building next to the airport, I ate a lunch of cream of mushroom soup and pasta with marinara sauce. The marinara sauce turned out to be ketchup with seafood.

This morning I heard what sounded like sporadic gunshots from the direction of the harbor. Later people out on the street told me that the harbor had been sealed off by a "leg fence" of Indonesian troops to ensure that none of the protesters would escape. The Morning Star flag had been taken down. Throughout the day I heard reports about how many people had been hunted down and killed. The numbers ranged from 2 to 60. One man told me that he saw large groups of people running through the streets that night, fleeing the police and military forces. The people had set up warning systems to let each other know when troops were coming. They would make noise by beating on oil drums. In the early afternoon I heard the loud report of a nearby gun. I peered around my door, and all the people whom I could see were staring across the road in the direction of the airport runway. A man had apparently just been shot at point-blank range. I ate dinner, rice and fried egg, at a small canteen in the airport. All the other customers in the canteen were soldiers. They wore green camo outfits and carried huge rifles.

Four years later I returned to Biak with the intent of piecing together a clearer picture of what happened at the Biak harbor on 6 July 1998. I approached survivors of the incident through Elsham, a human rights organization that supported my research. Some of the survivors agreed to meet me alone for an interview in the home of a trusted mutual friend. Others wanted to be interviewed together. To avoid attracting undue attention by hosting a meeting in someone's home, I organized a picnic at a remote beach. We quietly chatted in Logat Papua, a creole dialect of Indonesian, with my tape recorder running, while we roasted fresh fish over an open fire.

"Every morning my friends and I took food to the protesters," recounted one of these survivors, a woman from a church near the harbor. She told me about the first moments of the attack: "While we were carrying the food that morning, we saw several army trucks approaching. They told us to wait, but when we saw that they were military, we were afraid and began running with the food and water. They began chasing us with their guns blazing. We screamed, 'The enemy is here!'" (Anonymous 2002a).

As the attack started, Filep Karma roused his followers, all unarmed civilians, with a hymn. They held hands, sitting in a circle, under the water tower where the flag still flew. They were mowed down as they continued to sing. Another survivor told me: "There were Brimob police in riot gear, army troops (Kopasgad), a company of soldiers from the local Kodim barracks, as well as navy personnel. They formed a letter U around us and then shot at us repeatedly" (Anonymous 2002a). Another eyewitness reported that the Brimob troops who fired the first shots were ethnic West Papuans. He recognized them as local troops stationed in Biak (Anonymous 2002b). During the initial assault, Filep Karma was shot twice – once in each leg – but he survived the incident. Many of his followers were not so fortunate and were killed instantly. 29 people were killed in this initial assault, according to Karma and a secondhand report from a low-ranking soldier.[21]

Some of Karma's followers, who took his words literally about using the Bible and hymns as weapons, believed that they were miraculously protected. One participant in the flag raising told human rights investigators that he had escaped the violence by clutching his Bible and pointing it at his attackers. He told the Indonesian soldiers: "If you all know religion and are the children of God, then continue to shoot." A soldier leveled his gun at this man's chest as he spoke. The soldier fired. By the account of this believer, the bullet miraculously left the gun barrel, swerved under the man's armpit and embedded itself in the concrete at the base of the water tower where the Morning Star flag was still flying (Elsham 2008, 22). This account of a miracle amid a massacre might also be read as an example of collaboration across enemy lines. Perhaps this soldier was a God-fearing man, who deliberately missed his target after being hailed by the man's biblical language.

Scores of people were loaded onto navy ships that had docked at the harbor. I took pictures of these ships from the hotel where I was staying. One group investigating the incident concluded that "one hundred thirty nine people were loaded on two frigates that headed in two directions to the east and to the west and these people were dropped into the sea."[22] A woman who narrowly escaped this ordeal told me: "I was taken by the troops to a navy ship. The number on the side of the ship was 534AL. Several of my friends had already been taken aboard. They beat us. Some were already dead. There were women raped right next to me. One soldier, he was from Toraja, saved me. The ship was still close to shore, and he told me to jump. I jumped off the back of the ship, and I swam back to the place where it had been tied up. There I found a hiding place and I waited, from 8:00 in the morning till 8:20 that night" (Anonymous 2002a). Fleeting collaborations, alliances among enemies, created moments of hope in the face of disaster.

At least 32 decaying bodies later washed ashore on Biak (Elsham 1999, 56–8). Indonesian government officials explained that these corpses were transnational travelers: they belonged to victims of a tidal wave that hit the coast over six hundred kilometers away in the neighboring country of Papua New Guinea on 17 July 1998 (Anonymous 1998). However, the official explanation does not match the facts. Four bodies washed up on the beaches of Biak on 10 July (Elsham 1999, 60). This was four days after the police opened fire on the demonstrators and one week before the tidal wave struck. Some cadavers were missing their heads, hands or genitals. One man's body still had a Morning Star flag painted on its chest (red, white and blue in contrast to the black, red and yellow flag of Papua New Guinea), and a corpse of a child was found still embracing its mother's body (Polet 1998).

The bodies of people who were shot under the water tower were heaped into a small cargo truck. Some of these people were not yet dead. Several eyewitnesses reported that the truck was filled with corpses. It left the harbor and then returned for another load. "I counted 15 people in the first load," one eyewitness told me. "The truck came a second time, and I counted 17 people inside. When they opened up the truck bed, I could see lots of blood. In that small truck there was lots of blood" (Anonymous 2002b). Human rights investigators could not determine what happened to the dead and wounded people who were transported in this truck. Filep Karma, who is now an Amnesty International prisoner of conscience, told me about how to find one mass grave, but forensic archaeologists have not yet visited this site.

West Papuan human rights workers were themselves frightened of possible government reprisals as a result of their investigations into the Biak massacre. Their work proceeded quietly as they gathered up information bit by bit. A pastor who began investigating the 6 July massacre the very next day recounted his emotionally taxing efforts: "I ran into someone from Manero at the market. He asked, 'Father, can you come with me?' 'Where?' 'To Manero, to see the body of a person that washed up on the beach.' Only the body was there. They didn't know where his head had gone. I dug a hole and neatly buried him and I cried."

In contrast to the 1991 Dili massacre in East Timor, which was filmed and photographed by international journalists, little mention of the July 1998 Biak massacre was made in the international media. Few reports emerged. CNN did not cover the event, despite the rumors at the protest. According to the official Indonesian version of this two-day siege, only one person died: "The National Commission of Human Rights and the Armed Forces said one activist died in the incident. He was identified as 27-year-old Ruben Orboy" (Anonymous 1998). Elsham, the rights organization, produced a 69-page report in Indonesian about the massacre titled "Names without Graves, Graves without Names" (1999). The report called for an international investigation, but no international human rights organizations followed up on their call.[23]

Tuesday, 7 July 1998

My connecting ferry to Nabire came into the harbor this morning. On my way out of town, I changed money at Bank Exim and then wandered around the harbor and market. People were just starting to come back to their offices, where they were inspecting the damage done by the demonstrators and the army. Desks had been ransacked, and documents littered the floor in a thick layer. Graffiti covered the walls. I went looking for a pay phone, and someone, not thinking, directed me to the building below the water tower where the Morning Star flag had been flying. I found the phone, but the mouthpiece had been ripped away from the handset. The mouthpiece hung, limp, from a few wires. The buildings under the water tower, which looked like government offices, were reduced to hollow shells spray-painted with flags and slogans. It looked like this had been the primary base for the protesters. Bullet holes riddled the walls at chest height. I continued toward the market, where I found a phone. A few market stalls were open. In the street – in between the market and the water tower – stood a disabled truck. All the tires were flat, and the doors had been ripped halfway off their hinges. When I headed back toward the harbor to board the ferry, a host of troops and government officials had arrived to inspect the damage at the water tower. Another group puzzled about what to do with the truck that had been destroyed by protesters in their initial clash with security forces.

Rather than marking an apocalyptic ending, a definitive break with the past, the security forces' use of raw violence to quell the protest became evidence of continuity.[24] The same old tactics of state violence from the Suharto era were being deployed in Indonesia's new era of supposed reform. At the same time, these old tactics were no longer working. As Indonesian security forces deliberated and tried to destroy freedom dreams with spectacular violence – launching joint operations involving the navy, army and police – the movement exploded with activity. In July 1998, West Papuans were evading Indonesian authorities by staging events in multiple places all at once. Even as the protests I witnessed in Jayapura and Biak were disrupted by security force violence, flag raisings were also taking place in Sorong, a city in the Bird's Head region of West Papua, as well as Wamena in the highlands.[25] The struggle for freedom was spreading underground. It was on the move, evading detection by authorities. In a word, the movement was operating according to principles of the rhizome.

Rhizomes, in a botanical sense, are stems that spread laterally in the topsoil and send down roots. In the lexicon of Gilles Deleuze, a French philosopher, and Félix Guattari, a psychoanalyst, rhizomes are different from roots. Rhizomes, for Deleuze and Guattari, are figures of political resistance: they ceaselessly establish connections among organizations of power, social struggles and other heterogeneous forms. These forms are extremely difficult to disrupt or kill. When plants with rhizomes are mowed down, they grow back. When chopped up and left for dead, they resprout. "A rhizome can be cracked and broken at any point," observe Deleuze and Guattari, but "it starts off again following one or another of its lines, or even other lines (Deleuze and Guattari 1983, 17–18).

"The rhizome itself assumes very diverse forms," write Deleuze and Guattari, "from ramified surface extension in all directions to concretion into bulbs and tubers [...] The rhizome includes the best and the worst: potato and couchgrass, or the weed" (Deleuze and Guattari 1988, 8–9). Messianic figures are like the potato or tuber form of the rhizome: they temporarily collect and stabilize revolutionary activity and dreaming. During the long decades of the Suharto regime, figures of the messianic multiple were largely hidden underground, with activists furtively coming together in hideouts, scattering like a swarm of ants at the slightest hint of danger. When Filep Karma stepped forward to lead a public struggle for freedom in July 1998, he momentarily embodied the messianic spirit.[26] After Karma was shot and hauled off to prison, the spirit flitted away to animate new objects, figures and future events.

Expecting the unexpected, without desiring anything in particular, Derrida worked to keep rhizomorphic potatoes and tubers out of his own messianic desert. Derrida tried to protect the notion of messianicity without messianism from the tools of deconstruction that he helped create with his early work. Deconstruction, in short, means taking apart a symbolic system to show that it contains several irreconcilable and contradictory meanings. If the messianic spirit is emptied of all content, Derrida reasons, then it cannot be taken apart. "The figures of messianism would have to be [...] deconstructed as 'religious,' ideological, or fetishistic formations," writes Derrida, "whereas messianicity without messianism remains, for its part, undeconstructible, like justice" (Derrida 2002, 253). With his work on messianicity, Derrida intended to politicize the masses.[27] But his ideas about waiting for nothing in particular have not inspired mass political movements. Contentless messianicity, an empty promise, goes nowhere.

Trying to keep political and messianic movements beyond the reach of deconstruction is a mistake. Alliances and ideological formations are constructed, and are often deconstructed or reconstructed, as contingencies change (Clifford 2001, 481). Rather than Derrida's empty messianicity, people who joined West Papua's movement for freedom were hoping for many different things – a messianic multiple. Even as survivors of the massacre in Biak remembered fleeting glimpses of the messianic spirit – the fiery light in Filep Karma's eyes, the Pelni ocean liner appearing on the horizon – their collective imagination danced away to alight on other events, objects and figures.[28] When raising a flag on the water tower did not result in the recognition of West Papua as a sovereign nation, the central prefigured event for the crowd, visionaries refigured hopes and desires. Dreams about a messianic multiple, with new figures for probing future horizons, generated hope even in this moment of post-revolutionary disappointment.

The logic of the messianic multiple – an expectation of the unexpected that is not fixed on any single thing – gave West Papua's vibrant social movement flexibility amid shifting historical contingencies. When a specific object of desire failed to materialize or figures leading the movement disappeared behind bars, new content rushed in to take their place. As a new era of free speech dawned in Indonesia, the messianic spirit of West Papua's movement for freedom came to alight on increasingly stable, publicly recognizable figures of hope. Burrowing under the noses of Indonesian authorities, the movement entered key nodes in the matrix of power. West Papuan activists penetrated institutions of domination and linked up with other freedom dreams. Surprising alliances were forged, and the boundaries between enemy and ally began to break down as the infectious spirit of freedom captured the imaginations of West Papuans from all walks of life. The Biak massacre did not mark a violent end to the world in West Papua. Instead it set the stage for a new historical era.

Notes

1 Derrida also regards messianicity "as *promise* and not as onto-theological or teleo-eschatological program or design" (Derrida 1994, 74, italics in original).
2 The messianic spirit was animating a secular political formation, rather than a religious ideology. Kenelm Burridge, a student of indigenous history and politics in New Guinea, writes: "faith is faith whether thought of as religious or secular" (Burridge 1969, 7). See also Derrida (1994, 167).
3 Words are "like drops of liquid mercury splashing about, moving in any direction", writes Chinese poet Gu Cheng (Weinberger 2005, 42). Like liquid mercury, *merdeka* is difficult to contain. It runs through figural holes and travels abroad in unlikely disguises. All manner of heterogeneous, and seemingly contradictory, elements are contained in the fluidity of *merdeka* – hopes for national independence, capitalist wealth, socialist equality, Christian salvation and indigenous sovereignty. These imperfect equivalencies allowed a massively popular grassroots movement to coalesce in West Papua after the fall of Suharto. (My thanks are extended to Katie Peterson and Li Dong for bringing Gu Cheng's work to my attention during our time together at Deep Springs College.)
4 The multitude, a swarm of creative agents is distinct from my notion of the messianic multiple – a revolutionary logic that can work in the imagination of an individual

visionary. When the spirit of the messianic multiple catches hold of a crowd, anything can happen at any time.

5 "From a millenarian perspective, things are always getting worse," writes Donna Haraway. "Oddly, belief in advancing disaster is actually part of a trust in salvation, whether deliverance is expected by sacred or profane revelations, through revolution, dramatic scientific breakthroughs, or religious rapture" (Haraway 1997, 41).

6 Many specialists on Indonesia will likely disagree with me on this point. The student activists who were at the political vanguard of the Indonesian Reformasi movement looked upon indigenous prophecy, and messianic hopes grounded in religion, as unhelpful superstition (Aspinall 1999, 213). These secular revolutionaries had faith that was not tied to religion. Still, they believed in profound transformations to come. My intention is to stretch meaning of the word messianic – to blur the boundaries between secular and religious desires. I am working to reclaim the political possibilities contained in messianic desires (cf. Benjamin 1968; Derrida 1999; Haraway 1997; Jameson 1999).

7 The phrase "homogeneous, empty, time," which I use above to refer to the Suharto era, has also been purloined from Benjamin (1968, 261). Benedict Anderson also uses this phrase: "The idea of a sociological organism moving calendrically through homogeneous, empty time is a precise analogue of the idea of the nation, which also is conceived as a solid community moving steadily down (or up) history" (Anderson 1991, 26).

8 "During the 1990s, apocalypticism, and, somewhat less flamboyantly, its millennialist twin, have become a constant and unavoidable presence in everyday life" (Stewart and Harding 1999, 289–90).

9 See J. Clifford, "Saving Indigenous Time" (2005). Paper presented at Saving Time: An Interdisciplinary Conference on Memory and Memorialization. Cowell College, University of California Santa Cruz.

10 In written testimony for a US congressional hearing about West Papua, Pieter Drooglever suggested that the New York Agreement ruled out the possibility of a referendum on the issue of independence:

> There were certainly no clear plans for a plebiscite on the basis of universal suffrage and individual vote – which would have been hardly practicable in the isolated but densely populated highland areas. Instead the documents stipulated that an Indonesian-style *Musyawarah*, or "traditional consultation," would be an essential part of the Act of Free Choice. This 'consultation' allowed for manipulation from above. Thus, the foundations for the inadequate Act of Free Choice were already laid down in the agreement itself. (Drooglever 2010, 2)

My knowledge of the New York Agreement text (informed by lively debates in the early twenty-first century among West Papuan intellectuals) leads me to suspect that a *musyawarah*, or "traditional consultation," was not the only practical option available to the parties charged with implementing the treaty. The original text of the New York Agreement suggests that all West Papuans should have been eligible to participate. Indonesia was responsible for ensuring "the eligibility of all adults, male and female, not foreign nationals to participate in the act of self-determination to be carried out in accordance with international practice" (Subandrio et al. 1962, art. 18).

11 This text and the ones that follow are excerpts from my field notes that have been condensed and rewritten.

12 The student who had been shot in the head later died in the hospital (Associated Press Worldstream 1998).
13 Rutherford points us to this quote from George Orwell's essay "Shooting an Elephant," about a crowd in Burma who became "all happy and excited over this bit of fun." In Rutherford's collection of essays about West Papua, she uses Orwell's encounter with elephants and crowds in Burma as an opportunity to explore ideas about sovereignty (Rutherford 2012).
14 According to Anna Tsing, "[r]umors offer a clue to knowledge not yet generally established by suggesting where powerful centers may shift [...] Like changing market prices, rumors cannot be ignored where quick evasions are necessary for survival" (Tsing 1993, 91).
15 This army is described in Judges 4. Years later I interviewed several members of the Deborah and Barak prayer group, on the condition of strict anonymity. In the Biak language the word *barak* also refers to supernatural power that pilgrims sought from the Sultan of Tidore during the period of indirect colonial rule (Rutherford 2002, 17).
16 Reviewing Derrida's work, Fredric Jameson writes: "We ought to be able to distinguish an apocalyptic politics from a messianic one, [...] which might lead us on into some new way of sorting out the Left from the Right, the new International in Marx's spirit from that in the world of business and state power. The messianic is spectral, it is the spectrality of the future, the other dimension, that answers to the haunting spectrality of the past which is historicity itself. The apocalyptic, however, announces the end of spectrality" (Jameson 2009, 63–4).
17 The people of Biak, in Danilyn Rutherford's words, "fetishized the foreign" (2002, 4). Her ideas about the fetish exceed the associations of popular parlance – mystical qualities attached to inanimate objects, the sexual attraction to objects or body parts not conventionally regarded as erotic, or even the commodity fetishism described by Karl Marx. The fetish analytic, as elaborated by Marx and Freud, looks for misplaced concreteness. In Rutherford's argument, "the foreign" is not a specific fetish object but something more expansive and elusive. She suggests that the Biak people "turned what is foreign into a source of agency and an object of desire" (Rutherford 2012, 56; see also Haraway 1997, 146–8; Marx 1978, III:165).
18 The messianic multiple is at play in the borderlands where hope meets desire. Departing from Vincent Crapanzano, who maintains a distinction between hope and desire, I suggest that the slippage between these two sentiments generates revolutionary possibilities. When generalized feelings of collective hope become articulated to multiple specific objects of desire – coming events, material concessions or historical figures – mass movements begin to gain political traction (Crapanzano 2004, 103–4, 146).
19 Peter Worsley, who studied messianic movements in New Guinea in the aftermath of the second world war, distinguished "movements which anticipate that the millennium will occur solely as a result of supernatural intervention, and those which envisage that the action of human beings will be necessary" (Worsley 1968, 12).
20 Divine violence is an element of all revolutions, according to Benjamin, but it is never possible to pinpoint the order-destroying moment. "Divine violence," he concludes, "which is the sign and seal but never the means of sacred execution, may be called sovereign violence" (1978, 285). For Rutherford, this Biak protest contained the potential of divine violence – the potential of destroying the order of Indonesian law. When the crowd rallied behind Filep Karma's demands for independence, many people undoubtedly wondered if God would mark the event with a divine seal (Rutherford 2012).

21 First Infantry Lieutenant Hermanus Yeninar reportedly burst into tears when he told a close family member the number of people killed in the initial assault (Elsham 1999, 31, 34).
22 I did not attempt to systematically verify this number, but from my interviews with other eyewitnesses, it is within the realm of possibility. The source is a faxed appeal to Dr Kofi Annan, from the Komite Solidaritas Rakyat Irian Kosorairi, which cites eyewitness accounts as well as reports from the largest Protestant church in West Papua (GKI) of dead bodies appearing on the beaches of Biak. This faxed appeal was posted on the West Papua Newsgroup (Polet 1998).
23 Elsham's report was published in July 1999, several months after preliminary reports by journalists, Human Rights Watch and Survival International. Rutherford has compiled an extensive list of reports about the event that emerged on the Internet and in the press (Human Rights Watch 1998; Rutherford 2012, 39–40).
24 My line of argument here is made in counterpoint to Rutherford's interpretation of the same event. She writes that the Biak protesters "envisioned international acknowledgement of the West Papuan nation as leading to an eschatological transformation." Eschatology, according to the *Oxford English Dictionary*, is "the department of theological science concerned with 'the four last things: death, judgment, heaven, and hell.'" Rutherford suggests that Biaks were waiting for an "eschatological moment [that] was – and remains – a focus of longing and hope." There is little evidence that the people who gathered in the harbor longed for death, judgment and hell. The collective imagination of the crowd settled on clear figures of hope. Certainly protesters were "waiting for the end" of Indonesian rule, and anxiety about a possible crackdown by Indonesian security forces was also at play in the crowd. The charismatic leaders who rallied the crowd did not seek redemption through death but looked for political and theological transformations through peace. Like the Indonesian students who had willed Suharto out of office, these West Papuan protesters were waiting for a seemingly impossible event. They were waiting to be granted independence (Rutherford 2002, 25; 2012, 54).
25 Demonstrators destroyed the Sorong government offices and mosques, as well as shops, restaurants, hotels and drugstores owned by Indonesians. In response, Indonesian troops opened fire on the crowd, killing a pregnant woman and a man (Alua 2001, 8).
26 When I interviewed Melkianus Awom, a distant relative of Permenas Ferry Awom, he confirmed that Filep Karma was not involved with his group of guerrilla soldiers.
27 In a normative, even programmatic, passage in *Specters of Marx*, Derrida insists on embracing "emancipatory desire," which he regards as "the condition of a re-politicization" (Derrida 1994, 74–5).
28 In *Imaginative Horizons*, Vincent Crapanzano suggests that we can take pleasure in the unreality of imaginary hinterlands – the possibilities and the play it facilitates (2004, 100–102).

References

Alua, A. 2001. *Dialog Nasional Papua dan Indonesia 26 Februari 1999*. Jayapura, West Papua: Biro Penelitian STFT Fajar Timur.
Anderson, B. 1991. *Imagined Communities: Reflections on the Origin and Spread of Nationalism*. London: Verso.
Anonymous. 2002a. Tape-recorded interview in Indonesian. Biak, Indonesia, 3 September.

———. 2002b. Tape-recorded interview in Indonesian. Bosnik, Biak, Indonesia, 5 September.

Aspinall, E., H. Feith and G. Van Klinken, eds. 1999. *The Last Days of President Suharto*. Clayton, Victoria: Monash Asia Institute.

Associated Press Worldstream. 1998. "One Student Killed in Clash with Security Personnel," Jakarta, 3 July.

Benjamin, W. 1968. *Illuminations*. Edited and with an introduction by Hannah Arendt, translated by Harry Zohn. New York: Harcourt, Brace & World.

———. 1978. "Critique of Violence." In *Reflections: Essays, Aphorisms, Autobiographical Writings*, edited and with an introduction by Peter Demetz, translated by Edmund Jephott. New York: Harcourt Brace Jovanovich.

Bird, Judith. 1998. "Indonesia in 1997: The Tinderbox Year." *Asian Survey* 38, no. 2: 168–76.

"Bodies Found Near Biak 'May Be Shooting Victims.'" 1998. *Jakarta Post*, 30 July.

Burridge, K. 1969. *Tangu Traditions: A Study In the Way of Life, Mythology and Developing Experience of a New Guinea People*. Oxford: Clarendon Press.

Clifford, J. 2001. "Indigenous Articulations." *Special Issue: The Contemporary Pacific* 13(2): 468–90.

———. 2005. "Saving Indigenous Time." Paper presented at Saving Time: An Interdisciplinary Conference on Memory and Memorialization, Cowell College, UC Santa Cruz, 18 November.

Crapanzano, V. 2004. *Imaginative Horizons: An Essay in Literary-Philosophical Anthropology*. Chicago: University of Chicago Press.

Deleuze, G. and F. Guattari. 1983. *On the Line (Foreign Agents Series)*. Translated by John Johnston. New York: Semiotext(e).

———. 1988. *A Thousand Plateaus: Capitalism and Schizophrenia*. Translated and with a foreword by Brian Massumi. London: Althone Press.

Derrida, J. 1994. *Specters of Marx: The State of the Debt, the Work of Mourning and the New International*. Translated by Peggy Kamuf. London: Routledge.

———. 1999. "Marx and Sons." In *Ghostly Demarcations: A Symposium on Jacques Derrida's Specters of Marx*, edited by M. Sprinkler. Brooklyn: Verso.

———. 2004. "For a Justice to Come." Interview with Ris Orangis. Transcribed by Maï wenn Furic, translated by Ortwin de Graef. *The Brussels Tribunal*, 19 February.

Drooglever, P. J. O. 2009. *An Act of Free Choice: Decolonization and the Right to Self-Determination in West Papua*. Oxford: Oneworld.

———. 2010. "Crimes Against Humanity: When Will Indonesia's Military be Held Accountable for Deliberate and Systematic Abuses in West Papua?" US House Committee on Foreign Affairs Hearing, 22 September.

"Drought Disaster and Snowfall." 1997. *Kompas*, 23 October. West Papua Archives 2007. Online: http://www.converge.org.nz/wpapua/The-archives-1997.html (accessed 30 March 2012).

Elsham. 1999. "Nama Tanpa Pusara, Pusara Tanpa Nama." Unpublished report, Jayapura, West Papua, July.

Giay, B. 2007. "Eben Kirksey's Thesis in West Papuan History." Personal communication to author, Washington, 23 November.

Haraway, D. 1997. *Modest-Witness@Second_Millennium.Female_Meets_Onco Mouse: Feminism and Technoscience*. New York: Routledge.

Harding, S. 1994. "Imagining the Last Days: The Politics of Apocalyptic Language." *Bulletin of the American Academy of Arts and Sciences* 48(3): 14–44.

Hardt, M. and Antonio Negri. 2004. *Multitude: War and Democracy in the Age of Empire*. New York: Penguin.
Hill, H. 1996. *The Indonesian Economy since 1966: Southeast Asia's Emerging Giant*. Cambridge: Cambridge University Press.
Human Rights Watch. 1998. "Indonesia: Human Rights and Pro-Independence Actions in Irian Jaya." 10(8, C). New York, 29 December. Online: http://www.hrw.org/news/1998/12/27/indonesia-human-rights-and-pro-independence-actions-irian-jaya (accessed 30 March 2012).
Jameson, F. 1999. *Postmodernism, or, the Cultural Logic of Late Capitalism*. Durham, NC: Duke University Press.
———. 2009. *Marx's Purloined Letter: Valences of the Dialectic*. London and Brooklyn: Verso.
Lioe, F. 1998. "Indonesia on the Boil." *Far Eastern Economic Review*. February.
Orwell, G. 1936. "Shooting an Elephant." *New Writing* 2.
Pemberton, G. 1987. *All the Way: Australia's Road to Vietnam*. Sydney: Allen & Unwin.
Polet, Anthonie. 1998. "Human Rights Violations in West Papua." *Jakarta Post*, 12 August.
Rutherford, D. 2002. *Raiding the Land of the Foreigners: Power, History and Difference in Biak, Irian Jaya, Indonesia*. Princeton: Princeton University Press.
———. 2012. *Laughing at Leviathan: Sovereignty and Audience in West Papua*. Chicago and London: University of Chicago Press.
Saltford, J. 2003. *The United Nations and the Indonesian Takeover of West Papua, 1962–1969: The Anatomy of Betrayal*. London: RoutledgeCurzon.
Stewart, K. and S. Harding. 1999. "Bad Endings: American Apocalypsis." *Annual Review of Anthropology* 28: 285–310.
Subandrio, J., H. van Rouen and C. W. A. Schurmann. 1962. *The New York Agreement*. Original document in UN archives in New York. Online: http://en.wikisource.org/ and http://www.indonesia.hu/bulletin/pr1902irjalamp.htm (accessed 21 June 2003).
Timmer, J. 2000. "The Return of the Kingdom: Agana and the Millenium among the Imyan of Irian Jaya, Indonesia." *Ethnohistory* 47(1): 29–65.
Tsing, A. L. 1997. "Indigenous Voice." In *Indigenous Experience Today*, edited by M. de la Cadena and O. Stern, 33–68. Oxford: Berg.
———. 2003. *In the Realm of the Diamond Queen: Marginality in an Out-of-the-Way-Place*. Princeton: Princeton University Press.
"UN Envoy Due in Indonesia on East Timor Conflict." 1998. *Deutsche Presse-Agentur*, 4 July.
Vidal, J. 1997. "Poison Fog Blanket Threatens World." *Guardian*, 27 September.
Walters, P. 1997. "Malaria Compounds Irian Jayans' Misery." *Weekend Australian*, December 6–7.
Weinberger, E. 2005. *What Happened Here: Bush Chronicles*. New York: New Directions Books.
Worseley, P. 1968. *The Trumpet Shall Sound: A Study of "Cargo" Cults in Melanesia*. New York: Schocken Books.

Chapter 3

LINCOLN, THE MINISTERS OF RELIGION AND THE AMERICAN JEREMIAD

Jonathan Keller

Introduction: An Almost Chosen People

On 21 February 1861, president-elect Abraham Lincoln appeared before the New Jersey State Senate – after seven southern states had already seceded from the Union, and four more were preparing to follow suit – and described Americans in a curiously idiosyncratic manner:

> I am exceedingly anxious that this Union, the Constitution, and the liberties of the people shall be perpetuated in accordance with the original idea for which that struggle was made, and I shall be most happy indeed if I shall be an humble instrument in the hands of the Almighty, and of this, his *almost chosen people,* for perpetuating the object of that great struggle. (Lincoln 1992a, 280; emphasis mine)

This was the only time Lincoln ever spoke of Americans as a "chosen people" – strange indeed for an orator already legendary for his unparalleled ability to frame political conflict in biblical terms.[1] And yet he says Americans somehow were only "almost" chosen.[2] In biblical terms, that is more or less like saying that Esau was "almost Jacob," or Jonathan was "almost David." Lincoln's ambiguity is especially puzzling during this era. As David Blight explains, by the 1850s a powerful conception of American "chosenness" became a "central unifying myth of nineteenth century America," and had firmly entrenched itself in public discourse (Blight 1989, 104).

But whether Lincoln meant to disavow two-and-a-half century old Puritan narratives likening America to the biblical Israel of the scriptures, a second "light unto the nations,"[3] or instead that America had gone wayward from an assumed sacred national purpose and could somehow *reclaim* its chosen status, is impossible to say.[4] Either way, the sixteenth president's deliberate ambiguity points us toward a historically capacious anxiety that has persistently haunted the American project. Sociologist Robert Bellah argues that these peak historical moments – "times of testing," he calls them – are revelatory, in that they reveal the "civil religion" of the nation (1967, 3).

In the mainline Protestant pulpit, there was also a "time of testing," but of a parallel sort. The following essay discusses how the slavery question divided jeremiads of America's exceptionalist origins and meaning into two groups, representing two different notions of American chosenness. I begin with a discussion of the "American Hermeneutic," a type of biblical literalism shared by both Northern and Southern preachers prior to the Civil War. Next I explain how the controversy over slavery radically disrupted this hermeneutic, sending ministers north and south of the Mason–Dixon Line onto different exegetical trajectories. Each side maintained a notion of "chosenness," however, based on its version of biblical literalism. I conclude by comparing them both with Lincoln's idiosyncratic jeremiad, which ironically demonstrated greater fidelity to the prophetic literature of the Bible than did the ministers.

In *The Civil War as a Theological Crisis*, historian Mark Noll argues that the pulpit presents a great irony of the American Civil War: the most highly influential ministers, while both learned and steeped in biblical understanding, oddly "did not engage in any actual biblical exegesis" when making the case for or against slavery (Noll 2006, 3). But while their sermons may have lacked proper analysis of the biblical texts, as Sacvan Bercovitch and Andrew Murphy have argued, their rhetoric always resembled the long-established rhetorical form, the jeremiad, a forceful exhortation to reform the community in the name of Godly ancestors that is modeled on the rhetoric of the Old Testament prophets, and occurred within a particular American context of interpretation (Murphy 2009). In short, while an otherwise naturally evolving exegetical debate was reframed around the most divisive issue in American history, ministers North and South still clung fiercely to what they understood to be literalist approaches.

The American Hermeneutic

Civil War preaching, both Northern and Southern, was based on the fundamental religious premise, generally accepted in pre-Darwinian America, that God controlled the universe and everything and action in it. Further, North and South shared common language, law, heritage of the revolution, political institutions[5] and the Union itself as an organizing myth. Both sides saw the Union as having transcendent worth, with grandiose perceptions of

America's mission in the world. However, although the Bible was ostensibly at the center of the debate, historian Mark Noll explains that:

> The hermeneutical crisis of the Civil War – the crisis arising from the full deployment for more than two generations of a common set of reformed and American assumptions, about how to read, interpret and apply the scriptures – was a crisis on two levels. The obvious crisis that bore directly on the fate of the nation was that "simple" reading of the Bible yielded violently incommensurate understandings of Scripture with no means, short of warfare, to adjudicate the differences. The less obvious crisis was more directly theological; it concerned the fate of biblical authority itself. (Noll 1998, 49)

In the pre-Darwin era[6] very few Americans could distinguish between the Bible and the Bible as read in America, because of a certain kind of hermeneutic described by British observer James Sterling in 1857 as "the notion that every direction contained in its pages is applicable at all times to all men" (Noll 1998, 46). What we now understand as biblical literalism was far more popular in the United States than in Europe, by this point, and this broad notion shaped the debate over how to read the Bible, when it came to chattel slavery.

It would in fact be more accurate to call it a hermeneutic of the "Reformed" approach – from the remainders of Calvinist churches. This theological bent was most prevalent among New Englanders and mid-state Presbyterians, as well as Scottish, English and Dutch forms of Protestant Reformers (Noll 2006, 47), and was characterized by three overarching principles: first, *scriptura sola* (by scripture alone); second, the "regulative principle," which held that people are required to do what the Bible commands and not do what the Bible is silent about; third, what Noll and Hatch call "The Third Use of the Law" (Noll, Mardson and Hatch 1989, 76), meaning that scripture not only demonstrates the individual's need for salvation, but provides a blueprint for how the Christian should live out her/his entire life. As one might imagine, when this collided headlong with the simmering debate over chattel slavery, it caused enormous theological disagreement. Noll contends that this hermeneutic developed because of two factors: first, because varieties of Reformed Protestantism composed the bulk of American churches; second, because they occurred within a context of continual social transformation: "the engine that drove this hermeneutic was 'social transformation' – from hierarchy to democratic, ideological antihierarchy – a revolution which created a distinct American form of biblicalism" (Noll, 2006, 26) – the notion that anyone could understand the Bible, which inevitably led to new sects and churches.

While the combination of these broad principles and the democratizing tendencies of Jacksonian America made agreement on the meaning of specific scriptural imperatives next to impossible, ironically it had the effect of elevating the authority of the Bible itself. In Nathan Hatch's terms, "the Bible saved people from the din of sectarian confusion" (Noll 1998, 48). American Protestants generally did not attempt to defend their interpretative practices with direct appeal to scripture. The reformed literal hermeneutic grew instead from particular American circumstances, and a simple confidence in the Bible itself. While this idiosyncratic elevation of biblical authority was not rooted directly in literal *use* of scripture, it nonetheless became the norm, both before and during the Civil War. "Literalism without the text," as it were, helped generate a stable, consistent notion of American chosenness, on both sides of the Mason–Dixon Line.

Abolitionists and Anti-Biblical "Chosenness": Theodore Parker and Henry Ward Beecher

Opponents of slavery who were also churchmen faced a serious conundrum when attempting to wield the Bible as a weapon. They seemed to have only four options, all of them unappealing. They could simply admit the Bible sanctioned slavery, and abandon the Bible when they went on the attack against slavery. This option was by far the least popular, but had the notoriety of luminary abolitionist figures William Lloyd Garrison and Gerrit Smith to recommend it. Ultimately, however, this option was too problematic, as it put the otherwise extremely pious (like Garrison, a strict Sabbatarian and Sunday school teacher before he became a radical abolitionist) in an awkward position, and left religious moderates like Smith extremely vulnerable to charges of heresy.

Alternatively, they could conclude that since the Bible sanctions slavery – as in several books in both the Old and New Testaments[7] – they should also accept it in the United States. But that did not mean it should be supported as a positive good. One might want to reform it, and eliminate its cruelest practices. This view was most popular amongst Southerners around the time of the American Revolution, but after the British manumission of most slaves throughout the empire in 1833, this position appeared far less frequently.

Third, the most complicated position: a recognition that the Bible only sanctions a particular form of slavery, but not necessarily American slavery. This approach required moving away from the Bible itself, to a discussion of how the Bible should be applied to modern life via analogy and other more flexible means of interpretation. This smacked of an antiliteralism that the ministers rarely would admit to (but frequently practiced) during this era.

Finally, one could draw a general distinction between the letter and the spirit of the Bible itself, arguing, as many abolitionists did, that to be a literalist meant fidelity to immutable principles, not particular sections of the Bible which clearly condoned, or at the very least recognized, slavery as a legitimate institution of the ancient world.

Options three or four posed a very serious problem: supporting either risked being an infidel in attacking the authority of the Bible itself. Any way the abolitionists tried to frame it, the notion that overarching principles drawn from inference are more authoritative than literal passages from the Bible was a very difficult sell. Therefore, in the end these positions were ultimately reduced to just two: "orthodox" and pro-slavery versus "heretical" and antislavery.

Thus, if one were strictly following the exegetical debate during this period, the South would seem to have captured the debate over slavery in the Bible. Black, Christian abolitionists tended to shy away from Talmudic weighing of competing biblical passages, choosing the more vocal registers of the prophetic tradition instead, in order to dramatize the conflict in moral terms. Frederick Douglass, for instance, sounded like a nineteenth-century millenialist when he emphasized eschatological symbolism, God's Second Coming, and retributive justice, all enveloped in the American sense of mission as a redeemer nation (Blight 1989, 8). Like Douglass, most influential mainline Northern ministers, such as Theodore Parker and Henry Ward Beecher, appeared to move away from a literalism of textual fidelity, and toward a fidelity to universal biblical principle, which in their minds clearly condemned American chattel slavery.

Theodore Parker (1810–1860) was arguably the most outspoken antislavery minister in the North between 1841 and 1860. Chosen to lead the Twenty-Eighth Congregational Society of Boston in 1846, his congregation grew to 7,000 and included luminaries William Lloyd Garrison, Julia Ward Howe and Elizabeth Cady Stanton. While he was famous for sermons of declensive moral anxiety that rivaled his Puritan forerunners, his earlier contribution to the concept of "natural" or "moral law" was equally significant to the abolitionist movement.

Like most Northern preachers before the war, Parker would never begin a sermon with slavery. First he would talk about temperance. Then impiety and infidelity, idol worship and the like. Eventually, when he reached a fever pitch, he would end with slavery – which, like all sins, was ultimately rooted for Parker in the quintessential prophetic distinction between eternal law and conventional man-made law – in his terms, "business" versus "duty":

> Certain artificial demands are made of men, which have no foundation in the moral nature of man; these demands are thought to represent duties […] hence comes no small confusion: the conventional and official

obligation is thought to rest on the same foundation as the natural and personal duty. (Chesebrough 1991, 40)

Then Parker would immediately link this philosophical meditation on the American situation to broad clarion calls for justice from Exodus:

A statute was once enacted by King Pharaoh for the destruction of the Israelites in Egypt [...] it was made the official business of all citizens to aid in their destruction. Which should he obey, Lord Pharaoh, or the Lord God? [...] I make no doubt that the priests of Osiris, Orus, Apis, Isis and the judges [...] and the members of Congress at that time, said, "Keep the king's commandment." (Chesebrough 1991, 43)

When confronted by a choice between obeying the laws of convention, or the eternal law of God which applied to all but especially his chosen nation, Parker held that "right alone shall last for ever and ever." In the meanwhile, he warned prophetically, "since '76 our success was never so doubtful as at this time" (Parker 1969, 314).

Parker's denunciation was directed especially at men such as Daniel Webster, who were willing to postpone grappling with slavery in order to preserve the Union. This position, according to Parker, was one which disavowed America's *intrinsic* and timeless purpose. As he explained in the sermon "The Destination of America" (1848):

Now, while each nation has its particular genius of character which does not change, it has also and accordingly a particular work to perform in the economy of the world, a certain fundamental idea to unfold and develop. This is its national task [...] a genius for liberty: the American idea is freedom, natural rights. Accordingly, the work providentially laid out for us to do seems this – to organize the rights of man. This is a problem hitherto unattempted on a national scale, in human history. (Parker 1969, 124–5)

While it is true, he declares, that this purpose has not always been so apparent, that the American has sometimes seemed to "spurn liberty" and "tramples, knowingly, consciously, tramples on the most unquestionable and sacred rights," in the end, while our national course may look "as crooked as the Rio Grande, but nothing comes out with such relief as this love of freedom, this idea of liberty, this attempt to organize rights." This, he says, is "secured in the great charter of our being" (127). Parker would return to this theme again in his jeremiads, wondering aloud why "Southern slavery is an institution which is in earnest," but "Northern freedom is an institution that is not in earnest" (Chesebrough 1991, 57).

Henry Ward Beecher (1813–1887) was the most popular preacher in mid-nineteenth-century America and, some said, the most famous man in America. As historian William G. McLoughlin put it:

> For at least three decades Beecher was the high priest of American religion. His pulpit was the nation's spiritual center [...] Millions read him, millions heard him, millions believed in him. Beecher was the first American clergyman to attain a national audience which acknowledged him as its spokesman; the first to make it part of his regular practice to speak out on every significant social and political issue; the first to make a point of being seen with Presidents, to campaign for Presidents – in short, our first self-appointed national chaplain. (McLoughlin 1959, 252)

Unlike Parker, Henry Ward Beecher initially favored separation from the South. But like many of his contemporaries, after the first shots were fired at Fort Sumter on 12 February 1861, he quickly changed his mind and was fully in support of the war, delivering several of the most full-throated jeremiads of the era. But Parker and Beecher were alike on a more fundamental level: both men preached again and again that the North was the truly American region, and that its society was superior to the South, morally, culturally and intellectually.

Beecher's developing position on the war occurred in two stages. First he moved from ambivalence to strongly favoring going to war with the South, but only in order to force the Confederate states back into the Union. But over time he came to see the war very differently, particularly after the North experienced severe losses in early battles and a crisis of confidence and morale. After the Union's bruising defeat at the Battle of Bull Run in Manassas, Virginia in 1861, Parker gave a series of guilt-ridden "sermons of humiliation," wondering aloud whether God was punishing the North because its purpose in going to war was not noble enough. Secession was hardly an offense against God, he argued, whereas, in his mind at least, slavery most certainly was.

In this sense, the development of Beecher's sermons is typical of this era: early losses on the battlefield deeply influenced Northern perceptions of the war in the Protestant pulpit. There was a great period of introspection following these early losses, particularly before the decisive battles of Gettysburg and Vicksburg tipped the course of the war permanently (May–July 1863). Lincoln's Emancipation Proclamation, issued on 1 January 1863, came to be seen as responsible for the North finally regaining God's grace. At long last, Northerners had purified themselves, and the course of the war shifted.

In his famous Thanksgiving Day Sermon of 1860, Beecher began with Luke 4:17–19 (where the young Jesus points to the verses in Isaiah he claims prophesy his arrival), explaining that this shows Christ coming to save the world, "not laws, not governments, not institutions, not dynasties, but *the people*" (Chesebrough 1991, 65). But then as the sermon continued, Beecher talked more and more about the chosen status of the Americans, and what providential purposes God had in mind for them. Even though "prophets are dead, and God no longer tells us beforehand what he is going to do," when looking at the course of the world's history, one cannot help but be struck by the fact that, as Tocqueville noted, nations based on tyranny are in decline, and liberty is increasing. "While we cannot know the end of all this," Beecher continued, "it would seem that God chose us for a pivotal period on which ages turn, barbarism or civilization" (Chesebrough 1991, 69).

In the conclusion of the sermon, however, Beecher made an unusual rhetorical move – he directly criticized the founders. First he laid blame on that heroic generation: "The Southern States and the Northern alike found poisonous seed sown in colonial days. The North chose to weed it out. The South determined to cultivate it, and see what it would bear. The harvest-time has now come. We are reaping what we sowed." Then he exhorted the crowd – on Thanksgiving, a day usually reserved for honoring the past – to *exceed* the framers: "Are you wiser than your fathers? Yes! [...] we may know now, better than they did then, what their wisest course would have been. While France and Italy, Germany and Russia, are advancing toward the dawn, shall we recede toward midnight?" (Chesebrough 1991, 78).

Southern Religion: Pessimism, Slavery and Biblical Literalism

The religion that dominated mid-nineteenth-century America was in the midst of significant change, which paralleled larger democratizing currents within Jacksonian America (Goen 1985, 6). In short, as C. C. Goen and Mark Noll have argued, the Calvinism of the Puritans, with its elitist emphasis on the absolute sovereignty of God and the helplessness of man, was becoming less and less palatable to American religious tastes on both sides of the Mason–Dixon Line. Two controlling principles emerged, albeit inconsistently: the rights and dignity of man, and the self-improvement of mankind.

Political sermons in the antebellum and Civil War periods reflected these developments. As David Chesebrough argues, however, these tended to reflect rather than shape the opinions of Southern congregations and the broader currents within the Protestant world. The evangelical impulse of the Second Great Awakening to reform was pitted against the interests of "Bible experts" – learned ministers interested in protecting their authoritative status. But the slavery question ultimately dominated the debate within the three major sects. Fifteen years before the first shots were fired on Fort Sumter (1861), the Methodist, Presbyterian and Baptist churches all experienced schisms which were not wholly sectional in their origins, but increasingly became so as slavery moved front and center in the theological debates (Chesebrough 1991, 2). The biblical status of chattel slavery supervened on a host of key theological and political questions: sectionalism; war; assigning guilt and blame; theologies of victory versus the "religion of the lost cause" after the war. All of these themes ultimately revolved around the question of "American chosenness."

Because of the South's "peculiar institution," these notions would always be constrained within the larger racial order in the South, whereas in the North there could be greater flexibility of doctrine. As historian C. Vann Woodward explains, because of the South's preoccupation with justifying slavery, it tended to reject

> such popular American ideas as the doctrine of human perfectibility, the belief that every evil has a cure, and the notion that every human problem has a solution [...] In the most optimistic of centuries in the most optimistic part of the world, the south remained basically pessimistic in its social outlook and its moral philosophy. (Woodward 1993, 21)

Nevertheless, two major changes occurred in Southern Protestantism after 1830. First, it became evangelical: the Second Great Awakening caused the slow replacement of the Church of England. By 1830, Baptists and Methodists predominated in increasing numbers. By the time of the Civil War, 82 percent of churches in the 11 Confederate states were Methodist or Baptist (Goen 1985, 134). Second, whereas after the American Revolution many Southern religious leaders were actually opposed to slavery, by 1830 most of them had adopted strongly pro-slavery positions.

Stringfellow, De Bow and Palmer

Thornton Stringfellow (1788–1869) was pastor to a large congregation in Culpepper, Virginia, which was half black, a majority of whom were slaves (Faust, 1977). He was very well off financially, both owning and inheriting slaves. He published frequently on slavery and theology, in newspapers, *De Bow's Review*, etc. Most importantly, he strongly supported the Southern Baptist separation from the North, in 1845, over the issue of appointing slaveholding missionaries. At the end of the Civil War, he was held captive in his home for two months by Yankee soldiers. He lost between 60 and 70 slaves when the war ended (Faust 1977, 3).

Stringfellow's views about slavery were not independent from his other theological and ecclesiastical commitments, however. Specifically, the official split between Northern and Southern Baptist churches in 1845 had three interrelated elements: first, the tension between educated ministers versus uneducated evangelicals. Although there is no record of his formal education, Stringfellow valued education in the ministry, and sided with the elites in this controversy.[8] Second, the centrality of "Mission." He always believed in social activism over predestination. Before his involvement as a defender of slavery, he was an active sabbatarian, temperance advocate and Sunday school promoter. Third, sectionalism: he always argued that the South was the "true conscience of the nation."

In his infamous *Slavery in the Light of Divine Revelation* (1860), Stringfellow addressed all three. First, he made it clear that slavery's biblical status cannot be left up to individual conscience; second, he called parishioners to action, in the name of scriptural truth, to defend the ancient and holy institution. Finally, he presented the South as redemptive of the nation *as a whole*. Stringfellow's sermon offers four justifications for slavery: the sanction of the Almighty in the patriarchal age; that slavery was incorporated into the only national constitution that emanated from God; that it was legally recognized and its relative duties recognized in the New Testament; and that it is full of mercy.

Stringfellow began by explaining that slavery existed in the patriarchic biblical age, so it would make no sense to see figures like Abraham and Jacob as sinners, because God clearly did not. These patriarchs have been singled out by the Almighty as objects of his special regard, "whose character and conduct he has held up as models for future generation." Quoting Genesis IX:22–7, he made the common pro-slavery argument about Noah's son Ham: "here language is used, which God would exercise to the posterity of Shem and Japheth, while they were holding the posterity of Ham in a state of abject bondage" (Stringfellow 1860, 141). All this because Ham had "looked upon" his unclothed, drunken father (Noah), and somehow, American chattel slaves are understood to be the descendants of Ham (Canaan).

After foregrounding the discussion of slavery's justification in the patriarchal age of the Bible, mentioning that the Gospels are silent on the issue and explaining that the Pauline tradition justifies it outright, his argument comes to fruition with the advent of America. The United States, he said, "incorporated it into the only National Constitution which ever emanated from God" (Faust 1981, 139).

J. D. B. De Bow (1820–1867) was the editor of *De Bow's Review*, a widely circulated Southern magazine in the mid-nineteenth century (1846–1884). De Bow would often write articles in his publication, the most famous of which was "Slavery and the Bible" in 1850. In his account, De Bow conspicuously left out the Ham story, dwelling extensively instead on the patriarchs Abraham and Moses, the Book of Exodus and several books of the New Testament. But he too concluded that American chosenness lay at the heart of slavery's continuation into the modern era in the United States. Slaves are consistently presented as property in the Bible, he contended; Abraham not only owned slaves, but was explicitly ordered by God to circumcise them.[9] In Joseph's story, slavery is presented as a background condition of society – their lot is clearly hereditary. Finally, there are specific rules about how one is supposed to treat his slaves, with very specific punishments – including manumission – for gross mistreatment.[10] Finally, he argued that Abraham was chosen by God to do great things and to bear the progeny of the nation of Israel – so he asks: why would God select someone who was behaving in an evil manner?

Next follows De Bow's interpretation of Exodus – the quintessential story of revolution in the Bible. He argues that Hebrews were slaves in Egypt, and that God allowed this. Moreover, once the Hebrews were freed, and wandering in the wilderness, they were given laws which specify the bringing in, buying and inheriting of slaves. These laws were meant to be carried forward into the promised land, once they arrived there. In De Bow's view, the Israelites are a people meant to dominate other races – and, by extension, own slaves.[11]

Finally, in the New Testament, De Bow contends, both Paul's epistles and Timothy clearly encourage slaves to obey their masters (slavery is much worse in ancient Rome than in the American South, he argues). Why would they have said that, if they thought slavery so evil? Both the Old and New Testaments, he concludes, affirm slavery. God permits, recognizes, even commands it. That which God has permitted, he argues, cannot be inconsistent with His will.

From here it was not a stretch to reach Benjamin Palmer's "National Responsibility Before God" (13 June 1861), which was very similar to Beecher's criticism of the framers, yet for precisely the opposite reasons: "We bewail then, in the first place, the fatal error of our Fathers in not making a clear national recognition of God at the outset of the nation's career" (cited in Chesebrough 1991, 207). The Confederate Constitution does recognize slavery's sanctification by the Almighty, he argues, in making two significant recognitions: first, that "there were always two nations in the American womb" (Chesebrough 1991, 220). Second, and more importantly, the Civil War is the ultimate battle, of even greater historical importance than the Revolutionary War. Its principles are "broader and deeper than those which underlay that of the Revolution" (Chesebrough 1991, 218). Only by righting this fundamental wrong can America, born a "helpless orphan," achieve the "great national act of incorporation […] which connects the old American nation with the Providence and Government of Jehovah" (Chesebrough 1991, 208).

Return to Lincoln: Idiosyncratic Jeremiad

Unlike Parker, Beecher, De Bow, Stringfellow or Palmer, Abraham Lincoln was careful to explain that he did not think we could know God's true will, let alone what actions should be taken, with any kind of certainty. He said as much in 1865, four years after Palmer's pronouncements, in his second inaugural address, after 620,000 Americans had died during the Civil War:

> It may seem strange that any men should dare to ask a just God's assistance, in wringing their bread from the sweat of other man's faces; but let us judge not that we not be judged. The prayers of both could not be answered; that of neither has been answered fully. The Almighty has his own purposes. (Lincoln 1992b, 450)

There is an obvious temptation to be cynical about Lincoln's frequent invocations of the Bible. After all, he knew his nineteenth-century audiences well. But we should also take note of panegyrics such as the one below, by Episcopal theologian William J. Wolf:

> Lincoln is one of the greatest theologians of America – not in the technical meaning of producing a system of doctrine, certainly not as the defender of some one denomination, but in the sense of seeing the hand of God intimately in the affairs of nations. Just so the prophets of Israel criticized the events of their day from the perspective of the God who is concerned for history and who reveals His will within it. Lincoln now stands among God's latter-day prophets. (Wolf 1963, 24)

We might agree that Wolf goes too far here. Perhaps he does. His comparison remains apt, however, if we consider that he could just as easily have compared Lincoln to an heroic political *leader* in the Bible, say King David, or Moses. Instead he says Lincoln's greatness lay in his ability as a "seer" and a "critic," the two basic characteristics of Old Testament prophets that are also claimed by American ministers (Heschel 2001). But these seers and critics – both in the Bible and America – are also great orators who appear in moments of crisis, reminding us again of Bellah's "time of testing" (1967, 3).

If we consider again the speech Lincoln gave to the New Jersey State Senate on 21 February 1861, we see him as an outlier:

> I am exceedingly anxious that this Union, the Constitution, and the liberties of the people shall be perpetuated in accordance with the original idea for which that struggle was made, and I shall be most happy

indeed if I shall be an humble instrument in the hands of the Almighty, and of this, his *almost chosen people,* for perpetuating the object of that great struggle. (Lincoln 1992a, 280; emphasis mine)

As I mentioned at the outset, perhaps Lincoln was merely updating well-worn Puritan narratives, by then nearly two-and-a-half centuries old, which always assumed that Americans have a sacred status, akin to the ancient Israelites of the Old Testament, and that America's future is destined to unfold according to the cyclical Hebraic model of ascendance, tragic decline, failure, and eventually redemption. For instance, in "A Model of Christian Charity" (1630), John Winthrop excoriated his shipmates on board the Arbella for their moral transgressions – which hadn't even happened yet – as the biblical patriarch Moses had, during the descent at the very end of his life.[12] In this interpretation, God's gift, it seems, remains perpetually underappreciated. But like in Genesis, it can never be withdrawn. The "humble instrument" Lincoln mentions above expresses a similar idea to what he wrote to Kentucky editor Albert Hodges in April 1864: "I claim not to have controlled events, but confess plainly that events have controlled me" (Lincoln 2009, 330).

On the other hand, we might interpret the "near miss" here as an exhortation to recover our chosenness. Here we have to continually be *urged on, to work, to show that we are deserving* – "perpetuation" in Lincoln's terms (a word that appeared frequently in his speeches) – but always "in accordance with the original idea for which the struggle was made," and with "the object of that great struggle" (Lincoln 1992a, 280). Robert Bellah has called this the "Civil Religion of America,"[13] the notion that, in America, it is understood that "God's work must be our own" (1967, 2).

Some recent scholarship that attempts to zero in on Lincoln's religious beliefs definitely supports this interpretation. Richard Carwardine attempts to put Lincoln's theological views into perspective:

> Lincoln's Calvinistic frame of thought prompted him to conceive of the Almighty as the ruler of nations as well as of men, to identify nations as moral entities equally as guilty of transgressions against the divine law as the individuals who composed them [...] The calamity of the Civil War, the sacrifices and the suffering had to be seen as punishments [...] Americans had a duty to "confess our national sins," to repent, and to pray for God's clemency. (Carwardine 2008, 238)

Alternatively, we could also read Lincoln's words here as closer to those of the young lawyer of "The Lyceum Speech" (1837), delivered in the fading afterglow of the American Revolution. Here a young Lincoln laments the passing of an era of revolutionary heroism, and fixes our sights on less inspiring sources of correction, as the country drifts towards lawlessness. Here we might still have important tasks as a nation, but they pale in comparison to those of the ancient Hebrews of biblical Israel. Americans are left with a perpetual, but permanently second-order (secular) struggle, which can never be wholly redemptive – the way, for example, the eternal "City upon a Hill" is rendered in the Gospel of Matthew.[14]

Other recent scholarship would seem to bolster this conclusion. Historian Allen Guelzo suggests that, although the Whigs (Lincoln's party before he helped form the Republican party) was forged in part by close ties with Evangelicals, Lincoln himself always had a more traditional bent – although it is well-documented that he never was a member of a church.[15] His position was best summed up by Civil War historian Allen Guelzo as Enlightenment rationalism, harbored within the shell of a residual Calvinism:

> Lincoln's concept of God [...] was not the orthodox trinitarian God of Father, Son, and Holy Spirit described by the Old School theologians but a truncated one with God the Father – remote, austere, all-powerful, uncommunicative – and neither Son nor Spirit. (Guelzo 1999, 153)

Finally, there is a fourth possibility, which gets us closer to Lincoln's exceptionalism. Perhaps Lincoln meant that we should not assume that God has any special affection for America at all. By "almost chosen," he meant something closer to what that would mean in the Bible – nothing. While that would be an unusual notion for an American president to have, he expressed this more than once, albeit usually privately. After the Union had suffered another defeat at Bull Run (August 1862), and Lincoln had seriously begun to ponder the radical step of proclaiming the emancipation of Southern slaves, he penned a "Meditation on the Divine Will," which his secretaries later recalled was meant for Lincoln's eyes alone:

> The will of God prevails. In great contests each party claims to act in accordance with the will of God. Both *may* be, and one *must* be wrong. God can not be *for*, and *against* the same thing at the same time. In the present civil war it is quite possible that God's purpose is something different from the purpose of either party – and yet the human instrumentalities, working just as they do, are of the best adaptation to effect His purpose. I am almost ready to say this is probably true – that God wills this contest, and wills that it shall not end yet. By his mere quiet power, on the minds of the now contestants, He could have either *saved* or *destroyed* the Union without a human contest. Yet the contest began. And having begun He could give the final victory to either side any day. Yet the contest proceeds. (Noll 1997, 8)

Only once did Lincoln say he was acting directly on the will of God – when, after months of perseverance, he finally issued the Emancipation Proclamation of 1863. The rest of the time, Lincoln sought to remind Americans that "the Almighty has his own purposes" (1992b, 450). The difference was always that President Lincoln never presumed to know what those purposes were.

Notes

1 Although he never identified with any particular Protestant sect, Lincoln knew his King James Bible well, and was renowned for his ability to use biblical metaphors to describe political events.
2 New Jersey never chose Lincoln, incidentally. In both 1860 and 1864, it was the only northeastern state Lincoln failed to carry.
3 Isaiah 49:6 (King James Bible).
4 Another interpretation could be that Lincoln was positioning himself as an American Moses, the divine "instrument" who would rescue the nation from the precipice of impending collapse, and redeem and renew its sacred covenant.
5 There were several differences between the American Constitution of 1789 and the Confederate Constitution of 1861. Most relevant to my purposes here were changes to the Preamble: the phrase "more perfect union" is replaced with "permanent federal government." The words "invoking the favor and guidance of Almighty God" were added to the Confederate Constitution.
6 *The Origin of Species* (1859) first appeared in America in 1860. Ronald Numbers argues that it was not taken seriously in the American scientific community until approximately 1870. Thus the religious leaders of the time saw no need to respond to it. See R. L. Numbers, *Darwinism Comes to America* (Cambridge, MA: Harvard University Press, 1998).
7 See Corinthian 7:21; Deuteronomy 20:10; Genesis 14:4; Leviticus 25:44 and many others.
8 Stringfellow received honorary degrees in theology from Columbia and Richmond Colleges.
9 Genesis 17:11.
10 Genesis 37–50.
11 This is an important distinction, as the status of imperialism and slavery are separate moral questions.
12 "For I know that, when I am dead, you will take to infamous practices and turn aside from the way which I told you to follow. In days to come, disaster will befall you, for in doing what is wrong in the eyes of the lord you provoked him to anger" (Deuteronomy 31:29 (King James Bible)).
13 In *Civil Religion in America*, Bellah explains that this universal is a generic, non-sectarian, Protestant position (he quotes President Kennedy's inaugural address to make the point).
14 This is the phrasing of John Winthrop in "A Modell of Christian Charity" (1630). The original phrasing in the King James Version of Matthew reads "A city that is set on a hill cannot be hid" (5:13). President-elect John F. Kennedy cited the passage correctly in a speech on 9 January 1961. Ronald Reagan, however, famously added the word "shining" before "city" on at least two occasions – first in his presidential renomination speech in Dallas in 1984, and again in his Farewell Address on 11 January 1989.

15 Lincoln frequently attended Sunday services, however, first at the First Presbyterian Church in Springfield, Illinois and later with his wife Mary at New York Avenue Church in Washington, DC – both Old School Presbyterian churches.

References

Bellah, Robert. 1967. "Civil Religion in America." *Daedalus* 96(1): 1–21.
Blight, D. W. 1989. *Frederick Douglass' Civil War: Keeping Faith in Jubilee*. Baton Rouge: Louisiana State University Press.
Carwardine, Richard. 2008. "Lincoln's Religion." In *Our Lincoln: New Perspectives on Lincoln and His World*, edited by Eric Foner. New York: W. W. Norton & Co.
Chesebrough, D. B. 1991. *"God Ordained this War": Sermons on the Sectional Crisis, 1830–1865*. Columbia: University of South Carolina Press.
———. 1996. *Clergy Dissent in the Old South, 1830–1865*. Carbondale: Southern Illinois University Press.
Faust, D. G. 1981. *The Ideology of Slavery: Proslavery Thought in the Antebellum South, 1830–1860*. Baton Rouge: Louisiana State University Press.
———. 1977. "Evangelicalism and the Meaning of the Pro-Slavery Argument – The Reverend Thornton Stringfellow of Virginia." *Virginia Magazine of History and Biography* 85(1): 3–17.
Genovese, E. D. 1985. *Slavery Ordained of God: The Southern Slaveholders' View of Biblical History and Modern Politics*. Gettysburg: Gettysburg College.
Goen, C. C. 1985. *Broken Churches, Broken Nation: Denominational Schisms and the Coming of the American Civil War*. Macon: Mercer University Press.
Guelzo, Allen C.1999. *Abraham Lincoln: Redeemer President*. Grand Rapids: W. B. Eerdmans.
Lincoln, Abraham. 1992a. "Address to New Jersey Senate at Trenton, New Jersey. 21 February 1861." In *Abraham Lincoln: Selected Speeches and Writings*, edited by Don E. Fehrenbacher. New York: Vintage.
———. 1992b. "Second Inaugural Address. 4 March 1865." In *Abraham Lincoln: Selected Speeches and Writings*, edited by Don E. Fehrenbacher. New York: Vintage.
McLoughlin, W. G. 1970. *The Meaning of Henry Ward Beecher: An Essay on the Shifting Values of Mid-Victorian America, 1840–1870*. New York: Knopf.
Murphy, A. R. 2009. *Prodigal Nation: Moral Decline and Divine Punishment from New England to 9/11*. New York: Oxford University Press.
Noll, Mark. 1997. "The Singularity of Lincoln's Faith in the Era of the Civil War." *Journal of the Abraham Lincoln Association* 18(1): 1–26.
———. 1998. "The Bible and Slavery." In *Religion and the American Civil War*, edited by Randall Miller, Harry S. Stout and Charles Reagan Wilson. New York: Oxford University Press.
———. 2006. *The Civil War as a Theological Crisis*. Chapel Hill: University of North Carolina Press.
Noll, Mark, Nathan O. Hatch and George M. Marsden. 1989. *The Search for Christian America*. Colorado Springs: Helmers & Howard.
Parker, T. 1969. *The Slave Power*. New York: Arno Press.
Wolf, W. J. 1963. *The Religion of Abraham Lincoln*. New York: Seabury Press.
Woodward, C. V. 1993. *The Burden of Southern History*. Baton Rouge: Louisiana State University Press.

Chapter 4

SPIRITUAL VIOLENCE: MAX WEBER AND NORBERT ELIAS ON RELIGION AND CIVILIZATION

Bryan S. Turner

Introduction

In a famous passage from the *Ynglingsaga*, we hear about the comrades of Odin who "went without shields, and were mad as dogs or wolves, and bit on their shields, and were as strong as bears or bulls; men they slew, and neither fire nor steel would deal with them; and this is what is called the fury of the berserker" (Morris and Magnusson 1893, I:16–17). This passage could usefully function as a preface to either *The Civilizing Process* or *Economy and Society*. We can interpret Norbert Elias's theory of the civilizing process as, amongst other things, a history of the decline of the warrior stratum in European feudalism and the rise of the court society. The emergence of a pacified court society and the technological development of weapons employing gunpowder eventually transformed the social functions and status of feudal warlords and their followers. These changes in civility also chart the formation of the nation-state and the centralization of institutional power. The transformation of the emotions is also an important feature of this history. In the discussion "On changes in aggressiveness," Elias (2000, 161–2) provides an important account of how violent passions in the early feudal period were slowly regulated as the civilized forms of court society evolved. In this chapter, I develop an argument that there are important parallels between Max Weber's account of the routinization of charisma in military bureaucracies and Elias's analysis of the decline of militarized feudalism. The routinization of charismatic force in society brings about a predictable social environment in which risk and passion are routinely managed. However, I want to criticize Elias's historical sociology for its neglect of religion and the relationship of religion to military institutions and culture. In developing this interpretation of war and civilization, I shall coin the expression "warrior charisma" in order to extend Weber's analysis of types of authority.

Despite their shared interests in the historical sociology of power relations and state institutions, there are relatively few published commentaries by Elias on Weber's sociology. However, Weber was clearly important in the development of Elias's historical sociology. There is, for example, an extended discussion of Weber in the *The Court Society*. Elias criticized Weber effectively for developing a unidimensional and ahistorical notion of rationality, and pointed out that patterns of rational behavior would be specific to different social contexts. While Weber had in mind primarily "bourgeois-capitalist" forms of rationality, Elias argued that the court had its own style of rational norms of action. Thus "[c]ourt rationality is generated by the compulsion of the elite social mesh; by it people and prestige are made calculable as instruments of power" (Elias 1983, 111). In *The Civilizing Process* (Elias 2000, 469), Weber is criticized for his static view of "the individual," and for his inability to reconcile the analytical tensions between "the individual" and "society." Elias (2000, 472) treats Weber's failure to deal successfully with this artificial and static division as part of a general weakness of sociological theory, and argues that Weber and Parsons belong to "the same provenance." The same argument occurs in *The Society of Individuals* (Elias 1991, 164) where it is claimed that human society is not a loose collection of individuals or groups as "depicted in some older sociological theories, including Max Weber's theory of action." Elias's solution was to analyze the two concepts of individual and society as social processes "in conjunction with empirical investigations" (Elias 2000, 473). In *The Court Society* (Elias 1983, 21) Weber is discussed with approval in relation to the problem of luxury in the court society, but his "ideal type" method is rejected as historically inadequate, especially in Weber's treatment of patrimonialism.

My argument is broadly that Weber's "rationalization process" in which legal-rational norms of conduct come to dominate social interaction is parallel to the civilizing process in which civil norms of self-restraint come to dominate social interaction. The routinizing process and the civilizing process have similar analytical functions and occupy the same space within the theoretical structure of Weber's macro-sociology and Elias's figurational sociology. In addition, much of Elias's criticism of Weber (and Parsons) is misplaced. Weber did not accept a static, ideal-typical analysis of the historical patterns of authority, but more importantly his sociology is not based on a rigid division between society and individual. The concept of the social actor in both Weber and Parsons was an analytical construct that emerged from their critical engagement with economic theory. By contrast, in his sociology of religion, Weber developed the sophisticated idea of "personality" and "life orders" in which a personality structure is not a given, but is cultivated through education and discipline. "Personality" stands frequently in opposition to the "life orders" of the economy and the state, and with the growth of capitalism, personality is threatened by the regulatory impact of the practical rationality of this secular world (Hennis 1988). Different cultures have different regimes that produce these personalities. The violent personalities of medieval society are replaced by the new life orders that emerge with new social technologies. In his studies of the Protestant sects, Weber examined the historical development of the ascetic personality in relation to the life orders of an emerging capitalist society. One can argue that the articles on European and American sectarianism were part of a larger project on the sociology of life conduct (*Lebensfuhrugt*) (Baehr 2001). It is not possible therefore to interpret Weber's sociology as yet another conventional dichotomy of the individual and society; the question for Weber was thoroughly anthropological and historical. Similar arguments might be developed in relation to Parsons who thought of personality as a type of institution and hence did not conceptualize society as simply a collection of individuals. Neither Weber nor Parsons adopted a behavioral epistemology of the individual, and both assumed that religion had historically played an important part in shaping the "individual" as an historical construct (Bourricaud 1981).

Charisma, and especially warrior charisma, is important because it occupies a social and historical niche that appears to challenge the social practices that bring about civility and civilization. Charisma is opposed to the normalizing process of tradition and incompatible with the rationalizing processes of the legal-rational bureaucracies in the modern state. Bureaucratization occurs in societies where the disruptive effects of charismatic claims have been contained and suppressed by the political power of the "office" over "the person," and by the centralizing of state power (Shils 1975). Civilizational processes in court society are parallel to the routinizing of charisma into the authority of office, and, while the habitus of the court and the office are very different, they are both incompatible with charismatic frenzy. The self-restraint of both settings is far removed from the warrior intoxication of the berserk warrior and the growth of military discipline and training as techniques for producing a mass army. The training of the body in the feudal court and the monastery are early models of body techniques that were developed by educational and military institutions in the creation of professional training (Foucault 1977; Vigarella 1989).

The modern state emerges as an institution that secures a monopoly over legitimate violence, and hence it relies on specialized training and military discipline to produce professional men who are able to carry out their tasks in a spirit of neutrality and disinterest. The calling of the modern soldier does not include the sheer enjoyment of killing that was characteristic of the feudal warrior or the "noble savage." Although women in the modern army may not necessarily be combat troops, the fact that women are recruited into the military is an important indication that the emotional structure of the military, and of modern warfare, are consistent with a professional rather than a charismatic culture. In this chapter, I want to modify Weber's argument in two directions. In many "primitive societies," warrior charisma is also a form of spiritual ecstasy in which the warrior is transformed out of an earthly and profane role into a sacred domain. I shall take the Cheyenne Plains tribes of North America as an illustration. Charisma, while commonly understood to be a spontaneous eruption into normal social relationships, is still governed by norms, roles and customs. In this sense, it is already partly "cultivated" and hence partly "civilized." This issue is related to the problem in Weber's account in *Ancient Judaism* (1952) concerning the difference between true and false prophets. Can charisma be simulated and manufactured, or is it a blind force of the sacred? My second elaboration of Weber's sociology is that, while Weber's argument is correct that charisma is a rare form of authority in modern societies, charisma is increasingly manufactured and transformed into celebrity. In modern societies, charisma is democratized, and as a result of commercial routinization appears as popular celebrity. In the world of popular entertainment, any trivial and mundane activity of celebrities has charismatic worth, but the contents of the original notion have completely disappeared. The contrast with the intoxicated fury of the charismatic warrior could not be more profound and hence this discussion of warrior charisma provides a theoretical platform for examining the historical and social relationship between religion, discipline and (organized) violence.

Weber's development of the concepts of personality and life order can be understood as a sociological contribution to the study of character as a form of discipline. We can reasonably interpret Weber's notion of personality as an institutionalization of the individual, and thereby make some sensible comparisons with Michel Foucault's contribution to the "technologies of the self" (Foucault 1997). The military training of the Cheyenne was designed to construct a technology of the self that was set within the sacred. Their mode of warfare can be defined as a form of spiritual violence, because warfare was bound up with religious norms of conduct and their military interaction was highly ritualized. War was a deadly serious game. Cheyenne warriors had a reputation for extreme forms of violence, but their mode of warfare was also a highly controlled ritual. The basic idea was to show how the training of the body as technology of the self-produced a capacity to define the warrior as (socially) dead prior to conflict. These spiritual technologies are therefore an important illustration of military technologies of self-creation.

There is no doubt that Elias produced one of the most influential theories of the transformation of violence in human societies in terms of the civilizing process. His argument is well known. In summary, it states that with the transformation of feudal society, the rise of the bourgeois society and the development of the modern state, interpersonal violence was increasingly regulated by social norms that emphasized self-restraint and personal discipline. The theory can be regarded as a moral pedagogy of the body in which raw passions and emotions are self-regulated through disciplinary regimes. The theory shows how developments in social institutions (such as the court, the state and the bourgeois family) are important for and interact with the emotions and dispositions of individuals. Personal civility and civilizing institutions are bound together in a dynamic historical process. As a result, in contemporary societies, social restraint and social order require the development of self-attention in which through self-reflection (imagining what others think of us) we exercise self-surveillance and personal control (Barbalet 1998, 86). In this sense, we can regard the theory of the civilizing process as an historical psychoanalytic of violent emotions within the sociological paradigm of the modern state.

Given the important exposition of the contrast between culture and civilization in the introduction to Elias's major work, it is odd that he chose the title "the civilizing process," because his argument is in fact about the cultivating process. Elias's historical study of the social processes that cultivate behavior through the development of a culture of restraint occurs within the context of an established European debate about the contrast between *Kulture* and *Zivilisation*. Through this discussion, Elias begins to establish the sociology of morals, where different social classes are involved in a competitive struggle over the meaning and value of ethical conduct, and where different systems of training and discipline are seen to be appropriate to the cultural production of character. These differences were not only about the cultural conflict between the social classes, but also between nations and national character. The theory of Zivilisation was interpreted as part of an international struggle between Anglo-Saxon, specifically American industrial, society and Germany. This perception of profound differences in national character was an important aspect of actual politics and social theory. Pessimism about intercultural conflict was evident in Weber's inaugural Freiburg Lecture on social conflict as a Darwinistic struggle, in the pessimistic cultural analysis of the decline of the West by Oswald Spengler and in the literary works of Thomas Mann (Herf 1984). Elias was sensitive to these historical struggles in the evolution of the notion of culture, and he argued that the dichotomy between (technological) civilization and (moral) cultivation was gradually transformed from a social distinction between social classes to a national distinction as the German bourgeoisie rose in social power. Elias's sociology of morals is concerned therefore with the complex historical relationship between the production of character and the production of culture. This sociological concept of process is a major criticism of the traditional dichotomy of the individual and society that has dominated and frequently frustrated the development of sociological theory.

While this theory has been distinctively influential, it has also been subject to systematic criticism. In this chapter, I shall outline three obvious lacunae in Elias's theory. Firstly, the theory does not provide any adequate account of the role of religion in controlling human violence. Once can develop this critical observation through a commentary on charisma and the sacred in human society, namely on the nature of sacred violence. Secondly, Elias had relatively little to say about the interaction between technology, particularly military hardware, and interpersonal norms. Against Elias's theory of the civilizing process, modern technology has made it possible, both in peace and war, for the state and modern military institutions to exercise control over instruments of mass destruction that were unimaginable in less civilized societies. Elias's analysis of the importance of constraints in terms of interpersonal violence is, however, consistent with the view that modern technology has obviously enhanced the capacity of the means of violence in civilized societies. The "de-personalization" of violence is obviously consistent with Elias's civilization theory, and it is clearly compatible with Weber's discussion of rationalization. While the Holocaust raised basic questions about the civilization of Europe, the destruction of Jewish communities can be interpreted as the rational application of the means of violence to an administrative objective (Bauman 1989). It was an aspect of "the banality of evil" (Arendt 1994) that Nazi officers like Adolph Eichmann went about their bureaucratic tasks with clinical calmness. My point is that Elias has very little to say about technology as such. Thirdly, apart from Elias's interest in art in African society, possibly as a consequence of his teaching appointment in Ghana (1962–64), his theory was primarily concerned to explain aspects of social change in European society. My examination of the evolution of violence and warrior charisma among American Plains Indians, especially the Cheyenne, is intended to be an elaboration of the discussion of self-restraint in Elias's historical sociology. Elias made some important comparisons between contemporary societies and Native American tribes in terms of the importance of self-restraint and time discipline in *Time: An Essay* (Elias 1992), and I shall draw upon this discussion in what follows.

Weber and Elias on Religion and Civilization

In the history of sociological theory it has been commonplace to compare Elias's work favorably with the work of Talcott Parsons on the grounds that Parsons neglected historical processes, because his structural-functional analysis made static assumptions about the properties of social systems rather than historical transformations. The intention here is not to reassess Parsons' functionalism, but rather to explore an important difference between Elias and Parsons in order to develop a sociological account of charisma, the sacred and violence. While Elias gave special emphasis to military conflicts and social violence in his study of the civilizing process, he almost completely neglected the historical and comparative importance of religious cultures and institutions. *The Civilizing Process* is largely silent about the role of religious norms and institutions in European history in the regulation of social behavior. By contrast, the centrality of the sociology of religion in Parsons' sociology was in part a consequence of his intellectual encounter with the legacy of Weber (Turner 1999). Parsons was steeped in Weber's sociological project, and recognized that the question of religion was the continuous thread in Weber's economic and political sociology. For example, Parsons translated *The Protestant Ethic and the Spirit of Capitalism* (Weber 1930), wrote an influential introduction to *The Sociology of Religion* (Parsons 1966) and edited *The Theory of Social and Economic Organization* (Parsons 1947). The absence of any sustained discussion of religious institutions in any part of Elias's oeuvre is remarkable, and provides a definite contrast with the sociological legacies of both Weber and Parsons. Parsons' criticisms of simple secularization theories and his recognition of the generic importance of religion to the building of institutions were major foundations of his sociology as a whole.

The fact that Elias showed no interest in the regulative and restraining functions of religious norms in the historical process of civilizing military violence, the court and the bourgeois household is a significant problem in his treatment of the institutional matrix of Western nation-states. Sociologists who are sympathetic to Elias's historical sociology have claimed that it was simply not possible for Elias to deal with all aspects of the civilizing process, and that in any case his analysis was specifically concerned with secular institutions and processes (Russell 1996). This defense is not convincing because, from a sociological and historical perspective, religion is fundamental to social regulation. Religion, to paraphrase Durkheim, includes the rites and rituals that bind people together into a moral community, and exercises constraint over their affective drives. Religion, to paraphrase Weber, disciplines the person, especially through ascetic practices, and creates life orders and personalities. Weber's sociology of religion can be read as a contribution to the idea that religion has been important in regulating the instinctual life in the interests of social order (Turner 1987). Freudian psychoanalysis, for example, was preoccupied with the tensions between instinctual gratification and religious asceticism, and the analysis of the relationship between psychic regulation and social requirements in *Civilization and its Discontents* (Freud 1930) was an important anticipation of the critical theory of Herbert Marcuse in such works as *Eros and Civilization* (1955). The notion that religious norms play an important part in creating and establishing social order has been fundamental to social and political theory.

There are linguistic, philosophical and theological arguments that we separate and distinguish violence from the sacred, but further reflection shows that this separation is unwarranted and historically complex. The psychoanalysis of ritual indicates the falsity of this cultural separation. In *Violence and the Sacred* (1988), René Girard showed how sacrifice was the root of religious ritual and the social contract. Sacrifice is a collective ritual that obscures the origins of religious practices in actual murder and physical violence. Sacrifice can be interpreted as a collective celebration that ritually undermines the prohibition or taboo on murder, especially of relatives and kinfolk. In general, collective rituals typically undermine and reverse the normal order of society to release charismatic powers that become available to the social group. Freud had almost unwittingly (re)discovered the true connections between sexual abstinence, sacrifice and the Oedipus complex in *Totem and Taboo* (1913). Primitive religious ritual is organized around the killing of a surrogate victim, and involves a fusion of opposites – violence and the sacred. The historical evolution of rituals typically obscures these primitive origins. The crucifixion of Christ was yet another sacrifice of the offspring in order to release the charismatic powers of the Father. From this psychoanalytic vantage point, Elias's theory might also obscure this relationship, and allow us to argue that the evolution of the civilizing process involves the suppression of primitive violence behind the shield of civility.

The periodic revivification of the social order requires a release of charismatic powers through what Durkheim called a collective effervescence. When these rituals are separated for any length of time, their celebration "sometimes attains to a sort of frenzy" (Durkheim 1961, 391–2). The study of these ritual practices led Durkheim to conclude that religion was the wellspring of social life, because "nearly all the great social institutions have been born in religion" (Durkheim 1961, 466). These lasting institutional forms required a periodic restoration through moments of collective frenzy. It is appropriate to call this social frenzy a "collective charisma." In ancient cultures, warrior cults and military leaders were thus a common feature of religious organization (Wach 1944, 255).

In "primitive society," there is no clear institutional differentiation between violence and the sacred, but with the rise of Christianity these spheres are distinguished in Christian theology, which had a clear understanding of "the world" and religion. Augustinian theology established a categorical separation of the secular world of violence and the Christian world of *agape*. The City of God was characterized by justice and forgiveness, whereas the secular world of the pagans was violent and cruel. But Augustine, partly as a result of his struggle with the Donatist sect, was compelled to compromise in recognizing the validity of the concept of the just war (Weithman 2001). This attempt to reconcile imperial Rome and Christianity as a religion of salvation produced a profound reaction against the materialism of secular society, namely Christian monasticism and mysticism. Augustine was critical of the alleged virtues of the pre-Christian empire, arguing that the military advances of the empire were not motivated by true virtues. He rejected Cicero's view of the glorious origins of Rome, and championed Christian virtue as the foundation of a civilized society based on love of neighbors. Augustine hated civil disturbance and war, and was compelled to accept the state as a necessary regulation of society.

Medieval political theory moved in a very different direction and was concerned to find some institutional reconciliation between church and state and, in particular, ecclesiastical teaching returned to a conception of the prince as religious leader who ruled wisely and, where necessary, forcefully. The problem specifically was to develop a view of feudal kingship as, at least potentially, a religious institution. This theological trajectory was eventually established by Charlemagne (768–814), who was crowned the emperor of the Romans in 800 by Pope Leo III in St Peter's basilica. In the resulting Carolingian theory of rulership, theocracy was combined with some degree of popular consent. We can identify this amalgam in the writings of Charlemagne's teacher Alcuin, who claimed that the emperor had two swords, one to keep the church internally free from heretical belief and the other to quell its external pagan enemies. In the tradition of the biblical King David, Charlemagne embraced the roles of ruler and priest.

With the creation of the Holy Roman Empire, an institutional fusion of religion and imperial power was achieved, but theologians still struggled to determine Christian norms of conduct that would regulate key areas of life, especially sex and the family, the economy and exchange, and war. In feudalism, religion provided an important institutional check on interpersonal violence by integrating the warrior into society. Christianity legitimized the social role of the knight as a necessary aspect of human society and redirected that military violence outwards during the Crusades. Religious norms clearly played an important part in the development of the tradition of the chivalrous knight and were a significant component of the social regulation of violence in medieval society. In *The Canterbury Tales*, Chaucer's knight is the classic example of the warrior who has been civilized by the values and culture of Christendom (Chaucer 1969). For example, the knight who has recently returned from a military campaign undertakes a pilgrimage to offer thanks to a saint for his safe return. The regulation of such warrior traditions involved a complex and often contradictory mixture of secular, feudal values of hierarchy and duty, and Christian norms, such as respect for the honor of noble women.

Although Elias was clearly aware of such religious norms, ecclesiastical institutions did not play any significant part in his account of civilizing processes. However, this absence raises a more general issue about the relationship between spiritual and secular powers, and between charismatic force and military violence. In his account of power, Weber compared the role of the state that seeks a monopoly of spiritual or symbolic violence within a given territory, and the church that aims at a monopoly of spiritual or symbolic violence in human society. For example, the excommunication of heretics and sinners was a form of symbolic violence that excluded people from access to divine grace. The history of Western society can be interpreted as an unstable balance between these two systems of authority. As a liberal political theorist, Weber regarded the political system of caesaropapism, where religion and secular power are institutionally united, as the principal foundation of secular absolutism.

The symbolic capital of ecclesiastical institutions was closely connected to Weber's general theory of authority in which charisma remained a potent challenge to traditional forms of institutional regulation. Charisma is a theological concept that has been widely used in the social and religious sciences to describe the hierarchical organization of religious roles, social movements based on religious inspiration, and authority and leadership in society generally. In its religious context, charisma means a divinely conferred power. Charismatic power is tied to the sacred as an irresistible force in human societies, and people who possess charisma are thought to have extraordinary talents such as healing or prophecy. In shamanism, charismatic authority depends on a capacity to have visions and to perform healing (Eliade 1964). Weber's sociology of religion was particularly concerned to understand the tensions between the informal authority of charismatic leaders and formal bureaucratic authority of established religious institutions (Werbner and Basu 1998). As a result, charisma is conceptually part of an analytical framework that understands the dynamics of large-scale changes in religious institutions and the foundations of authority as outcomes of the violent impact of the sacred on the profane (Lindholm 1993).

In *Economy and Society* (Weber 1978, I:241), charisma is "applied to a certain quality of an individual personality by virtue of which he is considered extraordinary and treated as endowed with supernatural, superhuman, or at least specifically exceptional powers or qualities." In the rise of religions, certain individuals have been recognized as having a capacity to experience ecstatic states that were perceived as the pre-condition for healing, telepathy and divination (Weber 1965, 2). Such charismatic power is either acquired by extraordinary means or inherited as a natural endowment. Often this religious capacity is conceived as an actual substance that may remain dormant in a person until it is aroused by ascetic practices or by trance. In everyday life, charismatic possession is a form of sacred intoxication that is not widely available to the masses (Eisenstadt 1968). Charisma is the foundation of claims to leadership over persons who become disciples or over groups that become as a result "charismatic communities." In "primitive communities," these extraordinary forces were "thought of as resting on magical powers, whether of prophets, persons with a reputation for therapeutic or legal wisdom, leaders in the hunt, or heroes in war" (Weber 1978, I:241).

Although Jesus Christ, Muhammed, Napoleon, Stefan George and the Chinese emperor were all treated by Weber as charismatics, Weber was primarily concerned with religious charisma in the Old Testament prophets (Clements 1997). It is from his analysis of the war prophecy in ancient Judaism that I want to develop the idea of warrior charisma to designate the role of sacred force in military leadership. Such forms of charisma are very common in pre-modern society where the authority of military leaders was based on their charismatic capacities as illustrated by their power over enemies and their ability to avoid injury and death. Weber was particularly interested in the charismatic ecstasy of the Old Testament prophets who were called to defend the relationship between the Jewish people and their jealous God, Yahweh, in times of external threat and adversity. For example, Weber (1952, 98) drew attention to Saul who was "seized by ecstasy and went around naked, spoke madly and for an entire day was in a faint." He also compared Saul who was possessed with an "explosive fury" to "a warrior ecstatic like Mohammed."

These forms of charismatic powers are by definition "uncivilized" in the sense that this power is conferred on individuals as a result of the action of a divine force that cannot be easily controlled or cajoled. The early warlike charismatics were not in control of their actions and their intoxication was an indication of their extraordinary powers. Charisma is always spilling out of the institutions that are designed to house and domesticate it. Charisma thus is always imagined as breaking through and disrupting human relations, bringing confusion, conflict and violence in its train. This religious intensity has clear psychological consequences because "religious life cannot attain a certain degree of intensity without implying a psychical exaltation not far removed from delirium. That is why [...] the men whose religious consciousness is exceptionally sensitive, very frequently give signs of an excessive nervousness that is even pathological" (Durkheim 1961, 258). Among the American Plains Indians, such warrior charisma was associated with transitions to manhood status where tribal rites of passage produced experiences of possession, trance and vision. Charisma erupts into human society, albeit in the context of rituals and institutions of liminal transition. While the training of the knight inculcates norms of bodily deportment, uprightness and chivalrous dispositions, shaking, convulsive and vibrating bodies mark the presence of charisma. Although warrior charisma is often manifest in the controlled body, it is important to recognize that frenzied behavior typically takes place in the context of ritual prescriptions and expectations. There are shared norms about the ritual context within which frenzy will occur, and also assumptions about which persons may enter such social roles.

Weber's sociology of charisma is useful in understanding the social strains that have faced traditional societies in their encounters with Western colonialism and postcolonialism. Charismatic leadership has also played a significant role in those new religious movements that have been a response to the social and economic disruptions associated with the decolonization of the Third World (Worsley 1970). For example, charismatic renewal has been a common theme of diverse religious movements in "primal societies" (Wilson 1973; 1975). The collapse of aboriginal or tribal societies under colonial settlement resulted in the spread of charismatic movements against the supremacy of white-settler societies such as the Ghost Dance among the Cheyenne and Sioux tribes of the American Plains in the 1880s (Niezen 2000). A Paiute prophet called Wovoka had received a vision in which through ritual dance the dead would return to restore the pristine culture of native societies (Brown 1970, 433). This anti-white charismatic movement subsided after the murder of Sitting Bull and the destruction of his followers at Wounded Knee in December 1890. It is interesting that the beliefs associated with the Ghost Dance movement actually discouraged war and ritual practices associated with it, such as the war and scalp dances (Mooney 1996, 145). They also proscribed the mutilation of the body that was a traditional aspect of mourning.

Military Techniques and Charisma: The Cheyenne

Early historical records of the Cheyenne from the seventeenth century indicate that they were living west of the Mississippi River in Minnesota. The name "Cheyenne" is an approximation of the name given to them by the Lakota or Dakota people and means a people whom the Lakota could not understand but were not enemies. Living on the edge of the Plains and equipped with primitive weapons, the Cheyenne were hunter-gatherers, being dependent on gathering wild rice and stalking buffalo. The archeological evidence suggests that the Cheyenne constructed fortified villages and lived in earth lodges in the eighteenth century on the Cheyenne River in North Dakota on the site known in the scientific literature as Biesterfeldt (Wood and Liberty 1980). This village was attacked and burned by a Chippewa war party around 1790. By the end of the eighteenth century, Cheyenne groups were migrating southwestward onto the Great Plains where they became nomadic tribes dependent on hunting buffalo from horseback (Grinnell 1962). The history of the modern Cheyenne is bracketed by two tragedies, Wounded Knee I, when the Seventh Cavalry massacred a large band, and Wounded Knee II, when members of the American Indian Movement (AIM) came into bloody conflict with supporters of tribal leader Dick Wilson (Frazier 2000, 61).

Although the Plains Indian tribes shared a number of common war practices, the Cheyenne perfected and made explicit their underlying "spiritual" and ritualistic characteristics. The Cheyenne, who became famous among white settlers and military for the (alleged) practice of cutting off the arms of enemies as trophies, were renowned among native tribesmen for their concentrated use of ruthless violence against their enemies, and the spread of horses through the Plains region converted them into a formidable mobile military unit. Like other forms of ritualization of violence, Cheyenne warrior practices involved a remarkable discipline of the self to bring about the maximum effect of violence (real and symbolic) on an enemy. From a brief description of Cheyenne fighting protocols, we can learn something more generally interesting about the discipline of the body as a technology of the self to produce through specific institutions a spiritual violence.

Because people living in the militarized societies of the Plains had to face the prospect of an early and violent death, often accompanied by horrific torture, young children were trained to experience pain stoically. The ideal warrior could undergo torture without any expression of pain, and would sing proudly about the military prowess of his own tribe as his captors tore flesh from his body. Plains warriors took great delight in humiliating their enemies through the grotesque torture of prisoners, and as a result they too had to prepare themselves for an equally protracted and violent end. Elias (1992, 155–60) makes the important point that, in our nuclear age, modern military systems can destroy whole societies, but our social codes prohibit enjoyment of torture and regard interpersonal violence as uncivilized. In "pre-state societies," individuals enjoyed a wide margin of personal freedom because they were not subject to time constraints, but such freedoms were set within a militarized environment in which they might anticipate a violent death.

These social codes trained men in the stoical acceptance of death. The fundamental point of Cheyenne military culture was that warriors already counted themselves among the dead prior to violent engagement, and hence they were spiritually oblivious to the danger of their own death. They prepared for battle by saying farewell to their relatives, dressing as for a funeral and singing their death songs. Having ritually consigned themselves to death, they were as a result surprised to survive such encounters. Plains warfare was organized by a definite set of formal procedures. Warriors would line up to face their foes, and then issue taunts and other gestures calculated to humiliate the opposition. The men would dress in their buckskin and ornaments as if they were already prepared for death. Because Cheyenne warriors had already accepted death, their indifference to suffering and death was calculated to cause the maximum psychological terror. Taunts and insults preceded most engagements. Those warriors who had great medicine or warrior charisma would challenge the enemy to shoot them by riding in front of them.

Cheyenne tactics involved a ritualized sequence of attacks. There were firstly 'suicide boys' who were typically unarmed. They sought suicide because they had experienced some loss of face within their own community, or a woman had rejected them, or they were grieving over a lost relative. These young men, with the encouragement of the mature warriors, threw themselves upon their enemy in an effort to tear them apart with their bare hands. The death of such boys was an indication that the Cheyenne had no concern for casualties. The next wave involved the "dog rope men" who denied themselves the possibility of flight by fixing themselves to the ground with a sash tied to a stake. They fought from this ground position with long lances, clubs and bows and arrows. Singing their death songs, they invited the enemy to kill them. These men were often able to break up a mounted attack of the enemy. These preparations were followed by a genuine Cheyenne cavalry attack in which the soldiers concentrated their force on a single point in the enemy line. Once this attack was complete, the Cheyenne would remorselessly pursue those who attempted to escape the battlefield. Military engagements normally concluded with victory songs expressing their joy and triumph over their enemies. Their tactics, which expressed a spiritualized approach to symbolic self-destruction prior to battle, had the consequence of making the Cheyenne a dominant military force on the Plains (Moore 1999, 107–8). The Cheyenne were ferocious opponents who sought to destroy their enemies rather than engage them only in ritualized confrontation. Plains warfare in other tribal cultures often involved ritualized harassment of the enemy such as stealing horses or counting coup by striking an enemy with a stick as a form of humiliation.[1] Cheyenne warfare was more determined and systematic. It is claimed that they once exterminated a tribe (the Owuqeo) in a form of tribal genocide (Moore 1999, 113).

The military victories of the Plains Indians over General Crook on the Rosebud River and George Custer at the Little Big Horn in 1876 were decisive. Cheyenne and Sioux warriors killed 254 members of Custer's troops and Custer's scalp became an important trophy. However, the retaliation of the United States troops was determined and ruthless, resulting in the dispersal of the Plains tribes and their final confinement to reservations by 1879. Reservation life had a devastating effect on people whose nomadic culture had been destroyed so rapidly and profoundly by the eradication of the buffalo herds, prolonged warfare and disease. In response, the Cheyenne joined the Ghost Dance movement of the 1880s, but Cheyenne involvement was terminated by the Wounded Knee massacre when approximately 300 men, women and children were killed by Hotchkiss machine guns. This sudden termination of their nomadic pattern of life was also the end of their warrior charisma, because the sedentary life of the reservation undermined the hunter-gatherer economy and the sacred rituals that produced it. By a strange fate, the extraordinary warriors of this period of modern history – Sitting Bull, Crazy Horse, Red Cloud, Little Big Man and Dull Knife – became legends of the encounter between civilization and savagery (Klein 1997). As a result, the Cheyenne and Sioux were drawn rapidly into the emerging entertainment culture of modern society. Warriors who had terrified white settlers in the 1870s became figures in popular culture by the 1880s. They became celebrities of "the Wild West" rather than charismatic warriors.

Warrior charisma flourished briefly, but in a highly technological context, when Plains Indians served in large numbers in the United States forces in the two world wars and in Vietnam. In these modern wars, Native Americans were still able to draw upon their tribal military cultures. Many Plains Indians became war heroes in the US forces. In *The Cheyenne*, Moore (1999, 108–13) recounts how Native American soldiers would count coup on surprised German soldiers during the Allied invasion of France, and how Roy Nightwalker, a Cheyenne chief, collected scalps from German soldiers that he had killed. These warriors of modern warfare were often welcomed back into their tribal communities with traditional ceremonies in which they received new names and tribal honors in respect of their bravery. Pima Ira Hayes, a Native American, was a member of the group of Marines who were photographed by the *Life* magazine reporter raising the American flag at Iwo Jima (Frazier 2000, 87). Native Americans also served in the Gulf War, but the occasions for warrior charisma are now limited by the growing dependence on high technology and the reluctance of the American government to sustain war casualties in an era of intensive media coverage.

A central aspect of Foucault's social theory was the recognition that in the Western tradition acquiring knowledge, recognizing moral truths and developing the self required a government of the body. Put simply, body training is a critical method of training the self (Foucault 1997). These various practices amounted to "techniques of the self." In particular, the warrior self is dependent on specific modes of body transformation through discipline. Don Levine (1991) has shown how the martial arts as a form of body training were linked to a specific educational regime. We might conclude from this research that the production of the self cannot be achieved without a corporeal pedagogy; in short, "characterology" requires a specific form of embodiment to achieve its effects.

We can identify a range of practices in the culture of Plains Indians that were designed to produce a special warrior character. Religious training of the warrior body involved a number of preparations for adulthood. These included the Sweat Lodge, dance, fasting and Sun Dance. These rituals also gave rise to specific religious experiences that typically involved a vision, and as a result a change of name. The frenzied behavior of charismatic warriors is a form of institutionalized violence. This behavior requires a certain amount of training preparation; it is organized into distinctive temporal sequences, for example, relating to initiation; the behavior is comprehensible to indigenous observers; and it is channeled in particular directions. Rape and pillage against women are often ritually controlled (Eliade 1958, 83). It may not count as "civilized behavior" but it is certainly cultivated. Furthermore, as we have seen, the violence between individuals is often regulated. The Cheyenne warriors would count coup against their enemies in terms of the rules of war.

It is obvious that in this account of Cheyenne spiritual violence I have sought to show the possible connections between Foucault's notion of the "technology of the self," Weber's "personality" and "life orders" and Elias's "civilizing process." Elias's theory can be seen as an application of this insight to a long-term historical process in which civilizational norms have achieved a transformation of character through the education of embodied practices. However, the theory was not equipped to analyze how religious experiences were crucial to sustaining violent but spiritual personalities. In fact, he has no real theory of ritual at all. In Elias's work, the civilizing process is primarily a secular history of manners whereby crude, vulgar and rustic behavior was converted into courtly dispositions. In particular, his approach was designed to explicate the normative regulation of the manners of the elite in European history. These processes contrast sharply with the meaning and intention of Cheyenne ritual which was constructed to sustain what we might call battle frenzy, where the warrior was induced to consider himself already dead. The civilizing process is designed to eliminate the forms of collective intoxication that produce warrior heroes in the Viking saga and Cheyenne folk memory. We might argue also that the civilizing process is related to the democratization of charisma that in its pristine form created a spiritual hierarchy of virtuoso religion. Whereas by definition charisma is in short supply, celebrity is subject to inflationary pressures, where everybody can be famous for 15 minutes. This conversion of charisma into celebrity also presupposes the democratization of personality, where spirit possession finds a substitute in narcotic addiction.

Conclusion

In this discussion of charisma and civility, I have drawn out some interesting and theoretically fruitful parallels between Elias and Weber in terms of their historical sociology of routinization and the civilizing process. However, while the analysis of religion was central to Weber's sociology as a whole, Elias was strangely silent about the macro-sociology of religious institutions in the formation of European society. Religion has played a major part in shaping the restraints on social behavior that make social life orderly and predictable. If we recognize that the appearance of warrior charisma is always an unpredictable and contingent event, then religion is important in making social interactions predictable. The actual relationships between military and religious institutions, as I have shown, are complex and contradictory. However, in their legitimation of the violence of knights, it is clear that religious institutions were important in the regulation of the scope and nature of violence. In this respect, my argument follows Weber closely in that warrior charisma was eventually routinized by the rise of a bureaucratic military. Although the lack of attention to religion is in my view a major and striking absence in Elias's otherwise comprehensive account of civility, it does not falsify his argument. There is no reason why the figurational paradigm could not include religious institutions in its account of civilizing processes.

Note

1 It was a common practice among Plains Indians to humiliate their enemies not by killing them but by striking them with sticks or other weapons. This practice of hitting or striking the enemy came to be described, from the initial observations of French explorers, as the practice of taking or counting coup. This practice further illustrates the fact that warfare resembled an elaborate game in which male aggression was channeled into ritualized combat (Hoxie 1996, 667).

References

Adorno, Theodor W. 1991. *The Culture Industry*. London and New York: Routledge.
Arendt, Hannah. 1994. *Eichman in Jerusalem: A Report on the Banality of Evil*. London: Penguin.

Baehr, Peter. 2002. Introduction to *The Protestant Ethic and the "Spirit" of Capitalism and Other Writings*, by Max Weber, ix–xxxii. New York: Penguin.
Barbalet, Jack H. 1998. *Emotion, Social Theory, and Social Structure: A Macrosociological Approach*. Cambridge: Cambridge University Press.
Bauman, Zigmunt. 1989. *Modernity and the Holocaust*. Cambridge: Polity Press.
Bourricaud, Francois. 1981. *The Sociology of Talcott Parsons*. Chicago and London: University of Chicago Press.
Brown, D. 1970. *Bury my Heart at Wounded Knee: An Indian History of the American West*. London: Book Club Associates.
Chaucer, Geoffrey. 1969. *The Prologue and the Three Tales*. Melbourne: Cheshire Publishers.
Clements, R. E. 1997. "Max Weber, Charisma and Biblical Prophecy." In *Prophecy and Prophets: The Diversity of Contemporary Issues in Scholarship*, edited by Y. Gitay, 89–108. Atlanta: Scholars Press.
Durkheim, Émile. 1961. *The Elementary Forms of Religious Life*. New York: Collier.
Eisenstadt, Shmuel N. 1968. *Max Weber on Charisma and Institution Building: Selected Papers*. Chicago: University of Chicago.
Eliade, Mircea. 1958. *Rites and Symbols of Initiation: The Mysteries of Birth and Rebirth*. New York: Harper & Row.
———. 1964. *Shamanism: Archaic Techniques of Ecstasy*. Princeton: Princeton University Press.
Elias, Norbert 1983. *The Court Society*. Oxford: Basil Blackwell.
———. 1991. *The Society of Individuals*. Oxford: Basil Blackwell.
———. 1992. *Time: An Essay*. Oxford: Blackwell.
———. 2000. *The Civilizing Process: Sociogenetic and Psychogenetic Investigations*. Oxford: Blackwell.
Foucault, Michel. 1977. *Discipline and Punish: The Birth of the Prison*. London: Tavistock.
———. 1997. "Technologies of the Self." In *Ethics: Subjectivity and Truth*, 225–51. London: Allen Lane.
Frazier, Ian. 2000. *On the Rez*. New York: Farrar, Strauss & Giroux.
Freud, Sigmund. 1913. "Totem and Taboo". In *The Standard Edition of the Complete Psychological Works of Sigmund Freud*, vol. 8. London: Hogarth Press.
———. 1930. "Civilization and its Discontents". In *The Standard Edition of the Complete Psychological Works of Sigmund Freud*, vol. 13. London: Hogarth Press.
Girard, R. 1988. *Violence and the Sacred*. London: Athlone Press.
Grinnell, G. B. 1962. *The Cheyenne Indians*. 2 vols. New York: Cooper Square.
Heidegger, Martin. 1977. *The Question Concerning Technology and Other Essays*. New York: Harper.
Hennis, Wilhelm. 1988. *Max Weber: An Essay on Reconstruction*. London: Allen & Unwin.
Herf, J. 1984. *Reactionary Modernism: Technology, Culture and Politics in Weimar and the Third Reich*. Cambridge: Cambridge University Press.
Hoxie, F. E., ed. 1996. *Encylopedia of North American Indians*. Boston: Houghton, Mifflin.
Klein, K. L. 1997. *Frontiers of Historical Imagination: Narrating the European Conquest of Native America, 1890–1990*. Berkeley: University of California Press.
Levine, Don. 1991. "Martial Arts as a Resource for Liberal Education: The Cost of Aikido." In *The Body: Social Process and Cultural Theory*, edited by M. Featherstone, M. Hepworth and B. S. Turner, 209–24. London: Sage.
Lindholm, Charles. 1993. *Charisma*. Oxford: Blackwell.

Marcuse, Herbert.1955. *Eros and Civilization: A Philosophical Inquiry into Freud.* Boston: Beacon Press.
Mooney, J. 1996. *The Ghost Dance.* North Dighton: JG Press.
Moore, J. H. 1999. *The Cheyenne.* Oxford: Blackwell.
Morris W. and E. Magnusson. 1893. *Heimskringla.* London: Sage Library.
Niezen, R., ed. 2000. *Spirit Wars: Native North American Religions in the Age of Nation Building.* Berkeley: University of California Press.
Parsons, Talcott. 1966. Introduction to *The Sociology of Religion*, by Max Weber, xix–lxvii. London: Methuen.
Ringer, F. 1969. *The Decline of the German Mandarins: The German Academic Community 1890–1933.* Cambridge, MA: Harvard University Press.
Russell, S. 1996. *Jewish Identity and Civilizing Processes.* Basingstoke: Macmillan.
Shils, Edward. 1975. *Center and Periphery: Essays in Macrosociology.* Chicago: University of Chicago Press.
Tocqueville, Alexis de. 1968. *Democracy in America.* Glasgow: Collins.
Turner, Bryan S. 1987. "The Rationalization of the Body: Reflections on Modernity and Discipline." In *Max Weber, Rationality and Modernity*, edited by S. Whimster and S. Lash, 222–41. London: Allen & Unwin.
Vigarello, G. 1989. "The Upward Training of the Body from the Age of Chivalry to Courtly Civility." In *Fragments for a History of the Human Body*, edited by M. Feher, 149–99. New York: Zone.
Wach, Joachim 1944. *Sociology of Religion.* Chicago and London: University of Chicago.
Weber, Max 1930. *The Protestant Ethic and the Spirit of Capitalism.* London: Allen & Unwin.
———. 1947. *The Theory of Social and Economic Organization.* New York: Oxford University Press.
———. 1952. *Ancient Judaism.* Glencoe: Free Press.
———. 1966. *The Sociology of Religion.* London: Methuen.
———. 1968. *Economy and Society: An Outline of Interpretive Sociology.* Berkeley: University of California Press.
Werbner, P. and H. Basu, eds. 1998. *Embodying Charisma: Modernity, Locality and the Performance of Emotion in Sufi Cults.* London and New York: Routledge.
Wilson, Byran R. 1973. *Magic and the Millennium: A Sociological Study of Religious Movements of Protest among Tribal and Third-World Peoples.* London: Heinemann Educational Books.
———. 1975. *The Noble Savages: The Primitive Origins of Charisma and its Contemporary Survival.* Berkeley: University of California Press.
Wood, W. R., and M. Liberty. 1980. *Anthropology on the Great Plains.* Lincoln: University of Nebraska Press.
Worsley, Peter 1970. *The Trumpet Shall Sound.* London: Paladin.

PEACE

Chapter 5

QUAKERS, THE ORIGINS OF THE PEACE TESTIMONY AND RESISTANCE TO WAR TAXES

Ana M. Acosta

> Whoever can reconcile this, "Resist not evil," with "Resist violence by force," again, "Give also thy other cheek," with "Strike again"; also "Love thine enemies," with "Spoil them, make a prey of them, pursue them with fire and the sword," or, "Pray for those that persecute you, and those that calumniate you," with "Persecute them by fines, imprisonments and death itself," whoever, I say, can find a means to reconcile these things may be supposed also to have found a way to reconcile God with the Devil, Christ with Antichrist, Light with Darkness, and good with evil. But if this be impossible, as indeed it is impossible, so will also the other be impossible, and men do but deceive both themselves and others, while they boldly adventure to establish such absurd and impossible things.
>
> Robert Barclay, 1678[1]

Introduction: Nonviolence and the Society of Friends

Robert Barclay's words, quoted above, have been echoed by Quakers since the seventeenth century and can still be found in the books of discipline and faith published by the Religious Society of Friends today. Barclay's statement followed the spirit of a letter sent in January of 1661 which had been signed by George Fox and many other prominent Quakers (Fox et al. 1660). It was intended to reassure the recently restored monarch, Charles II, of the harmlessness of the Friends, as they called themselves. The declarations made in this letter were not intended to demonstrate a quiet acquiescence on matters of conscience; on the contrary, they were issued as a testimony to the fact that their battle and their weapons were spiritual, not "carnall." After that date, many different Quaker preachers – women and men – elaborated, embellished and disseminated these core beliefs. In a letter of the previous year, 1660, Margaret Fell, one of the "mothers in Israel" of the early Quaker movement, had given the king her own version of this doctrine. In her letter we read, "This wee declare, that it is our principle life and practice to live peaceably with all men, And not to act any thing against the King nor the Peace of the Nation, by any plots, contrivances, insurrections, or carnall weapons to hurt or destroy either him or the Nation thereby, but to be obedient unto all just and lawfull Commands" (Glines 2003, 281 cited in Dandelion 2007, 43). The Peace Testimony, as it came to be known, resonates through the many extant diaries, testaments and pamphlets that Quakers have produced during their 350-year existence.

In the contents of these statements we can determine the way in which the early Quakers endorsed a separation of matters of public rule and matters of individual conscience. The difficulty in the years between 1660 and 1689, however, centered primarily on the fact that individual conscience was still defined as a question of government, and the establishment of a unified church was regarded as a particularly desirable means to guarantee stability and order. The doctrine of nonviolence eventually became one of the fundamental tenets of Quaker belief; it was often preached and frequently written up as an appeal to the spirit in every person to be expressed with zeal, and with sufficient legal liberty to allow individuals to follow the dictates of their own conscience.

Quakerism emerged in the middle of the seventeenth century as a popular movement where women figured prominently. It was without a doubt radical in its disregard of social and sexual hierarchies, and, in spite of the oft-made claim of noninterference in worldly matters, the early Friends were as clearly preoccupied with questions of social justice as of individual salvation. They engaged, if the anachronism can be excused, in a form of civil disobedience that prompted them in spite of severe persecution to refrain from taking oaths, paying tithes and removing their hats in the presence of their betters. The period under discussion in this essay saw the Quaker movement become an organized denomination; this article seeks to explore the various forms this doctrine took before it became fully codified in the course of the eighteenth century. In contradiction to the now accepted orthodoxy that Quakers were defeated into quietism after the Restoration, this chapter seeks further to demonstrate how the movement evolved to include refusing to pay taxes for war purposes. Moreover, it asks whether taxation destined for military use presented early Quakers with the kind of ethical dilemmas we see it pose for Quakers in our own time. It explores whether Quakers' reticence to pay tithes in the seventeenth century can be considered a precedent to resistance towards paying war taxes from the eighteenth century onward, and equivalent to the form in which present-day Friends have objected to paying war taxes.

Historians and the Quaker Peace Testimony

Much research was done in the years between the late 1950s and early 1980s in Britain on the radical religious sects – including the Quakers – that emerged in the middle decades of the seventeenth century, in particular the groundbreaking work of historians W. Alan Cole, Christopher Hill and, more recently, Barry Reay. This body of work changed the way in which the years of the civil wars and Commonwealth had been traditionally understood, but it was also deeply colored by its own historical specificity. Although most of this work remains exciting and inspiring, some of its fundamental tenets need to be reexamined.[2] The tenet that concerns this article is these theorists' evaluation of the Quaker Peace Testimony. For these historians the Quaker Peace Testimony came into being only after the Restoration in 1660 as a reaction to the political defeat of the Commonwealth, and was, therefore, motivated by a kind of social and political self-defense. They share one key assumption – perhaps the most problematic one – that pacifism is politically passive.[3] As a result, if pacifism was a survival strategy after the Restoration, then Quakers became passive after that date too. Christopher Hill unequivocally confirms this equation when he wistfully tells us:

> But treachery lurked in the inner light. In time of defeat, when the wave of revolution was ebbing, the inner voice became quietist, pacifist [...] Once the group decided this way, all the pressures were in the direction of accepting modes of expression not too shocking to the society in which men had to live and earn their living. (Hill 1991, 370)

It is not unlikely that on some level the desire to appease the new monarch was one of the motivations for this doctrine; if this was the case, it didn't work. Quakers were brutally persecuted in the years following the Restoration even after their Peace Testimony had been publicly declared. Moreover, their passivity was anything but quiet: it did not prevent them from preaching, meeting, writing and holding fast to their unorthodox beliefs. It is true that the Friends became organized and developed an administrative structure that encouraged uniformity, but, again, quietism and passivity don't seem to be the right adjectives. Hill in particular, has an unmistakable sympathy for antiestablishment views and tends to be wary of words such as organization, discipline and faith, all of them words that are central to Quakerism. Two other aspects need to be reinscribed into our evaluation of the Peace Testimony. First, the religious motivations of the Peace Testimony have been anachronistically downplayed; and, second, the concept of pacifism is also understood in this body of work from a modern perspective to the detriment of the ways it was experienced and understood in the late seventeenth and eighteenth centuries.[4] Thus, the commonly accepted and oft-repeated dogma that Quakers lost their revolutionary fervor – and their soul even after the Restoration (Braithwaite 1955, 521) – in a quietist and pacifist disappearance from the public sphere in the course of the eighteenth century needs to be reconsidered.[5] Here we will try to relocate pacifism in two contexts, in the seventeenth century and in our own time, before we can decide whether it is indeed quietist. Some work on this account has already been undertaken and most likely will continue in the years to come.

Pacifists and Quakers on Pacifism

From a different perspective, there is another significant body of scholarship on the Peace Testimony. It shares with the scholarship mentioned above the tendency to downplay religion and to impose the specific concerns of its own historical moment. Unlike the scholars mentioned above, however, this perspective regards Quaker pacifism not precisely as a form of defeatism but as the logical outcome of the progress towards liberal humanism. It places their pacifism in the midst of a global historical trend that includes such diverse movements as secular conscientious objectors during the two world wars in Europe, secular Tolstoyans, and the beliefs of and movement inspired by Gandhi. The historian Peter Brock is perhaps the most prolific and noteworthy proponent of this perspective. He writes from the standpoint of a non-Quaker conscientious objector briefly imprisoned during the Second World War, who then served by performing alternative service. After the war Brock worked as a volunteer with Quaker relief in western Germany and in Poland.[6] In his work on Quaker pacifism and regarding Hill's, Cole's and Reay's shared opinion that Quaker pacifism did not exist before 1660 and, therefore, was politically motivated, Brock has reservations. In order to address these reservations, he cites many cases of Quakers voicing objections to bearing arms both in Britain and the colonies during the 1650s, including George Fox himself and other early pacifists such as William Dewsbury (1990, 9–23).

Finally, and not surprisingly, the largest body of work comes from religious scholars, some but not all of whom are Quakers. Accordingly, in the early decades of the twentieth century we find the landmark work on the Peace Testimony of Margaret E. Hirst. Hirst's work antecedes the work of the historians we have been discussing in this section, and it is feasibly to her work and that of Geoffrey F. Nuttall, that emphasize religious experience over political and social factors, that Hill especially was reacting.⁷ At any rate, Hirst, like Brock, gives numerous examples of Quaker belief in pacifism before the Restoration (1923, 55).⁸

The Quaker Peace Testimony

> Do you bear a faithful testimony against bearing arms or paying Trophy Money, or being in any way concerned in privateers Letters of Marque, or in dealing in prize goods as such?
>
> Twelfth Query of the London Yearly Meeting 1758⁹

Early in his journal George Fox, who in 1650 had been imprisoned in Derby for blasphemy, had his first recorded opportunity to proclaim his newly held convictions about weapons and war. Fox tells how while he was in prison some soldiers tried to recruit him out of jail for the militia to fight on the royalist side.

> I told them I lived in the virtue of that life and power that took away the occasion of all wars, and I knew from whence all wars did rise, from the lust, according to James his doctrine. And still they courted me to accept of their offer, and thought I did but compliment with them, but I told them I was come into the covenant of peace, which was before wars and strifes was. (Fox 1952, 65)

This was one of the two recorded instances before the Restoration that attest to Fox's conversion to pacifism.¹⁰ The episode in Derby in 1650 has marked the official point of departure for Fox's and Quaker's pacifism generally even though there is an earlier episode narrated by William Dewsbury in his diary, where he explains how he arrived at his own conviction regarding the sinfulness of war in 1645:

> [T]he word of the Lord came unto me and said, Put up thy sword into thy scabbard [...] Then I could no longer fight with a carnal weapon, against a carnal man, for the letter, which man in his carnal wisdom had called the Gospel, and had deceived me; but then the Lord caused me to yield in obedience, to put up my carnal sword into the scabbard and to leave the Army. (Cited in Hirst 1923, 43)

There are other episodes such as these that delineate the process by which the early Friends arrived at the Peace Testimony, but it was primarily George

Fox's letter of 1661 to the king, mentioned above, that made these principles official. This letter became the basis of all future Quaker testimonies of peace. In the seventeenth and eighteenth centuries, as we have seen in Fox's and Dewsbury's cases, pacifism was understood primarily as a question of conscientious objection to bearing arms. Later on, especially in the nineteenth century, Friends became more active in the political arena by stressing conflict resolution before war. As Britain did not have conscription until World War I, the question of participating in militias had been the main arena in which Quaker resistance to violence and their beliefs were tested. Over the years, however, the question of how to define pacifism and what being a pacifist entails has been discussed by many and has developed to include active engagement in resolving conflict. Accordingly Wolf Mendl, in the 1974 Swarthmore Lecture *Prophets and Reconcilers; Reflections on the Quaker Peace Testimony*, stressed that peace does not mean absence of conflict and concluded that "Our responsibility is to participate in it [conflict] constructively and not to abolish it" (99). For Mendl, conflict is natural and therefore trying to imagine a world or even a person that is conflict-free is the wrong way to approach the question of the definition of pacifism. The three principal fields of action that Mendl recognizes are: the development of institutions to create a world system based on nonviolent conflict resolution, the study of the causes of war and violence to deepen our understanding of conflict and how best to approach it, and the application of nonviolent techniques to existing conflict situations (1974).

In our time, the Peace Testimony has seen Friends engage primarily in war relief. Moreover, as conscription presently does not exist in either Britain or the United States, the matter of conscientious objection has shifted to the problem of taxation for war purposes, and it is to this issue that we turn our attention in the following section.

The Question of War Taxes

Margaret E. Hirst tells us in her study of Quaker pacifism that from the start the question of taxation for war purposes was accepted in counter-distinction to conscription. She writes, "this distinction of taxation by the Government and the exaction of direct military service has been accepted by most later friends" (1923, 73). Hirst informs us of this acquiescence after discussing a journal entry about a poll tax that has been paid on behalf of both George and Margaret Fell Fox and, further, a letter by George Fox where he states:

> So in this thing, so doing, we can plead with Caesar and plead with them that hath our custom and hath our tribute if they seek to hinder us from our godly and peaceable life and then [if payment be not made] might

they say and plead against us, How can we defend you against foreign enemies and protect everyone in their estates and keep down thieves and murderers, that one man should not take another man's estate from him? (Cited in Hirst 1923, 78)

In her view, Hirst follows the Quaker historian William Braithwaite's assessment. In his magisterial work on early Quakerism Braithwaite includes an anecdote that provides an unambivalent endorsement of his position. He tells us that, in a conversation between Thomas Story and Peter the Great of Russia in 1697, Story upheld the view that Friends could pay taxes in the following words:

Though we are prohibited arms and fighting in person, as inconsistent we think with the rules of the gospel of Christ, yet we can and do by His example readily and cheerfully pay unto every Government, in every form, where we happen to be subjects, such sums and assessments as are required of us by the respective laws under which we live [...] We, by so great an example, do freely pay our taxes to Caesar, who of right hath the direction and application of them, to the various ends of government, to peace or to war, as it pleaseth him or as need may be, according to the constitution or laws of his kingdom, and in which we as subjects have no direction or share: for it is Caesar's part to rule in justice and in truth, but ours to be subject and mind our own business and not to meddle with his. (Braithwaite 1961, 601–2)

Of particular interest in Story's words is the conviction that subjects have no share or say in the way governments are run. It is an extreme application of Jesus's separation between worldly and heavenly affairs, and it is hard when reading his words not to agree with Christopher Hill's view that the radical sects were not just defeated after the Restoration, but that by the end of the century they had capitulated to a survivalist *Realpolitik*. On the other hand, during the 1690s and beyond, Story, who had become an itinerant preacher and had traveled extensively in the American colonies and the West Indies, was regularly preaching against slavery, demonstrating the incompatibility of Christian values with slave holding. Abolition would become one of the chief causes endorsed, and in some cases initiated, by Quakers in the eighteenth and nineteenth centuries.[11] Thus, although the separation of heavenly and earthly realms accompanied by a doctrine of nonintervention in the latter is consistent, it wound up being very narrowly defined. If a specific governmental policy infringed in any way on questions of conscience it was no longer understood as a secular matter. In view of this fact, we find in George Fox's works a consistent argument in favor of upholding governmental authorities *if* they perform their work justly.[12] A just magistrate, for example, is divinely appointed to punish evildoers while a corrupt magistrate is an agent of the antichrist and a lawful target for disobedience. But how is the particular status of the magistrate evaluated? It is determined by the inner conviction and the individual conscience of the true believer. In light of this position towards what pertains to Caesar, it becomes very difficult to defend outright the standard view of Quaker disengagement with the world; particularly so in the American colonies where the legal disabilities under which Dissenters lived in England throughout the eighteenth century did not apply. If, in England, Dissenters were barred from holding office, Quakers in the colonies were solicited and actively served in government (Weddle 2001, 144–52). In fact, it can be further argued that in England the inability of Quakers to participate in the political arena allowed them to champion unpopular causes (abolition, education of slaves, prison reform, sexual equality and, much later, universal suffrage) using their by-then well-established reputation for uprightness and their not inconsiderable wealth.

Returning to the question of war and taxation, Thomas Story in 1711 held fast to his position on the matter in Pennsylvania, where he was a staunch defender of the traditional view on taxation. According to Brock, in order to put down the revolt by some local Quakers who refused to pay the tax levied to raise money for Queen Anne's war efforts against the French, Story invoked as precedent Fox's position on taxes – which he dutifully paid – during the Anglo–Dutch Wars of the previous century, alleging that the responsibility for the war lay with the government of each country not with either English or Dutch Friends (Brock 1990, 186–7).

In the American colonies the question of taxation for war seems to have been a more pressing issue and more frequently debated than in England. In America it was raised on numerous occasions throughout the eighteenth century. In England, on the other hand, it seems only to have become a hotly debated issue at the end of the century with the advent of the Napoleonic Wars.[13] Greaves, however, presents us with some evidence of earlier Quaker objections to taxation for war. He states that as early as 1660 Friends had discussed the question of paying taxes destined for war: "John Whitehead, William Ames, and eight other Quakers sent Charles and his Council an affirmation of their obedience to magistracy and their readiness to pay taxes but not to contribute toward warfare" (Grieves 1992, 247).[14] Nevertheless, after this date, as we have seen, the question of withholding taxes seems to have been settled. It did not return until the middle of the eighteenth century in the American colonies with John Woolman and Anthony Benezet.[15] It is important to point out that holding on to these beliefs had made it well-nigh impossible for Friends to reconcile bearing witness to their principles with the pressing and worldly issues of running a colony. "It was, in particular, the emphatic testimony against war and against slavery," Hirst tells us, "that had stripped the Society of so many members, not a few among them Friends of standing and influence" (1923, 194). The passing of the Militia Bill in 1755 saw the Pennsylvania Quakers declare against war taxes (Hirst 1923, 376–8). From that period the issue would continue to resurface through the nineteenth and twentieth centuries, and remains very much a pressing issue for Friends today.

Quakers and the Question of War Taxes in the Last 40 Years

Since the Vietnam War, which was the last time the United States had a draft, the issue of conscientious objection to bearing arms in war has shifted from the issue of direct participation to the question of paying taxes destined for the military. Many Friends have expressed their belief that contributing to war either directly or indirectly is explicitly against God's will. Hence, the refusal to pay taxes that prolong and perpetuate war has been argued in courts on numerous occasions.[16] The case of Daniel Taylor Jenkins was decided in 2007. In 2005, the Tax Court had dismissed Jenkins' case and Jenkins then presented an amended petition in which he claimed that the Religious Freedom Restoration Act (RFRA) and the First and Ninth Amendments of the United States Constitution afforded him a right to retain the unpaid portion of his taxes on the basis of religious objections to military spending until such taxes could be directed to nonmilitary expenditures. The Tax Court had also imposed a penalty of $5,000 based on its conclusion that the petitioner's arguments were frivolous within the meaning of the statute. During the appeal of this decision Circuit Judge José A. Cabranes elucidated the court's conclusion in the following words:

> Although we do not doubt the sincerity of the petitioner's religious convictions, we conclude that his legal arguments are without merit. It is well settled that the collection of tax revenues for expenditures that offend the religious beliefs of individual taxpayers does not violate the Free Exercise Clause of the First Amendment. (*Jenkins v. Commissioner of Internal Revenue Service* 2007)

Moreover, Judge Cabranes cited *United States v. Lee* as a precedent. In *Lee* the principal argument rested on the premise that it is in the best public interest to sustain a sound tax system and that, therefore, maintaining a well-functioning tax system takes precedence over individual religious belief. In conclusion, the final decision upheld the view that "religious belief in conflict with the payment of taxes *affords no basis* for resisting the tax" (*Jenkins v. Commissioner of Internal Revenue Service* 2007; emphasis in original). The decisions in Jenkins' case rested on the 1999 case of *Adams v. Commissioner of Internal Revenue*, where, in the court of appeals, Circuit Judge Rendell affirmed the government's case. The final argument adduced in *Adams* was the threat to the viability of the government's proper function if objections to the ways in which taxes are distributed are allowed to prevail. On this point Judge Rendell provided the following rationale:

> On matters religious, it [the Tax Act] is neutral. If every citizen could refuse to pay all or part of his taxes because he disapproved of the government's use of the money, on religious grounds, the ability of the government to function could be impaired or even destroyed [...] There are few, if any governmental activities to which some person or group might not object on religious grounds. (*Adams v. Commissioner of Internal Revenue Service* 1999)

In the earlier case of Friend Rosa Covington Packard, the portion of the taxes she had refused to pay the Internal Revenue Service had been placed in an escrow account, the Peace Escrow Fund, established in 1991 by the Purchase New York Quarterly Meeting of the Religious Society of Friends, where the taxes withheld from the federal government and the corresponding interest on those taxes are held until the government should requisition the funds and allocate them to purposes not connected to the military.[17] This was likewise the procedure taken by Jenkins with his taxes (New York Yearly Meeting 2010.). As we have seen thus far, the United States judiciary has not been sympathetic to the fact that Friends have not literally reneged on their fiscal responsibilities but have "paid," if not to the government directly, the full amount of their taxes. The judiciary has continued to see the situation as more or less a question of tax liability and evasion. Because the different courts with a few minor exceptions have not contemplated as a procedural possibility the establishment of a fund where taxes can be withheld and earmarked for governmental activities not related to the defense budget, the organization Conscience and Peace Tax International has sponsored a bill in order to frame this issue as a legislative matter instead.[18] On 17 March 2011, a bill called the Religious Freedom Peace Tax Fund Act of 2011 was introduced to the Committee on Ways and Means.[19] The purpose of the bill is:

> To affirm the religious freedom of taxpayers who are conscientiously opposed to participation in war, to provide that the income, estate, or gift tax payments of such taxpayers be used for nonmilitary purposes, to create

the Religious Freedom Peace Tax Fund to receive such tax payments, to improve revenue collection, and for other purposes. (Conscience and Peace Tax International n.d.)

The bill highlights the need for consistency by extending the law to cover questions of taxation given that federal law recognizes conscientious objection to participation in war in any form based upon moral, ethical or religious beliefs with provision for alternative service, but does not provide "for taxpayers who are conscientious objectors and who are compelled to participate in war through the payment of taxes to support military activities" (H. R. 1191).

In fall 2011, the New York Quarterly Meeting posted on its webpage the statement of conscience of David Bassett of the Farmington-Scipio Regional Meeting.[20] In his statement Bassett declares that,

> [s]ince the Vietnam War era, I and my wife have been conscientiously opposed to paying military taxes. While the US government recognizes sincere conscientious objection to military service, it continues to require its citizens to pay for war, through federal taxes. This, in conscience, I cannot do. Thus I must (as my wife and I have done since 1970) act against the law (i.e., engage in nonviolent civil disobedience) by not voluntarily paying that portion of my (our) federal taxes which pays for the nation's current military expenses. Our government continues each year to extract those moneys, plus penalty and interest from our financial accounts, in this way denying our freedom of religious expression. ("Farmington-Scipio")

This statement of conscience presented to the meeting and recorded in its minutes is a clear example of the ways in which Friends today continue to express their sufferings.

It is not just individuals who have objected to paying war taxes. Quaker organizations have also supported individual Friends' refusals to pay taxes destined for military purposes. Therefore, on the New York Yearly Meeting's webpage we find that this organization refused to pay the federal telephone tax imposed to help finance the Vietnam War. Furthermore, in most if not all of the books of discipline and faith published for the use of their members, Quaker organizations have fully endorsed the belief in nonviolence and the need to resist the imperatives of war.[21] In Britain, the Religious Society of Friends issued the following statement regarding the Gulf War:

> Since its beginnings in the seventeenth century, [Quakerism has] borne witness against war and armed conflict as contrary to the spirit and

teachings of Christ. We have sought to build institutions and relationships which make for peace and to resist military activity. The horrific nature of modern armaments makes our witness particularly urgent. The Gulf War involved the substantial use of expensive modern weapons and technology, demonstrating that today it is the conscription of our money rather than our bodies which makes war possible. (Yearly Meeting of the Religious Society of Friends (Quakers) in Britain. 24.20.)

This same organization, the London Yearly Meeting, describes its own legal proceedings to redress the grievance posed by the question of war taxes.

In March 1982 Meeting for Sufferings considered the request by some London Yearly Meeting employees that the part of their income tax attributable to military purposes should be diverted to non-military uses. Tax was withheld from October 1982 until, in June 1985, the Appeal Court ruled that the action was unlawful. Meeting for Sufferings then decided to pay the tax withheld since the law had been tested as far as possible. At the same time it made a submission to the European Commission of Human Rights on the grounds of the right to freedom of thought, conscience and religion; in July 1986 the Commission ruled the case inadmissible. (Yearly Meeting of the Religious Society of Friends (Quakers) in Britain. 24.19.)

Some Conclusions

Peter Brock tells us that the Quaker Peace Testimony was the result of a "proto-democratic revolution." He affirms that Friends became some of the most "stubborn upholders of the freeborn Englishman's rights, whether at home or across the Atlantic. When a man's religion forbids him to bear arms, so [Quakers] argued, the state infringes his liberties requiring him to pay a 'tax' or perform some alternative service in exchange for permission to follow conscience, since to follow conscience without impediment is a free man's inalienable right" (1972, 477). This argument, as we have seen above, has been appealed to frequently with some degree of success. Friends have been successful as regards conscription, but have failed repeatedly regarding taxation. The right of Free Exercise guaranteed by the First Amendment has been invoked numerous times in tax cases in the last 40 years with little success. When the Religious Freedom Restoration Act (RFRA) was passed in 1993, many Friends felt a new way of arguing their case had been given them. This has also not come to pass. In fact, the RFRA has made no difference in the way their cases have been decided.

In the past, Quakers had on occasion accepted the paying of "mixed" taxes, meaning taxes devoted to all areas of government, but had refused to pay taxes explicitly destined to the military. In many of the recent cases, Friends have paid a part of their taxes and withheld that portion they have estimated to be destined by the government to war activities. The courts have dismissed this strategy and imposed penalties. These penalties are dutifully recorded by the Quaker organizations in their books of sufferings. Books like these have been kept by every Quaker meeting since the seventeenth century. But we know that the early Quakers, while conscientious objectors to bearing arms, did not object to paying taxes. Taxes became an issue only in the eighteenth century in the American colonies.

To offer a historical counter to Hirst's observation that, in the eighteenth and nineteenth centuries, it was the rigor and difficulty of holding fast to the Peace Testimony and the Quakers' objections to paying taxes that saw their numbers dwindle, in the middle of the twentieth century it was precisely these two fundamental tenets that attracted many new members (Heron 1995, 45 cited in Ceadel 2002, 25). Admittedly, their numbers again declined in Britain and the United States after World War II.

The question of taxation is central to the Friends' testimony and will not begin to be resolved until a court rules in their favor. This kind of antiwar activism may not have the revolutionary fervor that the early Quakers displayed during the turbulent decades in the middle of the seventeenth century in England, but it makes evident an unwavering commitment to a religious principle that, in principle, could have a considerable impact on how the American Constitution is interpreted. Taxation is without any doubt one of the most charged subjects in American politics and it is not surprising that since the eighteenth century this has been one of the focal points of Quaker activism.

What is more, Quaker pacifism, with its principles of bearing witness and civil disobedience as methods of registering opposition, has had a vital and influential second life in the West since the 1950s, within the context of the Cold War and afterwards. Quaker protests against nuclear development and weapons testing in the 1950s (primarily by the United States, Britain and the Soviet Union) evolved in the 1970s into the worldwide environmental movements we have today. Bearing witness, simply put, consists of recording moral or ethical opposition or disapproval by calling attention to an event through a person's presence. This method of protest was employed by Albert Bigelow in 1958. Bigelow, a Quaker, sailed in a boat called the *Golden Rule* to the Eniwetok and Bikini atolls in the Marshall Islands where the United States had planned a series of nuclear bomb detonations. In a letter to then-president Dwight Eisenhower, the Friends Committee for Non-Violent Action Against

Nuclear Weapons, of which Bigelow was a member, stated its intention to protest and bear witness against planned nuclear tests in the Pacific: "Four of us, with the support of many others, plan to sail a small vessel into the designated area in the Pacific by April 1st. We intend, come what may, to remain there during the test period, in an effort to halt what we feel is a monstrous delinquency of our government in continuing actions which threaten the well-being of all men" (quoted in Bigelow 1959, 42). The *Golden Rule* never arrived at its destination and Bigelow and the other three crewmen were arrested and jailed in Honolulu. Notwithstanding, the voyage of the *Golden Rule* inspired various similar protest ventures, including the voyage of the *Phoenix*, a later Quaker attempt (Hunter 1979, 8; Zelko 2004, 201–2). The most famous and the most enduring imitator of Bigelow and the *Golden Rule* has been *Greenpeace*. The *Greenpeace* sailed from Vancouver, British Columbia, to protest nuclear tests in Amchitka in the Aleutian Islands in 1971. Unlike the *Golden Rule*, the crew of the *Greenpeace* included several members of the Canadian media: Robert Hunter, a journalist with the *Sun*, Ben Metcalfe with the CBC and Irving Stowe with the *Georgia Straight* (Hunter 1979, 10). As Hunter succinctly expresses it: "Whereas the Quakers had been content to try to 'bear witness,' *Greenpeace* would try to make *everybody* bear witness – through news dispatches, voice reports, press releases, columns, and, of course, photographs" (Hunter 1979, 10; Brown and May 1991, 14; Weyler 2004, 104).

The Amchitka campaign was ultimately successful, primarily because it appropriated and reinvented the act of bearing witness as an effective strategy not just for Greenpeace, but for many environmental organizations since. There were many Quaker connections at the beginning of the movement: the Palo Alto and Oregon American Friends Service Committee provided some of the funding for the expedition, and four of the movement's founders – Irving and Dorothy Stowe and Jim and Marie Bohlen – were active Quaker pacifists. Greenpeace still references the Quakers on its webpage today: "The Quakers are a religious movement founded by the English, non-conformist, itinerate preacher George Fox in the 17th Century. A Quaker protest inspired the first Greenpeace voyage and the Quaker philosophy of 'Bearing Witness,' a form of non-violent resistance whereby someone protests simply by being at an objectionable scene, was adopted by Greenpeace" (Greenpeace, "The Quakers"). The continuing recourse to Quaker practice can be seen in *Greenpeace Witness*, a recent coffee-table book published by the organization that collects photographs documenting most of its campaigns to date as a powerful testimony of the effectiveness of bearing witness. Interestingly, this media-driven form of bearing witness has also limited Greenpeace's choice of which environmental issues to address.[22] Nevertheless, Greenpeace now counts more than 6 million members worldwide and has an annual budget of over 200 million dollars (Greenpeace 2011, 46). Arguably, this is the medium where Quaker pacifism has had its greatest and most enduring influence.

Due to its huge membership and considerable funds, Greenpeace has of necessity become more organized and also more corporate. Since the early 1990s, Greenpeace has added a science unit, a media unit, a lawyer, a political unit and a specialist actions unit (Rose 1993, 289). For some, Greenpeace may have lost its freshness and subversive appeal, its revolutionary fervor, as Christopher Hill deemed the Quakers had done following the Restoration of the Monarchy in 1660, on similar grounds (1991, 370). What I hope to have laid out in this article is that establishing a movement's successes and its capacity to effect change is not an all or nothing proposition and cannot be judged without taking into account its myriad incarnations over time.

Notes

1 *Apology for the True Christian Divinity* (1765), 491
2 Weddle (2001, 245–53) engages in a detailed assessment of the shortcomings of this position in the context of Quakers in the American colonies, specifically during King Philip's War. She rightly concludes that these historians' evaluation of Quakerism as passive is too categorical, and overgeneralizes in a way that fails to account for the myriad individual and group experiences of Friends both in Britain and its colonies before and after the Restoration (252–3).
3 For a reevaluation that expressly refutes the position of these historians on several grounds, see Greaves (1992, 237–59).
4 Hugh Barbour is a good example of a historian who has addressed this particular tendency. In his 1964 study he tells us that in the years of fierce persecution after the Restoration many Puritans, now more properly called Dissenters, urged each other to be meek and resist hating their persecutors. This was not the case with Friends, he explains, who "wrote fiery tracts and letters to and about their tormentors and made persecution a contest, and a means for growth in power." (210) For Barbour, dissenting was not about quiet resistance to oppression, since oppression was a sign of the Antichrist and clearly a target for the "Lamb's War" – the war of the godly against the ungodly. Therefore, the choice for Quakers was either persecution or conversion (210–13).
5 There is no doubt that in its beginnings the movement was far more socially and politically subversive and radical. But quietism and conservatism seem to gloss over too many complex issues. Another historian who has questioned this assessment is Phyllis Mack, who finds this polarization between radical and conservative simplistic. Mack regards the way in which the Society of Friends developed in the 1660s and 1670s as a complex synthesis between radical ideas and the practical need to codify the movement in order to guarantee its survival (Mack 1992, 273–80).
6 Brock's *Pacifism in Europe to 1914* (1972) and *The Quaker Peace Testimony 1660 to 1914* (1990) are his two most pertinent books on the subject of Quaker pacifism. Interestingly, *The Quaker Peace Testimony 1660 to 1914* is the primary source used by Friends to give a historical overview in their *amicus curiae* for the case of *Packard v. the United States* (discussed later in this chapter).
7 Nuttall was not a Quaker but a Congregational minister.

8 In this category we find the more recent works of Horace G. Alexander (1982) and Wolf Mendl (1974). Hirst's study remains the most comprehensive of these.
9 Hirst (1923, 195).
10 It could be argued – and it has been – that it is probable Fox used pacifism as an excuse to refuse to serve on the royalist side since his loyalties lay with the parliamentarians, but in his defense it can be countered that he also refused to serve during the Commonwealth as well, as can be documented in a 1657 letter to Oliver Cromwell.
11 Anthony Benezet (1718–84) is a good example of a Quaker abolitionist. He became an educator and devoted considerable energy to emancipation and abolition. At his death he willed his estate to support the education of African Americans and Indians (Gerona). It is worth mentioning that not all Quakers at the time were averse to slave holding. The issue was hotly debated and by the end of the eighteenth century the belief in slavery as immoral and inconsistent with Christian belief became official.
12 "One of Quakerism's foundation principles," Greaves tells us, "deals with this issue in deceptively simple terms: 'Obedience and subjection in the Lord belongs to Superiors [...]; but where Rulers, Parents or Masters or any other commandeth or requireth subjection in any thing which is contrary to God, or not according to him, in such causes all people are free, and ought to obey God rather than man'" (1992, 246). The words are Edward Burrough's (1660, 5).
13 This point is also made in Henry J. Cadbury's additional notes to Braithwaite's history.
14 Greaves cites from a document in the Library of the Religious Society of Friends: Spence MSS, vol. 3, nos. 4, 100, 107.
15 John Woolman, in a manner that characterizes the Quaker belief in following individual conscience, tellingly voices his discomfort with paying taxes in these words: "I was told that Friends in England frequently paid taxes, when the money was applied to such purposes. I had conferences with several noted Friends on the subject, who all favoured the payment of such taxes, some of whom I preferred before myself, and this made me easier for a time. Yet there was in the deeps of my mind a scruple which I never could get over, and at certain times was greatly distressed on that account. I all along perceived that there were some uprighthearted men, who paid such taxes, but could not see that their example was a sufficient reason for me to do so" (cited in Mendl 1974, 16).
16 Listed here are the most relevant cases involving Friends and the payment of taxes devoted to the war effort; they are listed in order from the oldest to the most recent (I am grateful to Gerald Neuman for helping me to track down these cases, and to Elizabeth Wang for advice on proper documentation practices): (i) Supreme Court of the United States. United States v. American Friends Service Committee et al. No. 73–1791. 29 October 1974. (ii) United States Court of Appeals, Sixth Circuit. Bruce and Ruth K. GRAVES, Petitioners-Appellants, v. Commissioner of Internal Revenue, Respondent-Appellee. No. 77–1188. Submitted 6 July 1978. Decided 7 July 1978. (iii) United States Court of Appeals, Sixth Circuit. Dr. Marjorie E. NELSON, Plaintiff-Appellant, United States of America, Internal Revenue Service, Defendant-Appellee. No. 85–3724. Argued 5 June 1986. Decided 15 July 1986. (iv) United States Court of Appeals, Second Circuit. Gordon M. BROWNE and Edith C. Browne, Plaintiffs-Appellants, v. United States of America dba Internal Revenue Service, Defendant-Appellee. No. 98–6124. Argued 26 February 1999. Decided 14 May 1999. (v) United States Court of Appeals, Third Circuit. Priscilla M. Lippincott ADAMS, Appellant v. Commissioner of Internal Revenue. No. 98–7200. Argued 14 January 1999. Decided

4 March 1999. (vi) United States Court of Appeals, Second Circuit. Rosa Covington PACKARD, Petitioner- Appellant, v. United States Respondent-Appellee. 1997. (vii) United States Court of Appeals, Second Circuit. Daniel Taylor JENKINS, Petitioner-Appellant, v. Commissioner of Internal Revenue Service, Respondent-Appellee. Docket No. 05–4756-ag. Argued: 22 February 2007. Decided: 6 March 2007.

17 "The total amount of delinquent tax for the two years involved in this case [Packard] was about $7,950, while the penalties assessed and then seized totaled about $1,465, approximately another 18%. The penalty amounts which the petitioner sought to recover by this refund action had been collected from her by levy, along with the principal amount of taxes due. The IRS deemed them delinquent, because in obedience to her Quaker religious conscience, she had refused to pay. Instead of making payment to the Internal Revenue Service, however, she had placed the full amounts due in an escrow account managed by her Quarterly Meeting of the Religious Society of Friends, in trust for the United States, as her letters disclosed" (Packard).

18 In *United States v. American Friends Service Committee* (1974), in which the Supreme Court decided against this Friends organization on questions of taxation, the one dissenting opinion came from Supreme Court Justice William O. Douglas, a strong advocate of First Amendment rights, who "stated that the First Amendment's free exercise clause permits no exceptions" (cited in Sagafi-nejad 2011, 101). Otherwise the courts in their decisions have been remarkably consistent.

19 This bill is sponsored by Representative John Lewis, Democrat of Georgia (for himself, Jesse Jackson Jr of Illinois, Raul Grijalva of Arizona, Lynn Woolsey of California, Pete Stark also of California and Rush Holt of New Jersey). They are all democrats with liberal records.

20 I am grateful to Nancy Black for directing me to David Bassett's testimony.

21 "Resistance to the war system is vital. We support the testimony of those who have refused to pay war taxes. The world's governmental investment in the technology of war dwarfs any similar investment in the technology of peace. We also continue to work for disarmament, and to root out the seeds of war in unjust economic and social practices. Building a peace system calls for us to educate ourselves and others and to be part of efforts to demonstrate the effectiveness of the technology of peace" (New York Yearly Meeting 2001, 51–2).

22 In his analysis of the different challenges facing the maturing organization Chris Rose (1990), program director for Greenpeace UK, observes that media success and media opportunities have also begun to limit the organization's involvement with less photogenic issues as well as estranging it from less glamorous grassroots activism. As a response to this self-identified problem, Greenpeace has added to its strategy of bearing witness different approaches, including exposés and investigations into environmental wrongdoing as well as work on enforcing solutions to identified problems such as ozone depletion and household appliances (Rose 1990, 292).

References

Alexander, Horace G. 1982 [1939]. *The Growth of the Peace Testimony of the Religious Society of Friends*. London: Quaker Peace & Service.

An Apology for the True Christian Divinity, Being an Explanation and Vindication of the Principles and Doctrines of the People Called Quakers. Birmingham, 1765. Early English Books Online (accessed 18 September 2011).

Barbour, Hugh. 1964. *The Quakers in Puritan England*. New Haven: Yale University Press.
Bigelow, Arthur. 1959. *The Voyage of the Golden Rule: An Experiment with Truth*. Garden City, NY: Doubleday.
Braithwaite, William C. 1961 [1919]. *The Second Period of Quakerism*. Cambridge: Cambridge University Press.
Brock, Peter. 1972. *Pacifism in Europe to 1914*. Princeton: Princeton University Press.
_____. 1990. *The Quaker Peace Testimony 1660 to 1914*. York: Sessions Book Trust.
Brown, Michael, and John May. 1991. *The Greenpeace Story*. Moorebank: Bantam.
Burrough, Edward. 1660 [1657]. *A Declaration to All the World*. Early English Books Online (accessed 18 September 2011).
Ceadel, Martin. 2002. "The Quaker Peace Testimony and its Contribution to the British Peace Movement: An Overview." *Quaker Studies* 7(1): 9–29.
Cole, W. Alan. 1956. "The Quakers and the English Revolution." *Past and Present* 10 (November): 39–54.
Conscience and Peace Tax International. Online: http://www.cpti.ws/ (accessed 16 September 2011).
Dandelion, Pink. 2007. *An Introduction to Quakerism*. New York: Cambridge University Press.
"Farmington-Scipio Regional Meeting of New York Yearly Meeting of the Religious Society of Friends." *New York Quarterly Meeting of the Religious Society of Friends*. 4 October 2011. Online: http://www.nyqm.org/ (accessed 10 October 2011).
Fox, George. 1952. *The Journal of George Fox*. Rev. ed. John L. Nickalls. Cambridge: Cambridge University Press.
Fox, George, et al. 1660. *A Declaration from the Harmless People of God Called Quakers. Against all Plotters and Fighters in the World*. Early English Books Online (accessed 15 September 2011).
Gerona, Carla. 2011. "Anthony Benezet." *Oxford Dictionary of National Biography*. Oxford: Oxford University Press.
Glines, Elsa. 2003. *Undaunted Zeal: The Letters of Margaret Fell*. Richmond, IN: Friends United Press.
Greaves Richard L. 1992. "Shattered Expectations? George Fox, the Quakers, and the Restoration State, 1660–1685." *Albion* 24(2): 237–59.
Greenpeace. "The Quakers." Greenpeace.org. Online: http://archive.greenpeace.org/comms/vrml/rw/text/def/quaker.html (accessed 18 September 2012).
_____. 2011. "Annual Report 2011." Greenpeace.org. Online: http://www.greenpeace.org/international/Global/international/publications/greenpeace/2012/AnnualReport2011.pdf (accessed 18 September 2012).
Heron, A. 1995. *Quakers in Britain: A Century of Change 1895–1995*. Kelso: Curlew Graphics.
Hill, Christopher. 1992 [1972]. *The World Turned Upside Down: Radical Ideas During the English Revolution*. London: Penguin.
_____. 1984. *The Experience of Defeat: Milton and Some Contemporaries*. New York: Viking.
Hirst, Margaret E. 1923. *The Quakers in Peace and War: An Account of Their Peace Principles and Practice*. London: Swarthmore Press.
Hunter, Robert. 1979. *Warriors of the Rainbow: A Chronicle of the Greenpeace Movement*. New York: Holt, Rinehart and Winston.
Mack, Phyllis. 1992. *Visionary Women: Ecstatic Prophecy in Seventeenth-Century England*. Berkeley: University of California Press.

Mendl, Wolf. 1974. *Prophets and Reconcilers: Reflections on the Quaker Peace Testimony*. London: Friends Home Service Committee.
Mulvaney, Kieran. 1996. *Greenpeace Witness: Twenty-Five Years on the Environmental Front Line*. London: André Deutsch.
New York Yearly Meeting. 2010. "Conscientious Objection to Paying for War." *New York Yearly Meeting*. Online: http://www.nyym.org/ (accessed 4 October 2011).
———. 2001. *Faith and Practice*. New York: New York Yearly Meeting.
Nuttall, Geoffrey F. 1958. *Christian Pacifism in History*. Oxford: Blackwell.
Packard, Rosa. "The Petition for a Writ of Certiorari." *Rosa Packard Peace Tax Witness and Conscientious Objection*. Online: www.rosapackard.org (accessed 5 October 2011).
Reay, Barry. 1985. *The Quakers and the English Revolution*. New York: Palgrave Macmillan.
Rose, Chris. 1993. "Beyond the Struggle for Proof: Factors Changing the Environmental Movement." *Environmental Values* 2(2): 285–98.
Sagafi-nejad, Nancy Black. 2011. *Friends at the Bar: A Quaker View of Law, Conflict Resolution, and Legal Reform*. Albany: State University of New York Press.
United States House Committee on Ways and Means. *Religious Freedom Peace Tax Fund Act*. 112th Congress. 1st sess. H.R. 1191. http://thomas.loc.gov/home/thomas.php (accessed 15 September 2011).
Weddle, Meredith Baldwin. 2011. *Walking in the Way of Peace: Quaker Pacifism in the Seventeenth Century*. Oxford: Oxford University Press.
Weyler, Rex. 2004. *Greenpeace: How a Group of Ecologists, Journalists, and Visionaries Changed the World*. Emmaus: Rodale.
Yearly Meeting of the Religious Society of Friends (Quakers) in Britain. *Quaker Faith & Practice*. 4th ed. 1995–2008 (accessed 3 October 2011).
Zelko, Frank. 2004. "Making Greenpeace: The Development of Direct Action Environmentalism in British Columbia." *BC Studies* 142/143 (Summer/Autumn): 197–239. Academic Search Premier (accessed 18 September 2012).

Court proceedings

United States Court of Appeals, Second Circuit. Rosa Covington PACKARD, Petitioner-Appellant, v. United States Respondent-Appellee. 1997. Westlaw: 15 September 2011.
United States Court of Appeals, Second Circuit. Gordon M. BROWNE and Edith C. Browne, Plaintiffs-Appellants, v. United States of America dba Internal Revenue Service, Defendant-Appellee. No. 98–6124. Argued 26 February 1999. Decided 14 May 1999. Westlaw: 15 September 2011.
United States Court of Appeals, Second Circuit. Daniel Taylor JENKINS, Petitioner-Appellant, v. Commissioner of Internal Revenue Service, Respondent-Appellee. Docket No. 05–4756-ag. Argued 22 February 2007. Decided 6 March 2007. Westlaw: 15 September 2011.
United States Court of Appeals, Sixth Circuit. Bruce and Ruth K. GRAVES, Petitioners-Appellants, v. Commissioner of Internal Revenue, Respondent-Appellee. No. 77–1188. Submitted 6 July 1978. Decided 7 July 1978. Westlaw: 15 September 2011.
United States Court of Appeals, Sixth Circuit. Dr. Marjorie E. NELSON, Plaintiff-Appellant, United States of America, Internal Revenue Service, Defendant-Appellee. No. 85–3724. Argued 5 June 1986. Decided 15 July 1986. Westlaw: 15 September 2011.

United States Court of Appeals, Third Circuit. Priscilla M. Lippincott ADAMS, Appellant v. Commissioner of Internal Revenue. No. 98–7200. Argued 14 January 1999. Decided 4 March 1999.

United States Supreme Court. United States v. American Friends Service Committee et al. No. 73–1791. 29 October 1974. Westlaw: 15 September 2011.

Chapter 6

A SACRED GROUND FOR PEACE: VIOLENCE, TOURISM AND SANCTIFICATION IN HIROSHIMA 1960–1970

Ran Zwigenberg

Introduction

"Each time I get near the Peace Park," wrote Kenzaburō Ōe in 1963, "I get the strong odor of politics" (1996, 45). And indeed the Hiroshima Peace Memorial Park in 1963 was a controversial and contested place. It is hard to believe it today, when the Peace Park, erected in 1955 to commemorate the site of the world's first use of a nuclear bomb, is largely a quiet and orderly memorial site frequented mostly by tourists and school groups, but in 1963 the park was the center of a worldwide radical antinuclear movement. This movement, though, was fast falling apart. With Gensuikyō (the Japanese Council Against Atomic and Hydrogen Weapons) split over the partial nuclear test ban treaty issue between pro-Chinese, pro-Soviet, liberal, radical and conservative factions, and with negotiations over a possible solution stalled, the antinuclear movement was on the verge of collapse. Many *hibakusha* and other activists were disgusted by the splits and factionalism.[1] Then, on the eve of 6 August, the park saw some of the worst violence in its history when radical students from Zengakuren (the all-Japan student union) stormed the stage of the Ninth World Conference Against Nuclear Weapons. The students were protesting Japanese Communist Party (JCP) resistance to the test ban treaty.[2] The Zengakuren called for an occupation of the conference of the "bankrupted Gensuikyō and the continuation of the struggle against nuclear weapons" (*Chūgoku Shinbun*, 7 August 1963). The communist delegates, in an act which was seen as the ultimate in hypocrisy by the students, called in the "bourgeois" police to clear the students.

The result was complete mayhem, with hundreds of students battling with police in front of the cenotaph, and the conference organizers' hopes for unity in tatters. The following morning, Hiroshima's newspapers were full of rage. The student violence was seen as a defilement of the park, and as "treading on Hiroshima's prayer." Hiroshima's citizens were "burning with anger." The anger however was not directed only against the students but against politics as a whole: "This kind of political conference," argued one Hiroshima resident, "should not be here, it should be in Tokyo." The mayor, claimed another respondent, "should have never given permission [for Gensuikyō] to use the Park" (*Chūgoku Shinbun*, 7 August 1963). And indeed, from 1964, the city denied political parties the use of the park. The city cited its wish to protect "the sacred nature" of the park as a "silent place of prayer," and the "peak in the tourist season" (*Chūgoku Shinbun*, 6 June 1964).

The 1963 violence marked the beginning of a process by which the city aimed at clearing the park from the "odor of politics." The main tool the city used in doing so was the language of the sacred and prayer in contrast with the violence and disruption of politics. The delegitimization of politics, especially of the leftist kind, has a long history in Japan (Gluck 1987).[3] But as the city's reference to the tourist season indicated, there was much more to the city's sanctification campaign, as it came to be called, than just aversion to politics. The 1960s were a time of enormous economic growth in Japan, which meant that many more Japanese (and foreigners – the 1960s were also a time of growing international travel) could now travel to Hiroshima. The city wished to capitalize on this and couple sanctification with commercialization. This sparked a sustained debate in Hiroshima throughout the 1960s about the relations of tourism, politics, violence and sanctification.

These debates however, did not observe a simple division between a politically committed "remembering camp" on one hand, and a "forgetting camp" of the powers-to-be on another. Befitting of the contradictory and ambivalent nature of the place, Hiroshima's memory wars were complex, and saw strange alliances and shifting commitments among the various forces that were vying for influence over the character of the Peace Park. The controversy touched on many of the topics and disputes surrounding Japan's troubled relations with its past. This essay will examine those debates through looking at the two campaigns which turned the Peace Park from a political space to a sacred ground: the campaign to preserve the A-Bomb Dome and the city's sanctification campaign. These campaigns illustrate the complexity of the eventual decision to preserve the dome. They illuminate the peculiar way in which the multi-layered conflicts between the groups ultimately had the unexpected effect of domesticating and sanitizing the memory of the bomb.

Preserving the "Temple of Peace"

The Atomic-Bomb Dome, located at the north side of the Peace Park in Hiroshima, is one of the few surviving buildings from the time of the bomb. It is the only one which was specifically preserved as a reminder of the bombing (Shono 1993, 267).[4] After 1945, the dome instantly became one of the symbols of the ruined city. It featured on countless posters, brochures, leaflets and books, and is marketed, alongside the temple in Miyajima, as one of the two main symbols (and prominent tourist sites) of the city.[5] In 1966, the city declared its intention to preserve the dome "for all eternity […] as a symbol of [Hiroshima's] vow to pursue the abolition of nuclear weapons and enduring peace," and campaigned vigorously to make it a world heritage site, which it became in 1996 ("A-Bomb Dome").

However, in the 1940s and 1950s, the dome only narrowly escaped demolition. A 1949 survey found that most residents (65 percent) wanted to see it destroyed, as it was "a reminder of the war and its destruction" (Nemoto 2006, 68).[6] A 1951 round-table discussion with Mayor Hamai Shinzo, the president of Hiroshima University and other prominent figures was in complete agreement as to the need to destroy the dome (Nemoto 2006, 68). Those who called for preservation of the dome were very much a minority in the 1950s. Lisa Yoneyama's assertion that the "survivors were known to be generally less supportive of retaining this painful visual reminder of the bomb, while the city administration clearly recognized its symbolic capital" (Yoneyama 1999, 70) is simply not true, as the issue split the hibakusha camp and city elites alike. The debate saw unusual alliances between peace groups, tourism officials and tour companies on one hand and, on the other, real estate interests (coveting the prime downtown spot) and other hibakusha who wanted it torn down. The debates over the dome were far from a simple "remembering versus forgetting" conflict. They illustrate the complexity of the preservation and the working of the dialectic process which domesticated and sanitized the memory of the bomb.

The dome's image was prominent in early peace movement literature, though it was not actually the movement but rather the Hiroshima Tourist Board that was the first to call for its preservation. The dome's tourist value was immediately recognized by the cash-strapped city and steps were taken to regulate its use, such as setting up an explanatory plaque, fencing, etc. (*Chūgoku Shinbun*, 30 April 2007).[7] The 1949 city plan recognized it as a historical site and called for further steps to preserve it "for its tourist and historical value" (Hiroshima City Archive 1950). As early as 1947, a Hiroshima guidebook (Yuichiro 1948) featured the Industrial Promotion Hall, as the dome was originally called, as one of the attractions of the city, next to a drawing of an "atomic bomb cloud" (Sasaki 1948). A 1949 article, Hiroshima's *Tourist Resources*, by a city official, Morihiro Sukeharu, who later became the director of the A-Bomb Memorial Museum, specifically called for its preservation as a "resource" (*shigen*).

The dome, until around 1955, seems to have been discussed exclusively in these terms and mostly in relation to tourism. Reacting to calls for demolition of the dome (Mayor Hamai's 1953 statement was the most prominent of these), hibakusha groups came together in 1954 with the Hiroshima Prefectural Tourist Association in a new organization: The A-Bomb Dome Preservation Association (Genbaku Domu Hozōnkai Dōmei). The association declared the dome to be a "symbol of Hiroshima's citizens' quest for peace," and that "it was needed for Hiroshima both as a historical site and as a tourist resource for a city with inadequate tourist resources" (Nemoto 2006, 69). Again, there was nothing too controversial in calling the dome a resource at the time.[8] The first reference to it in the city council records defined it as such, when then Mayor Watanabe said he would like to "preserve it for A-bomb tourism [...] as it became a symbol of Hiroshima and people come here to see it" (Hiroshima-shi 1988, 815).[9]

In 1960, however, the debate flared up. The immediate reason was the controversial relocation of the Hiroshima Chamber of Commerce to a lot opposite the dome.[10] The Chamber of Commerce's new shiny, modern building overshadowed the dome, and the construction process itself, with the use of heavy machinery and accompanying infrastructure work, was feared to put the dome in danger of collapse (*Asahi Grafu*, 25 August 1967). The chamber's move to this spot also sparked worries over land prices and land use in the downtown area. Hiroshima was experiencing a period of growth, and a construction boom downtown caused land prices to rise sharply. This led some to speculate that powerful business interests were behind the new campaign for the dome's demolition.[11] Business circles, however, were far from being the only ones arguing for its removal. A week after Hamai's interview, the *Chūgoku Shinbun* hosted a forum about the dome's preservation, eliciting some quite emotional pleas to remove the dome. One respondent, a hibakusha, asked: "Until when will we have this horrible reminder [of the bomb] among us?" Another one, using even stronger language, wrote: "This is simply selling our tragedy (*higeki o uru mono ni suu*). It is plain wrong." Other respondents argued for its removal as it was "plain ugly" and "destroys the beauty of our city." Others, including both hibakusha and non-hibakusha residents, defended the dome, using the familiar language of it being "a symbol for peace," a "reminder of the calamity" and the like (*Asahi Grafu*, 28 August 1960; see also Yagi 2005, 61).

In 1964, after a four-year hiatus, with the twenty-year anniversary looming and with general preparations for the foreign tourists expected for the 1964

Olympics, the issue of preservation came up again. The main reason this time was the city's move to block political use of the park.[12] The city's invocation of the sacred argument did not come out of thin air. Such language was present in Hiroshima from the very beginning. The same week that the city banned political gatherings, a visiting Soviet group called the park and the dome a "sacred ground for mankind" (*Asahi Grafu*, 20 April 1960). As we will shortly see, some activists rightly saw the "sacred ground" maneuver by the city as a cynical ploy by conservatives to co-opt hibakusha's legitimate requests to respect their feelings and expel the Left from the ceremonial heart of the city. This issue, like that of the dome's preservation, divided hibakusha between those who emphasized commemoration and respect for the dead, and those who sought to harness the tragedy for the cause of peace. Alliances and strategies shifted constantly as tourism officials, city planners, hibakusha groups and politicians worked sometimes together (as was the case with tourism and hibakusha groups) and sometimes at cross-purposes. Leftist groups within the pro-preservation camp often used the "sacred ground" language of argument in regard to the dome, but at other times rejected the formulation.

At the forefront of this campaign to preserve the dome, and a particularly good example of these contradictions, was the *Orizuru no kai* or Folded (Paper) Crane Society. The Crane Society was unique in its particularly neutral (one might even call it sterile) language, and its use of children and women as the ultimate symbols of Hiroshima's victimization.[13] The Crane Society launched its own campaign for the preservation of the dome in August 1960. A pamphlet from that year emphasized suffering and victimization, calling the dome a "pitiful thing [...] the dome is a forgotten monument, the only [place] in which our suffering is etched" (Nemoto 2006, 71). The society kept their campaign going through 1963, but did not garner much support among officials. That would change in March 1964 when, as part of preparations for the Olympics, and with the twentieth anniversary coming, the Hiroshima Tourist Board again called for funds for preservation and reawakened the debate (Yagi 2005, 60).[14] The Tourist Board was then joined by eleven peace groups. The groups' appeal was followed by a visit to the dome (*Chūgoku Shinbun*, 30 April 1965) by Kondō Yasuo, a well-known architect, and an appeal by a group of eight well-known intellectuals which included, in addition to Kondō, Tange Kenzō and Nobel Prize laureate and peace activist Yukawa Hideki. The appeal used the familiar "sacred" language, calling the dome "a memorial temple [*kinenseidō* – usually a term for a Confucian temple], crucial for saving the world from the bomb" (Hiroshima-shi 1988, 819).[15] Following these appeals, the city decided to commission an inquiry into the dome's structural weaknesses and the feasibility of preservations, but still refrained from committing to preservation.

In 1966, with no decision in sight, the debate intensified. Some commentators began voicing allegations that had been previously only implied. In an editorial in the magazine *Hiroshima no kawa*, Konishi Noboku wrote,

> [the demolition camp] points out that the Peace Park has been put in order, and now the dome matter should be dealt with concretely. Land in the vicinity of the dome is valued at 200,000 yen per tsubo (3.3 square meters), so it would be better to erect a commercial building that would bring revenue to the city [...] The A-bomb has become well known throughout the world, so it is best to tear the dome now. It only reminds us of dead people, anyway, and so on.

Konishi vehemently rejected these arguments:

> To these who say, "tear it down," I feel like thundering: "nonsense!" *We surviving victims have made a solemn pledge* that the same terrible disaster must never be repeated, and we should retain the dome as a monument dedicated to peace for all mankind [...] the preservation of the dome therefore must be considered from a worldwide point of view. (Ōe 1996, 105; emphasis mine)

Underlining the debate was the question of who would speak in the name of the hibakusha. What they wanted and how they "really" felt became the real sticking points. Both sides claimed they were speaking in the name of the survivors. The fact that some hibakusha were against the preservation cannot be disputed. Hamai himself was a survivor. A survivor talking to an *Asahi Grafu* reporter visiting Hiroshima argued that the money should be given, instead of to the preservation effort, to the A-bomb hospital; others repeated the oft-cited argument that the dome brought back old memories. This view was not limited to hibakusha; a veteran of the Burma campaign complained that it reminded him of the family and friends he lost. The man, however, although a Liberal Democratic Party (LDP) member of the city assembly, added that as a member of the administration he had to recognize the symbolic meaning of the dome and the fact that "it is a tourist asset and brings us a lot of money" (*Asahi grafu*, 5 August 1965). By that time, as we can see, even the conservatives and Hamai (an independent liberal) went over to the preservation side, according to Hamai, after appeals from the Crane Society children (Yagi 2005, 60). The rest of the political map in Hiroshima followed suit and after a number of revisions, a decision was passed in July 1966 to "preserve the dome for all times [...] as a barrier against the resumption of nuclear war and *in the name of the hibakusha and the spirits of the 200,000 that died*" (Hiroshima-shi 1988, 819; emphasis mine).

The decision, though, did not include any funding for the preservation and it was understood that a fundraising campaign would follow. Challenged on the issue in a debate on the floor of the city assembly in September, Hamai answered rather evasively, claiming that there were "some disagreements" in negotiations (with the Left), that the "movement [to preserve the dome] is a peace movement by itself" and that, thus, there was no need to consult with existing groups (Hiroshima-shi 1988, 824). Yonezawa Susumu, another socialist, challenged the mayor using much harsher language and alluding to his connections with the Chamber of Commerce. Yonezawa, like almost all other speakers, asserted that the "hibakusha want the dome preserved." The dome, he continued, "is the true proof of Hiroshima and the incredible cruelty committed so calmly by the Americans [...] the building of the chamber of commerce dwarfed the dome and diluted its impact. Hamai has been in power for all but four years since the bombing [...] isn't he responsible [for this]?" Hamai answered by again using the emotional argument that the dome evoked suffering and that he wanted it, like many other hibakusha, out of sight (Hiroshima-shi 1988, 825–6). At the end of this exchange, the assembly moved to vote and called for a fundraising campaign to be headed by the city. Media outlets like *Asahi* newspaper and NHK television joined in and, by December, the budget committee reported that a third of the money needed (40 million yen) was collected. By February 1967 the money was secured, and work on the dome started in May of that year.

The dome debates illustrate how fragile the status of the Peace Park was in the mid-60s. Very powerful interests and politicians were able to co-opt hibakusha suffering in their quest to remove the dome and "normalize" the city center. Both the Right and the Left used the language of the sacred and the hibakusha's suffering to their benefit. The Right, however, proved much more adept in this game and, as we will shortly see, was more successful in using hibakusha's sorrow in depoliticizing the Peace Park and expelling the Left from the ceremonial heart of the city, leaving it for tourists and for well-organized and smooth, if somewhat sterile, peace ceremonies. Still, this was the 60s, and the Left and others, especially the student movement, did not concede the park without a fight.

Hurling Bricks at the "Tourist City"

On 24 May 1967, Mayor Yamada Setsuo reported to the city assembly on the progress (or, rather, lack thereof) in the dome's preservation efforts. Yamada, who replaced Hamai in February 1967, campaigned on a platform for "restoring the peace city."[16] Just like Hamai, Yamada had to confront criticism over supposed hidden motives and stalling by the city administration. Yoshida

Jihei, again, was the one who pressed the mayor on the issue. Yamada's reply concentrated mostly on administrative details. In his conclusion, however, Yamada's comments went much further than the dome issue. "Today's Peace Park, the Nakajima Peace Memorial Park, is one unit [body], I believe it should be made into one sacred area, a sanctuary [a sacred or holy territory], and I would like to ask the Assembly to consider what concrete steps we could take [to achieve that purpose]" (Hiroshima-shi 1988, 836). In a matter of months, Yoshida's statement turned into official city policy. When a new monument and memorial tower were proposed, the committee responsible for the Peace Park (the oddly named Peace Infrastructure Committee) rejected it because, according to Tanaka Koichi, the chairman, "the Park is flooded [congested] with monuments [...] this is harmful for its character as a sacred space [...] and not proper for its air [atmosphere] of sacred ground [or sacred area park – *seichi koen no fuinkini fusawashi kunai*] (*Chūgoku Shinbun*, 12 September 1967). Yoshida's plan for the sanctification of the Peace Park (*seichika*) met immediate opposition. Opponents of Yoshida in the peace camp (Yoshida was initially backed by the socialists but moved more to the Right after his election) accused him of hypocrisy and of "trying to throw out the peace movement" from the park. Yamada, although portraying himself as a man of peace, did not necessarily deny these allegations. "The Park," Yamada said, "is a place for silent prayer [...] it should not be [a place] for waving red flags and screaming in pitched voices" (*Chūgoku Shinbun*, 30 July 1969). Indeed, one Yoshida's very first acts was to revoke permits for the annual May Day demonstration at the park. By 1969, the "sacred" argument had come full circle. The language once used as a rallying cry for the Left over the dome was now used against them. This did not mean they completely ceded this language to the Right.

What accentuated the Left's frustration and claims of hypocrisy was the city's decision to allow the Japan Defense Forces' Thirteenth Division, based in Hiroshima, to conduct their annual march through Peace Boulevard. The sight of tanks on Hiroshima's streets galvanized opposition to Yoshida. As in the dome debates, both sides were using the discourse of the sacred and notions of propriety to further their claims. The result, again, was the solidification of notions of sacred space, a development which led to further sanitization of the park, with youth "gangs," souvenir shops, concerts and ball games banned from the park's sacred ground. The only ones who did not participate in the "sacred" discourse were the radical students who came out in force against the "old" peace discourse in favor of a much more militant stand against nuclear weapons and US imperialism. The students' violence, however, was their undoing, as in the end their violation of the "sacred space" of the park led to further strengthening of the very notions the students opposed.

The Japan Defense Forces (JDF) parade was to include about 180 military vehicles, including tanks and howitzers, a flyover by F-86 jets and around 1,500 troops marching along Peace Boulevard, and it was to end in front of the A-bomb cenotaph with the division commanders paying respect to the dead. The announcement led to a storm of protest. The socialists, communists, hibakusha and student groups all sent protest letters to the city (*Chūgoku Shinbun*, 20 October 1965). The city, and Mayor Hamai in particular, seemed to be caught by surprise. Hamai managed to make the JDF slightly modify their plans to make them less offensive (such as not to carry weapons into the park itself) but claimed: "Legally, we cannot revoke [the] permit for use of [Peace Boulevard and the park]." In a further show of semantic virtuosity, Hamai argued that "since the JDF is not an 'aggressive' army, there should be no problem for them to march on Peace Boulevard" (*Chūgoku Shinbun*, 21 October 1965). Hamai's argument did not convince anyone on the Left. The fact that the city had just revoked the permit for leftist groups to hold their meetings in the park a year earlier enraged activists opposed to the JDF parade.

The prefectural socialists, the labor unions council and 13 other organizations appealed to the JDF directly to cancel its march, while six activists started a sit-in in front of the cenotaph, claiming that "the people of the bombed city do not want weapons-carrying soldiers in the Peace Park [...] they will not allow it" (*Chūgoku Shinbun*, 24 and 25 October 1965). In another case of linguistic acrobatics, so common in Japan where the army cannot constitutionally be called an army, the division's commander Watanabe Yoshie replied, "as the army division of the peace city, we want to respect the feelings of the residents" (*Chūgoku Shinbun*, 26 October 1965). The storm of protests continued, with students in Hiroshima University signing a petition and organizing a counter march. Unlike the more cautious Japan Socialist Party (JSP) and JCP, the students tied the march to the wider issues of the "US imperialism in Southeast Asia and the security treaty then negotiated with South Korea." The students' involvement unnerved many older residents. The fear of demonstrations, violent confrontations and "disturbance" (*konran*) permeated the whole debate. The students and New Left, whose presence on campuses was growing together with anti–Vietnam War sentiment, were the wild card everybody else was afraid of. The socialists themselves "threatened" that "although we do not want to see an anti-Vietnam demonstration in the Park, it will happen [if the march goes on] (*Chūgoku Shinbun*, 21October 1965). In the assembly, Hamai appealed to the JDF not to pass too close to the Peace Park so as to avoid "disorder," and to the army to respect the feelings of the citizens (*Chūgoku Shinbun*, 27 October 1965).

This was definitely not consensus view in Hiroshima, as many supported the march and denounced the Left's move to block it. Both sides immediately, almost reflexively, resorted to using the plight of the bomb's victims to support their side of the argument. A supporter of the march wrote: "Those who died [by the bomb] believed in Japan's mission, saved Japan with their sacrifice and would be pleased to see a peaceful and prosperous Japan" (*Chūgoku Shinbun*, 26 October 1965).[17] From the Left, as usual, there was talk about Hiroshima's "sacrifice for peace." An editorial in the *Chūgoku Shinbun* talked about the "insult" of seeing "military boots on this sacred ground, under which 200,000 are buried" (*Chūgoku Shinbun*, 23 October 1965).

As with the dome, using the sacred ground argument was a double-edged sword for the Left. In a press conference, Mayor Hamai argued that it was basically all for the best, as the debate over "bringing in weapons to the Park stimulated peoples' feelings and promoted the idea that it is a sacred site for Hiroshima citizens [*shimin no seichi kanjō shigeki*]." (The Left would have agreed with Hamai on that statement if it wasn't for his next move.) "The issue," Hamai continued, "was not the legitimacy of the JDF but the [status] of the park. In the same way that people were angry with the demonstrators in 1963 [they are angry now]. One should not enter the park with weapons and violence." Hamai then proceeded to confirm he would attend the parade (*Chūgoku Shinbun*, 28 October 1965). As it turned out, Hamai was using the controversy strategically to create a (false) equivalence between the peace camp and the army. Rather than debating the larger constitutional issue of Japan having a military in direct violation of its peace constitution, which manifested itself so concretely with tanks rolling down a "peace boulevard" in the self-proclaimed mecca of world peace, Hiroshima's politicians were playing with semantics and pointing fingers at the very people that tried to hold them accountable for their words. Turning the peace camp arguments on their head, the Right was using the Left's own rhetoric to expel it from the ceremonial heart of the city while allowing the military to claim it.

Hamai's and others' fears regarding the students and the Left, however, did not materialize, as the march went through the city relatively peacefully. The residents did not seem very distressed. Quite the opposite: the march saw only a few hundred demonstrators in the Peace Park but over 30,000 flag-waving spectators. The Left, however, was justified in its concern. Revealing the actual ideological agenda of the JDF and its backers, Watanabe said in a post-parade interview that "the current Japanese think about the world, or about themselves as individuals. In between, there are, the family and the nation, and I want people to appreciate this and teach more patriotism" (*Chūgoku Shinbun*, 1 November 1965).[18]

It was in this context that Yamada declared, shortly after his election, his plan for the sanctification of the park. Yamada was not very concerned with patriotism and the nation. Rather than at tanks and demonstrators, his move was aimed at accommodating the increasing numbers of foreign and domestic tourists. An *Asahi Grafu* reporter nicely caught the irony of the "peace city," depicting an anti-Vietnam War sign hoisted right next to a sign promoting Peace Cola (*heiwa kora*) (*Asahi Grafu*, 19 August 1965). Indeed, with Hiroshima once again serving as a launching pad for aggression on the continent (this time for the American involvement in Vietnam), the parade debates heightened the sense of danger and imminent revival of militarism in the Left.[19] The Left, however, was fast losing ground. The city was moving, if not more to the Right, then at least (with the exception of the students) away from politics and toward more "normal" preoccupations with consumerism and development. The past was fast becoming abstract, politicized and overused. Curiously, sanctification and forgetting (and the "normalization" of the city) went hand in hand, as the city confined the bomb and its memory into a sacred ground in the middle of city.

James Boon, a Nigerian journalist who visited Hiroshima in 1962, remarked that "[p]eople built this city in order to forget about the bomb [...] [They] are trying really hard to live just like people in other cities" (*Yumiyuri Shinbun*, 18 June 1962). In 1965, a *New York Times* reporter found teenagers using the strips of road surrounding the Peace Museum as a drag strip for car racing (*New York Times Magazine*, 1 August 1965). These bikers, complained a local resident in 1969, "ride around with flowing scarves, shouting at the top of their lungs, get drunk and make the residents' lives unbearable" (*Chūgoku Shinbun*, 21 June 1969). Another reporter who came to the city in 1967, when debate over the dome and the park still raged, echoed the prevailing rhetoric in his article's opening words: "Just like Mecca is for Islam, Jerusalem for Christians, Hiroshima is now a holy site for people who pray for peace worldwide: sacred ground of humanity." Immediately after this proclamation however, the reporter described watching in amazement as scores of people simply ignored the 6 August moment of silence, marked by sirens, and continued with their daily business. The reporter engaged in conversation with groups of young hippies, "Yankees" (Japanese slang for bike gangs and other young semi-criminal youth) and other youngsters on Hon Dori, the main shopping street, none of whom showed much interest in the ceremonies going on nearby (*Asahi Grafu*, 25 August 1967).

As part of its sanctification campaign, the city decided to crack down on these bike gangs, as well as dealing with other improper phenomena in the park. In June 1969, a major police operation was launched to stop bike hooligans (*bōsōzoku*). The following month, the city ordered all souvenir shops (most run by poor hibakusha) to close, as "it was not appropriate [to have these shops] according to the policy of sanctification" (*Chūgoku Shinbun*, 28 July 1969). The hibakusha owners of these booths, who sold books, snacks, etc., complained bitterly to the city. The souvenir shops and the bikers returned almost immediately (the bikers proving particularly confrontational: it took 120 policemen to dislodge them) and it was not until September that they were finally evicted (*Chūgoku Shinbun*, 28 September 1969). Other steps taken by Yamada administrators were mostly aesthetic and administrative.[20] The city plan for sanctification was supposed to be completed on 6 August 1970 (*Chūgoku Shinbun*, 30 July 1969).

Student radicals at Hiroshima University, however, had very different ideas for the 1970 ceremony. Anticipating trouble, the city called for all parties to display unity. The city focused the ceremony on the plight of the hibakusha. "We put the hibakusha in our heart" was the main slogan. Hibakusha compensation was one issue that all could rally around. In another conciliatory move the city also, for the first time, invited a *zainichi* (Japanese of Korean descent) representative to lay a wreath at the cenotaph (*Asahi Shinbun*, 6 August 1970). This was done in order to reduce tensions with the zainichi community. In April 1970, the memorial for the Korean victims of the bomb was forbidden from being located inside the Peace Park. The city pointed out the other memorials it had also banned, but Koreans and the Left quite rightly saw this exclusion as part of a decades-old history of discrimination and as a conscious move to deny Koreans' separate ethnic identity and memory (Yoneyama 1997, 207). The city's refusal to allow the sculpture to enter the park and its insistence on the universal and "sacred" nature of the park's message not allowing for ideological issues was clearly a case of ethnic nationalism.[21]

The inadequacy of such a reply and the problematic nature of Japan's peace movement were obvious, especially to those in the New Left who now sought to emphasize Japanese status as victimizers (*kagaisha*) rather than as victims (*higaisha*). Oda Makoto, the leader of Beheiren (Betonamu Heiwa o Shimin Rengo) – Citizens' League for Peace in Vietnam) was one of the first major public figures to confront the fallacy of victim consciousness and publicize the discovery that it blinded Japanese to their own responsibility for past victimizing (Orr 2001, 6). The Vietnam War revealed Japan's complicity in aggressions on the continent. Beheiren and other student groups vehemently opposed blanketing these historical and political realities under the usual abstraction. Directly challenging Yamada's administration and his newly instituted "tradition" of silent prayer, the students called for "a day of [moving] from prayer into struggle" (*Asahi Shinbun*, 7 August 1970). About 1,500 helmeted students marched from Hiroshima University campus to the Peace Park. Shouting slogans against US imperialism, discrimination against Koreans and the US–Japan security treaty, the students blocked traffic, snake danced and engaged in running fights with the police. The end of the day saw 11 arrests, countless windows smashed and a city in shock (*Washington*

Post, 7 August 1970). Many hibakusha could not understand the students. A *Washington Post* journalist pointed out the "generation gap" between the students and the older survivors (*Washington Post*, 7 August 1970). Already disillusioned by the politics of the Old Left, the new wave of radicalism and violence of the new student movement shocked many survivors even within the Left, who could not stomach the student use of *geba* (political violence (from the German *gewalt*)).[22]

In Hiroshima, as in the rest of Japan and, indeed, France, the US and other places which saw student unrest, the causes for student activism were a mixture of educational and political issues. Campus-related issues, however, were the main catalyst for expansion and the numerous campus occupations in the late 60s (Shimbori 1971, 151).[23] Exemplifying the initially non-political nature of these demonstrations was the fact that it was not humanities but medical students, whose exams and conditions were the harshest, who led many of these demonstrations. In January and May 1968, the Tokyo and Nihon University campuses exploded in protest over issues of entrance exam regulations and funding (Tsurumi 1968, 430–55). Similarly, at Hiroshima University, engineering and medical students were prominent among demonstrators (Hiroshima daigaku bunsho kan, 2008, 10). In a pattern which recurred all over Japanese campuses, when university administrations called in the police to tackle student demonstrations, non-political students and outsiders joined the more radical students (Shimbori 1971, 153). After the initial clashes in 1968, Hiroshima University was occupied up until 1969. Hiroshima was one of over a hundred and fifty campuses which were occupied at the time, and there, as in Tokyo, Kyoto and other cities, the campus occupation ended violently with riot police storming the campus and dozens of students wounded and arrested.

Beyond the campuses, the lines between "political" students and "non-political" citizens also blurred as the New Left repeatedly fought the security forces in the streets. As William Marotti has pointed out, the blurring of these lines caused much anxiety for authorities. As in the campuses, state violence led many *nanpori* (from the English "non-political") into activism and, indeed, transformed the very meaning of the word to suggest a "potential instability [...] and the possibility of political engagement" (Marotti 2009, 98). "The apparent paradox of *nanpori* politics," Marotti argues, "should actually alert us to an expansion of politics in practice that simply outpaced the conventional definitions of the term 'political'" (2009, 98). But the New Left was not only expanding the political, but also excluding and demarcating what kinds of politics were acceptable.

The old parties and the old peace movement were definitely outside of the New Left's definition of accepted politics. The students saw themselves as completely separate from the older peace movement and the style of politics of their parents' generations. As briefly noted above, the issue of victim consciousness (*higaishaishiki*) was one of the main reasons for this breach. While victimization and a feeling of betrayal by the state, as Oda Makoto and other intellectuals saw it, played a significant role in separating citizen and state and inserting a healthy measure of suspicion into citizens' relation to state institutions, by the 1960s the experience had been usurped by the state and made into a collective victim consciousness (Orr 2001, 8). The purest expression of this move was in Hiroshima, when the peace movement, seeking to expand its base following the "bikini incident," nationalized the hibakusha experience and turned all Japanese into *yuitsu no hibakukoku* (the only nation to have ever been bombed by nuclear weapons).[24] But being victims also meant forgetting the fact of being victimizers. Whenever notions of agency were articulated, they were divorced from "the people" or the "working class," who for the Old Left were beyond reproach and were as much victims of the "militarists" as other Asians were (Orr 2001, 8–9). Oda and others sought to go beyond such notions as part of a wider move of establishing an autonomous Japanese self, capable of resisting state authority and manipulation. In 1967, in a typical statement, student leader Shima Shigeru declared: "We believe there is a clear line of demarcation between ourselves and the communists of the pre-war days. Their primary motivation was the spirit of martyrdom. In contrast, our primary concern is the emancipation of ourselves as human beings" (Tsurumi 1968, 436).

Shima's use of the term "martyrdom" to denote the Old Left's attitude was no accident. Many of the first postwar generation of peace activists simply exchanged one form of radicalism (right-wing emperor worship) with another (peace activism). The gestures, language and emotional intensity stayed the same. Highlighting victimization and abstracting guilt beyond any concrete historic specificity was essential in facilitating this move. This lineage did not, however, mean that the 68ers parents' generation was wholly complicit. What Oda, Shima and indeed their whole generation forgot was that their concern with autonomy and "emancipation" had its roots in the *shutaisei* (subjectivity) debates which raged in the late '40s among left-wing intellectuals' "communities of contrition" (Orr 2001, 6). The reason for this blindness, in Japan as in Germany where students also blamed their parents for their complicity and silence, was generational. Oda was 13 years old when the war ended and did not experience the postwar intellectual moment. The generational difference was felt also on the other side of the divide, when older activists were dismayed by the violence displayed by the students, forgetting their own generation's violent confrontations with the police before the Korean War.

Violence played a special role in generational conflict. The students' style was very different from earlier movements. They wore helmets and came to demonstrations armed with long wooden staves, used to battle police. These students mythologized violence and its ability to transform individuals and society. They saw violence as a tool with which to unmask the violence and injustice of the state. Violence, as with other aspects of this debate, had in Hiroshima an even more symbolic significance. In a fascinating document, Teraoka Shōgo (2008, 11), a Hiroshima University student leader, writes of postwar Hiroshima as a "tourist city," which "fabricates its history" and buries its past. The rubble of the bomb was buried under the new shiny buildings and memorials and with it the memory of the bomb. "What is rubble?" asks Teraoka:

rubble – the destruction of Hiroshima by the bomb
rubble – an ugliness
rubble – where our history began
rubble – it exists in the now

It is the duty of students to pick up this rubble, to dig it out and hurl it (at the police). Smashing, through this act, the ignorance and indifference of the non-political masses and uncovering the true nature of Hiroshima, "not as a mistake but as a deliberate act," meant uncovering the true nature of the system and the way Hiroshima's memory was buried through the machinations of imperialism and capitalism.

This – for lack of a better word – fetishism of the hurled brick and aestheticizing of violence was very similar to the language employed by 1960s students worldwide.[25] But just like in May 1968 in France, the violent language notwithstanding, this revolution was one wherein nobody died.[26] The students' violence was a part of what Marotti (2009) rightly called "the theatre of protest." Snake dances, flying banners, masks and costumes were part of a street theater of violence. "Students," a Western journalist wrote in 1968, "opted for street dance and flamboyant melodrama […] but [the feeling was] that the students and the police will perform and society will go on" (Beer 1970, 44).

But if in Tokyo or Sasebo (where students clashed with police after a visit by the USS Enterprise) citizens could be onlookers, in Hiroshima they could not. The very term "citizens of Hiroshima" was politically loaded and was repeatedly used by the Left to denote the fundamentally "peace loving" character of the transformed Hiroshima. The Left or peace movement figures, rather than the LDP, were in control of the city and, thus, the clash between the old peace movement and the citizenry (conceived as one and the same by the former) and the New Left was much more pronounced. This resulted in head-on conflict and widespread hostility to the movement during the visit by Prime Minister Satō in August 1971 – the first ever by a Japanese prime minister at the peace ceremony. Although the students' violence did lead to some positive developments for the Left (for instance, the final cancellation of the JDF parades), its most significant development was the intensified solidification of the notion of sacred space and the end of the Peace Park as a political space.

Nuclear issues were major grounds for confrontation between the Satō administration and the students.[27] Satō endorsed Japan's three non-nuclear principles in December 1967.[28] The students saw it as a cynical ploy and, rightly, suspected foul play on the part of the government and the Americans, accusing the Americans of introducing nuclear weapons to Japan aboard US navy ships (Marotti 2009, 130). Most of the Old Left and the hibakusha movement, however, welcomed the LDP's endorsement of antinuclearism. Their support was not devoid of vested interests either. One of the main goals of the hibakusha organizations, if not their main goal, was getting compensation and special medical treatment from the Japanese government. The LDP endorsement also meant an increase in chances of a better deal for hibakusha. In fact, when the students declared their intention in early August to block Satō's visit, which many in the hibakusha movement saw as a historic victory and a step forward, many in Hiroshima were alarmed (Yokohara[29] 2010). The Crane Society, for instance, staged a vigil and spread paper cranes in front of the Children's Peace Monument "hoping to prevent disturbances in the ceremony" (*Chūgoku Shinbun*, 5 August 1971). The more radical students were taking little notice of these concerns. In an uncompromising statement, one faction called for the establishment of a nationwide organization to stop the prime minister's visit and called his stated concern with survivors' attendance of the ceremony "a pose, a transparent trial at evading war responsibility, and […] part of [the prime minister's] support for the re-invasion of Asia [i.e. Japan's support of the Vietnam War]" (Nemoto 2006, 161).

As the date of the prime minister's visit drew near, the New Left delivered on its promises of resistance. An organization called the Hibakusha Youth League (Hibakusha Seinen Renmei), which had some hibakusha support, tried to stage a sit-in in front of the cenotaph in late July. The city called in the police to remove them (*Asahi Shinbun*, 29 July 1971). As more and more students from *zenkyoto*, the *chukoku ha* and other organizations gathered in Hiroshima, tensions mounted. In preparation, Mayor Yamada declared the park a sacred zone and deployed police to stop demonstrations, and the prefectural and municipal police set up a special HQ (*Chūgoku Shinbun*, 6 August 1971). On the day of the visit, about 1,500 students converged on Hiroshima Station, where Satō was supposed to arrive. Luckily for the police, that same morning, a typhoon from Kyushu descended on Hiroshima. Battered by strong winds and rain, and facing an overwhelming force of riot police, the students could not prevent the prime minister from arriving at Hiroshima. At the ceremony itself, when the prime minister tried to lay a wreath at the cenotaph, four students burst into his route, threw firecrackers and tried to accost him. They were stopped by undercover police (*Mainichi Shinbun*, 6 August 1971). Outside the park, hundreds of students chanted that Satō should "go home" and other antiwar slogans. Even after the ceremony, during the fire lantern ritual, usually the most dignified and family-oriented part of the day, students played loud rock music and tried to interfere with ceremonies (Nemoto 2006, 164).

The response from Hiroshima citizens was almost overwhelmingly negative. Some hibakusha actually confronted the students, declaring "this is a place for prayer [...] you do not have the right to disturb our prayer [for the dead]." Others commented that they were saddened by the violence (*Chūgoku Shinbun*, 7 August 1971). The papers on the following days were full of anti-student sentiment. One citizen commented: "They only come here once a year [...] they do not know anything about [our suffering]." Another wrote: "I lost my wife and daughter that day [...] no one has the right to disturb [my mourning]." Another called the students "animals" (Nemoto 2006, 167). The Old Left, especially socialists and communist members of the assembly, also condemned the violence (*Chūgoku Shinbun*, 7 August 1971). There were some sympathetic voices pointing out that "prayer alone will not bring peace," and that the student anger was justified given that the government did nothing for the hibakusha, but they were few voices in a sea of condemnation (Nemoto 2006, 167).

Clearly, by 1971 the Yamada campaign for sanctification had succeeded in popular consciousness in turning the park into a sacred space in need of protection from the violence of politics. The students had played right into his hands. In his work on student violence, Marotti writes that "violence played an ambiguous role in uncovering state violence and bringing down the gap between regular *shimin* (citizens) and students [...] [and] created the conditions for non-violence" (2009, 128). Marotti argues that violence opened up space for different kinds of political groups and contributed to a restraining of police violence, which allowed citizen groups to reclaim the streets as political space. This was not the case in Hiroshima. Far from condemning police violence, most people accused the students of both physical and symbolic violence (defilement). The violence led to an affirmation of the park's sacred status and made any notion of the Left reclaiming it as a political space unthinkable, thus closing off rather than expanding important political space.

However, there are some signs that student violence had positive effects. The JDF parades through Hiroshima came under heavy criticism and legal challenges from the Left in 1972 and 1973. The courts rejected those, but it was the fear of student violence that pushed the governor of Hiroshima Prefecture and the JDF to cancel the parades. "I do not want," stated the governor, "to see the parade conducted [while] surrounded by riot police" (*Chūgoku Shinbun*, 26 May 1974).[30] The notion of sacred space was also still being mobilized by the Left to fight those other pernicious dangers: commercialization and tourism. The hotel that had stood in the park's grounds from its beginning was torn down in 1972 for being "inappropriate" and "violating the Peace Park law" (*Chūgoku Shinbun*, 1 February 1972).[31] These were some of the last victories of the Left in the '70s, as factionalism tore through the New Left and prosperity and co-option into the conservative system took the edge off the older union and party-based Left. With its campaign for sanctification of the park basically successful, the city moved to revamp the museum to make it befitting of "an international city of peace and culture." A 1970 tourist brochure for Hiroshima repeatedly made references to its being "a bright city, situated on the Seto Inland Sea, which is known as the Mediterranean of the Orient" (Hiroshima City, 1970). The brochure talks of beautiful beaches, girls in bikinis, and the many festivals and gay atmosphere in summertime Hiroshima. When the city's history is mentioned, the brochure calls Hiroshima "an international city of peace and culture [...] where the oneness of the world and unity of mankind can be achieved." The Peace Park is called "a symbol zone of peace and culture," and a "place of prayer." Images of crying hibakusha and religious ceremonies (of all faiths) complement the picture (Hiroshima City, 1970). Hiroshima tourist officials seemed at times outright annoyed by what one official called the "dark image" of their city, and opted instead to present the "beautiful industrial development and the bright Hiroshima of today." Another official declared: "We do not sell the bomb, but promote peace" (*Chūgoku Shinbun*, 30 April 1971). This was, of course, absurd. Unfortunately, by 1970, with the Left's power broken, not many in Hiroshima could mount a challenge to this view.

Conclusion

The sanctification of the Peace Park was not the result of policy decisions by Hiroshima City, its Tourist Board or hibakusha organizations. It was rather the result of a tortured process to which all groups – with the possible exception of the students – contributed whether intentionally or inadvertently. The more controversial and contradictory the process became, the more frequent were those invocations of the sacred. This was not surprising as the very nature of Hiroshima's project and its tragedy led to an almost reflexive usage of such language. For many people, religious language substituted for the incapacity of "normal" language and the pre-existing order of things to explain Hiroshima.

Mary McCarthy, in a devastating critique of John Hersey's *Hiroshima*, wrote of Hiroshima as "a hole in human history" (Treat 1996, 27). In a way, the whole ideological apparatus emerging after the bomb was a trial in reaffirming order, in filling up that hole. Religion, as Danièle Hervieu-Léger (2000) has argued, is especially adept in reaffirmation in its capacity to maintain community and continuity, and act as a "chain of memory."

Challenging the secularization thesis, Hervieu-Léger argues that religion has a stock of symbols, which can be utilized for modern projects – especially when secular projections are called into question (2000, 3). Hiroshima was just such a situation, and defenders of the status quo, both American and Japanese, lost no time in using religious language to describe Hiroshima (and Nagasaki – a Catholic city where such language was even more prevalent) as a "sacrificial lamb for peace" and praising hibakusha's silent resolve and lack of hate toward the Americans (Nagai 1949, 107).[32] What that kind of language masked was, of course, the severe censorship operated by Americans, which did not allow discussing the bomb in any negative terms, let alone speaking of revenge against the Americans or the immensely controversial nature of the bombing. This pattern continued into the '50s and '60s when hibakusha were turned into martyrs and Hiroshima into a sacred ground for peace.

Yamada and the Left saw themselves as acting with only the best of motives: trying to unify a divided country around the noble cause of peace. Nevertheless, the not-so-noble motives of capitalizing on Hiroshima's heritage as well as the uneasy past, which sanctification was trying to paper over, did not allow the process to go smoothly. Hiroshima's memory wars, in which radical students, the Old Left, independent liberals and conservatives all fought over who would speak in the hibakusha's name, made the transition of the Peace Park from a political center to a sacred space fraught with tensions and contradictions. Ironically, though, the more controversy the move generated, the more solid the notion of the park's sacredness became. Today, it is hard to imagine the Peace Park as a place of heated debate and violent clashes or, for that matter, JDF tanks rolling down Peace Boulevard. It is also hard to imagine, however, Hiroshima's sterile Peace Park having any remaining political role in what is still a dangerously nuclear-armed world. The sacred managed to triumph over violence in Hiroshima but it also, sadly, triumphed over politics as a whole.

Notes

I wish to thank Dagmar Herzog and Ana Belén Torres for reading and commenting on this paper. All translations, unless otherwise noted, are mine. For Japanese names, I have followed the Japanese convention and used the family name first.

1 *Hibakusha*, in Japanese, literally means a person who was exposed to the nuclear bomb. Lately, following Fukushima, hibakusha was expanded to include anyone who has been exposed to radiation.
2 In the inverted logic of the Cold War, the Chinese-backed JCP saw the ban as a way to keep nuclear weapons in the hands of the imperialists (i.e. Russia and the US) while denying them from "true" socialist countries like China.
3 The classic account of how politics were delegitimized in Japan is found in Gluck (1987).
4 The building's original name was the Industrial Promotion Hall. It was constructed in 1915 as a place for promoting the sale of goods produced in Hiroshima Prefecture. The building was designed by Czech architect Jan Letzel and, with its imposing European-style design, was already quite famous before the war. As Lisa Yoneyama has noted, the building in its current form serves as an ambiguous reminder of the failure of Japan's (first) quest for modernization. The building, conspicuous in its European features within the Japanese city, was a symbol of civilization and enlightenment (*bunmeikaika*) and of Japan's embrace of a European-inspired modernity; a quest which, along with science and modern architecture, also included scientific racism and imperialism. The bomb, of course, ended this phase in Japanese history. See Yoneyama's brilliant analysis of the building's multi-layered history in *Hiroshima Traces* (1999).
5 The dome's silhouette is everywhere in Hiroshima. It is prominent in posters, guides and tourist literature. Its image greets visitors when they get off the train in Hiroshima Station and is posted on the city tramlines.
6 I thank Nemoto Masaya for his generosity in sharing his thesis with me.
7 I thank *Chūgoku Shinbun*'s reporter Nishimoto Masami for informing me on these late 1940s efforts to preserve the dome.
8 For instance, the city already used the phrase "tourist resource" in its 1949 report: "The city outline," the city administrator stated, "[and] the many abandoned and ruined buildings in the downtown area are becoming our new tourist sites. Some of these are ground Zero [such as] the Industrial Promotion Hall, and [other sites] [...] From now on, international tourists who will be coming to Japan will put visiting the Hiroshima ruins on their schedule[s]." A 1953 report also included the dome as "tourist infrastructure and a representative of *Atom Hiroshima*" (Nemoto 2006, 69, see especially note 7; emphasis mine).
9 The exchange took place at the Hiroshima City Assembly Budget Committee on 15 March 1956.
10 The Chamber of Commerce moved into its new headquarters in October 1966. The move, the Chamber advocated, "represented their commitment to Hiroshima's progress and development" (Hiroshima Shōkō Kaigisho 1982, 569–70).
11 Hiroshima's Chamber of Commerce was quite alarmed by the rapid rise in real estate prices in the city center. The Chamber was also facing criticism over the use of what was formerly public land to build its headquarters building. With the support of Mayor Hamai, they formed a joint committee to examine the issue (Hiroshima Shōkō Kaigisho 1982, 575).
12 The preservation debates seem to have died down after 1960. The revision of the security treaty and other issues seem to have completely captured the attention of the Left, leaving little room for any other campaigns and, with the completion of the Chamber of Commerce building, ending fears of imminent collapse, the dome issue receded to the background. A cause for renewed interest was the aforementioned debate over the supposedly sacred nature of the Peace Park and its use by political groups. This debate will be further examined below.

13 Founded by a hibakusha named Kawamoto Ichiro and his wife, the society was inspired by the death of Sasaki Sadako and, as its name indicates, the millions of paper origami cranes folded by children worldwide for Sadako. The society was instrumental in the burst of activity for A-bomb children that followed and the making of the Children's Peace Monument (1958), and was particularly active among school children.
14 As Yagi noted, Hamai himself credited the Crane Society for changing his mind.
15 All these who signed were involved in nuclear issues in the past, Tange and Yukawa especially.
16 Yamada was, as a Diet member, instrumental in the passing of the law in 1949.
17 This was, as James Orr demonstrated, a pretty standard view among conservatives. The right wing in Japan routinely portrayed the loss and suffering of the war as a "sacrifice" which enabled Japan's postwar prosperity (2001, 137–8).
18 Furthermore, the ceremony was held in Hiroshima's local Defense of the Nation Shrine (Gokoku Jinja). These shrines, set up during imperial times to honor those who died in Japan's wars, were officially separated from state control in 1965 and run by a supposedly private body, the Shrine Shinto Association, which was formed after the war. This association retained powerful connections with the ruling LDP and continuously promoted conservative and nationalist values. Like the JDF as a whole, the association's and especially the National Defense Shrine's connection to the military are constitutionally suspect and have a history of covert right-wing agenda. For an overview of the issue, see Norma Field (1992). For a history of the association, see Franziska Seraphim (2006). The issue was even more sensitive in Hiroshima proper, as the site of the shrine was also the site of the former Imperial Headquarters which served Emperor Meiji in the First Sino–Japanese War.
19 Japan in general, and the Hiroshima region in particular, served as the launching pad for US army operations in Vietnam and Asia. For instance, the B-52 bombers that carpet-bombed North Vietnam flew to their mission from Japanese airbases. The Iwakuni air base next to Hiroshima is one of the largest in Japan. Also, Hiroshima shipyards and factories were engaged in contracts to supply arms, repair damaged vessels, etc. for the US army. Those connections dated back to the time of the Korean War.
20 These schemes included: banning entrance for cars, banning stepping on grass or playing on it (no ball games), new clover flowerbeds and a replacement of the concrete of the cenotaph with granite. Yamada also planned to get rid of the rest house and change the parking rules.
21 As Lisa Yoneyama argues, as with any national narrative, Japanese victimization was exclusive; it left out all but pure Japanese victims. The creation of the Peace Park meant also the creation of silences. The stories of Chinese and Korean forced laborers, American prisoners of war, Japanese Americans stranded in the city and all others who perished in the bombing were not mentioned. The entry of the Koreans would have been a reminder of Japan's wartime and imperial aggression and exploitation of Koreans, a reminder which was detrimental to the dogmatically "positive" message of the park.
22 By the late '60s, with cooperation and compromise becoming the norm at the increasingly affluent workplace, union and Old Left demonstrators, who were also physically older, apologized to citizens for the disturbance caused by strikes or demonstrations, and tried to work in cooperation with the authorities. The New Left was openly contemptuous of these unions' tactics.
23 In Tokyo University, for instance, issues of student union autonomy, high dorm expenses, students' freedom to choose roommates and the rigidity of the entrance exam placed the main student factions in conflict with the university. See Shimbori (1971, 151).

24 The Bikini Incident or *Daigo Fukuryū Maru* (*Lucky Dragon Five*) Incident was the irradiation of a Japanese fishing vessel, the *Lucky Dragon Five*, by radiation from an American nuclear test in March 1954. The incident sparked a nationwide antinuclear protest movement. Previous to that incident, the atomic bombing of Hiroshima and Nagasaki was not generally seen as an incident of victimization of all Japanese, but as more of a regional issue. The protest movement changed this and nationalized the issue.
25 See, among many others, Ross (2002) and the essays in Schildt and Siegfried (2006).
26 Later on, some did die. In the '70s the movement experienced an extremely violent stage. Student factions fought each other and among themselves. In the most famous incident, in 1972 the United Red Army faction, a Maoist splinter group, "purged" itself of traitors by killing 14 out of 25 members. This faction and others also turned to terrorism and engaged in plane hijacking and other activities.
27 Other reasons for dissent were his support for Vietnam and use of police order to disband a faction of Zengakuren.
28 On 11 December 1967, in a speech at the Diet, Satō introduced the Three Non-Nuclear Principles: vowing non-production, non-possession and non-introduction of nuclear weapons in Japan. This was an astute move on the part of the conservatives. With the antinuclear movement increasingly split and dysfunctional, the LDP aligned itself with the center-right factions and began to formulate its opposition to nuclear weapons, thus benefiting from popular antinuclear feelings in the wider public and making antinuclearism a mainstream goal. Soon after the 1967 declaration, Japan entered the Nuclear Non-Proliferation Treaty, and the Diet passed a resolution formally adopting the principles in 1971. Yoneyama and others rightly criticize this "nationalization of victimhood," seeing it as a cynical maneuver in deploying victim consciousness in the service of nationalist goals. As discussed above, being a nation of victims conventionally helped Japanese avoid consideration of their victimization of others.
29 Yokohara Yukio is former chair of the Gensuikyō organization. This interview took place in Hiroshima on 25 June 2010.
30 The JDF cited its wish to preserve fuel (the oil crisis had just hit Japan at the time). It was, however, widely acknowledged that the parades had become too controversial.
31 The city's auditor decided that "the presence of the Hiroshima Hotel within the Peace Park grounds is inappropriate and unlawful" and asked the mayor to remove it as fast as possible.
32 The full quote by Nagai, a Nagasaki survivor was, "Nagasaki, the only holy place in all Japan – was it not chosen as a victim, a pure lamb, to be slaughtered and burned on the altar of sacrifice to expiate the sins committed by humanity in the Second World War?" Similar language was used in Hiroshima. In General MacArthur's message on the second Hiroshima anniversary, he spoke of Hiroshima as a sober warning from God. The general, who incidentally had opposed the use of nuclear weapons in Japan (but not later in Korea), saw Hiroshima in firmly Christian terms (Ubuki 1992, 12).

References

"A-Bomb Dome." Hiroshima Peace Memorial Museum website. Online: http://www.pcf.city.hiroshima.jp/virtual/VirtualMuseum_e/tour_e/ireihi/tour_38_e.html (accessed 1 March 2011).

Beer, Lawrence W. 1970. "Japan, 1969: 'My Homeism' and Political Struggle." *Asian Survey* 10(1): 43–55.

Field, Norma. 1992. *In the Realm of a Dying Emperor.* New York: Vintage Books.
Gluck, Carol. 1987. *Japan's Modern Myths: Ideology in the Late Meiji Period.* Princeton: Princeton University Press.
Hervieu-Léger, Daniele. 2000. *Religion as a Chain of Memory.* New Brunswick, NJ: Rutgers University Press.
Hiroshima City. 1970. *Hiroshima, 1970.* Kyoto: Dai-Nippon Publishing. Online: http://sbarnhill.mvps.org/japan/attractions/hiroshima.htm (accessed 4 April 2011).
Hiroshima daigaku bunsho kan [Hiroshma Archive]. 2008. *Shōgen daigaku funsō: kikiteki jōkyō ni taisuru Hiroshima daigaku kyōshokuin no kiroku* [Testimonial of the Campus Strife: A Critical Evaluation of the Conflict According to Faculty Records] Tokyo: Gendaishiryō shuppan.
Hiroshima-shi. 1988. *Hiroshima shi shigikaishi: kiji shiryōhen.* [Hiroshima City Assembly History: Documents Section]. Hiroshima: Hiroshima-shi.
Hiroshima Shōkō Kaigisho. 1982. *Hiroshima Shōkō Kaigisho kyūjūnenshi* [Hiroshima Chamber of Commerce: 90 Years of History]. Hiroshima: Hiroshima Shōkō Kaigisho.
Marotti, William. 2009. "Japan 1968: The Performance of Violence and the Theater of Protest." *American Historical Review* (February), 143.
Morihito Sukeharo. 1950. *Hiroshima no kenko shigen: shintoshi* [Hiroshima Tourist Resource: A New City]. Hiroshima: Toshikei kaku kai.
Nagai, Takashi. 1994 [1949]. *The Bells of Nagasaki,* translated by William Johnston. New York: Kodansha International.
Nemoto, Masaya. 2006. "Hiroshima no sengo sanjunenkan ni miru genbaku hibakusha no hyoshō to jissen: chi, kenryoko to kukan" [Representations and Practices on the Catastrophe in Hiroshima during the 1945–1970s: Knowledge, Power and Space]. Unpublished master's thesis submitted to Hitotsubashi University, Tokyo.
Ōe, Kenzaburō. 1996. *Hiroshima Notes,* 1st ed. New York: Grove Press.
Orr, James J. 2001. *The Victim as Hero: Ideologies of Peace and National Identity in Postwar Japan.* Honolulu: University of Japan Press.
Ross, Kristin. 2002. *May '68 and its Afterlives.* Chicago: University of Chicago Press.
Sasaki, Yuichiro, ed. 1948. *Hiroshima Foto arubumu* [Hiroshima Photo Album]. Hiroshima: Hiroshima kenko busan kumiai.
Schildt, Axel and Detlef Siegfried, eds. 2006. *Between Marx and Coca-Cola: Youth Cultures in Changing European Societies, 1960–1980.* New York: Berghahn Books.
Seraphim, Franziska. 2006. *War Memory and Social Politics in Japan, 1945–2005.* Cambridge, MA: Harvard University Asia Center.
Shimbori, Michiya. 1971. "Student Radicals in Japan." *The Annals of the American Academy of Political and Social Science* 395(1): 150–58.
Shono, Naomi. 1993. "Mute Reminders of Hiroshima's Atomic Bombing." *Japan Quarterly* 40(3): 267–76.
Teraoka, Shōgo. 2008. "Gareki wo horiokose" [Hurling Bricks]. In Hiroshima daigaku bunsho kan, *Shōgen daigaku funsō: kikitekijō kyō ni taisuru Hiroshima daigaku kyoshokuin no kiroku* Tokyo: Gendaishiryō shuppan.
Tsurumi, Kazuko. 1968. "The Japanese Student Movement: Its Milieu." *Japan Quarterly* 15 (October–December): 430–55.
Ubuki, Satoro. 1992. *Heiwa Kinen Shikiten no Ayumi* [History of the Peace Memorial Ceremony]. Hiroshima: Hiroshima Peace Culture Foundation.
Whittier Treat, John. 1996. *Writing Ground Zero: Japanese Literature and the Atomic Bomb.* Chicago: University Of Chicago Press.

Yagi, Yoshihiro. 2005. "1965 nen mae no' Hiroshima" [Hiroshima before 1965]. In Arisue Ken, ed., *Sengo nihon no shakai to shiminishiki* [Postwar Japanese Society and Citizenship]. Tokyo: Keio daigakushupansha.

Yamada, Setsuo, *tuiso rokukan koiinkai hen* [The committee for the completion of materials for Yamada Setuo's biography]. 1976. *Yamada Setsuo Tsuisoroku* [Yamada Setsuo Recollections]. Hiroshima.

Yokohara, Yukio. 2010. Interview with author. Hiroshima, 25 June.

Yoneyama, Lisa. 1997. "Memory Matters: Hiroshima's Korean Atom Bomb Memorial and the Politics of Ethnicity." In *Living with the Bomb: American and Japanese Cultural Conflicts in the Nuclear Age*, edited by Laura Elizabeth Hein and Mark Selden, 202–31. Armonk, NY: M. E. Sharpe.

———. 1999. *Hiroshima Traces: Time Space and the Dialectics of Memory*. Berkeley: University of California Press.

Archives

Hiroshima City Archive. 1950. "Hiroshima heiwa to shaken setsukōsōan" [A Proposal for Building Hiroshima Peace City]. In *Hiroshima shiyakushō shichō shitu* [Hiroshima City Hall, Mayor's Documents], Fujimoto Collection, C–1993–800.

Newspapers/magazines

Asahi Grafu. 1960–1967.
Asahi Shinbun. 1970–1971.
Chūgoku Shinbun. 1963–2007.
Mainichi Shinbun. 1971.
New York Times Magazine. 1965.
Washington Post. 1970.
Yumiyuri Shinbun. 1962.

Chapter 7

THE SECTARIAN AS A CATEGORY OF SECULAR POWER: SECTARIAN TENSIONS AND JUDICIAL AUTHORITY IN LEBANON

Raja Abillama

Introduction

Sectarian tensions figure in contemporary commentaries on certain regions of the world as exemplary manifestations of religious violence or, among the more cautious ones, of its conditions. As the darker corollaries of religious diversity, the *bête noire* of an otherwise peaceful multiculturalism, they point to the bloody outcomes of unreason and intolerance evoked in age-old images of inter-religious slaughter. As such, sectarian tensions are a permanent trace of that forgotten past, its continuous din in the anxious ears of the self-proclaimed secular who sees a potential threat in any religious multiplicity.[1] In that capacity, they are seen to be propitious for the causes of dictators, who opportunistically exploit them for their own purposes, as an expert on Middle Eastern affairs writing about Syria has recently warned. "[I]t is now clear," he writes, "that Assad's strategy is to divide the opposition by stoking sectarian tensions" (Nasr 2011). They also occasion "consternation" and "condemnation" which, while "ultimately provid[ing] the main democratic guarantee against the narrowly factional exploitation of sectarianism" (Sen 1999, 5), may also entail a justification of political intervention. The same expert advises Washington that while it "can hope for a peaceful and democratic future [...] we should guard against sectarian conflicts that, once in the open, would likely run their destructive course at great cost to the region and the world" (Nasr 2011).

In public pronouncements on sectarianism, the "sectarian" in sectarian tension seems fairly obvious, enough to base a foreign policy on, or to predict the outcome of history. Indeed, the sectarian delineates a global geography, the vast landmass extending from West Africa, the Arab world, the fringes of Europe – Northern Ireland and the Balkans – Turkey, Iran, India and Pakistan. It presupposes "religious sects" to be universally valid, which makes it possible to encompass in a single category a series of disparate subcategories such as Christian, Muslim, Hindu, Copt, Druze, Maronite, 'Alawi, Shi'i or Sunni, to name a few, regardless of the respective historic and cultural specificity of each. Sectarian tensions refer to the relationships among various combinations of "sects" – Christians and Muslims, Copts and Muslims, Maronites and Druze, or Hindus and Muslims – of which a population or society consists. An essential criteria for the identification of sectarian tensions is the nature and quality of the power that governs those populations or societies. For instance, we are told about "Saudi Arabia's plan [...] to assuage sectarian tensions in the country" by a "state-backed economic aid package" worth "some $90 billion" (Gamble 2011), or that "[s]ectarian tensions have blighted Egyptian society because of the ill-advised policies pursued by the [...] [successive] regimes" (Harb 2010). Invocations of sectarian tensions tell us something about power.

In this chapter I focus on sectarian tensions as an instance of what the sectarian attribution privileges as distinctive: sectarian relations, violence, institutions, discourses, practices, sentiments and so on. I ask, what are we talking about when we talk about "the sectarian"? I address this question by tracing articulations of sectarian tensions in the context of Lebanese law, which, through the criminal category of "stoking sectarian tensions," enables the judiciary to authorize specific historical accounts that assign meaning to sectarian tensions. These accounts in turn provide the grounds to criminalize or sanction particular modes of signification, and to regulate public sentiments. An outcome of this judicial interpretation is the authoritative determination of what the political and ethical consist in. In that context, sectarian tensions are less phenomena or events emerging from the occasional collisions between religion and politics in non-secular states than occasions for the articulation of secular power. I argue that the meaning of the sectarian resides in the work it does in particular discursive contexts, namely to articulate the lineaments of that power. More generally, I suggest that the category sectarian belongs to a genealogy of secularism through which "politics," "religion," "history" and "ethics" are defined.

The rest of this chapter proceeds to offer an exposition of the notion of stoking sectarian tensions as it occurs in the Lebanese Penal Code, and to analyze its interpretation in particular criminal judicial cases. The essay consists of four sections, the first of which aims to highlight the ambiguity of the crime of stoking sectarian tensions in the Penal Code, a necessary ambiguity, I contend, for it extends the interpretive domain of judicial authority. That domain is explored in more detail in the sections that follow.

The second section analyses a case before the Lebanese Court of Publications in 1972. Sectarian tensions are articulated in terms of a republican historical script that pits a local spiritual nationalism, as it were, that unites Muslim and Christian "brethren" and "compatriots," against the cunning of colonial reason, which exploits missionary proselytism and religion to conceal its political and economic objectives. In the third section, three defendants are arraigned by the Accusatory Authority in Beirut in 2005, also for stoking sectarian tensions. This time the Lebanese Civil War of 1975–90, typifying the destructive consequences of sectarian tensions, serves as the historical script against which the Authority draws the line between legitimate political discourse that has a place in the present and illegal public declarations that belong to the Civil War, and by virtue of that risk stokes sectarian tensions – in other words, the Authority risks inviting the past back to dwell in the present. The fourth section presents a case appearing before the Single Criminal Judge in Beirut in 2007, in which the same Civil War and the concomitant necessity to avoid stoking sectarian tensions imposed an ethic or a mode of conduct honed to conform to the requirements of a plural civil society.

The Crime of Stoking Sectarian Tensions: Signification, Interpretation, Context

The crime of stoking sectarian tensions is not positively defined in the Lebanese Penal Code, but is nevertheless identified as a punishable crime. However, its outlines may be traced by its articulations with other sorts of crime, while its positive meaning is eventually defined by the judiciary in singular cases. In this section I summarize the crime of stoking sectarian tensions in the Penal Code of 1943 and some of its ambiguities. As I show in the subsequent sections, these ambiguities enable a process of judicial interpretation, the outcome of which is the production of historical, political and ethical domains through which emerges the meaning of sectarian tensions.

The Penal Code, issued during the last year of the French Mandate over Syria and Lebanon, explicitly links sectarian tensions to reasons of state through a particular sort of crime, stoking sectarian tensions. Acts that stoke sectarian tensions are classified as "crimes against the state's internal security" in a category that includes crimes "against national unity, or which disturb the peace among the components of the nation." They belong to the same class as crimes "against the Constitution," "usurping political or civil power, or a military command," "sedition (*al-fitna*)," "financing terrorism" and crimes against "[…] the state's financial standing." Article 317 stipulates: "Any act, text, and discourse (*khutāb*) meant to (*yuqsad biha*) stoke (*'ithārat*), or resulting in the stoking of […] sectarian (*madhhabiyya*) or racist (*'unsuriyya*) tensions (*na'arāt*), or to incite conflict among sects (*tā'ifa*s) [...] is punishable" (Penal Code [henceforth PC] 1943, bk II, pt 1, sec. 2, art. 317). Stoking sectarian tensions and crimes against religion belong to two different categories of crime. Unlike the former, the definition of which is left open and is largely taken for granted, "the religious" is specified in detail and encompasses religious sentiments (arts 473–5), conversion, marriage (art. 476) and death (arts 477–82). Crimes against religious sentiments, for example, include "blasphemy against the name of God (*al-lāh*) in public," "denigrating public religious practices (*al-sha'ā'ir al-dīniyya*)," "interrupting religious ceremonies" and "demolishing, destroying, defacing, desecrating (*dannasa*), polluting (*najjasa*) places of worship or anything honored by the members of a religion or a group of people." Crimes against the dead include "obstructing funerals," "stealing or mutilating a corpse," "taking possession of, dissecting, or using a corpse for scientific or educational purposes without informing the rightful party," "degrading and desecrating the sacredness of cemeteries and mortuaries" and "desecrating, demolishing, destroying or vandalizing anything that relates to mortuary ceremonies."

It is worth comparing the Lebanese Penal Code with the Ottoman Penal Code (OPC) of 1883 (Walpole 1888). The latter mentions "worship and religious ceremonies" in article 132, chapter XI, entitled "Restriction on Free Worship – Injuries to Monuments." The article stipulates that "[w]hosoever shall interfere with the course of worship and religious ceremonies of any sect of His Imperial Majesty's subjects who are permitted the free exercise thereof, or who shall restrain the same by any act or threat, shall according to the gravity of the offence be punished with imprisonment for from one week to three months." It occurs in Book I, "Of Offences against the State, and Punishment of the Same," in which are also included "Offences against the Internal Security of the Ottoman Empire" under chapter II. In the 11 articles of that chapter, religion or sects are never mentioned. Instead, the code refers to the "subjects of the Ottoman Empire" (OPC 1883, art. 55), the "inhabitants of the Ottoman Empire" (art. 56), "community of persons" (art. 62) and the "citizens or inhabitants" (art. 66) (Walpole 1888). The point is that the internal security of the Ottoman state is not seen to be under threat by tensions or conflicts among them. The very notion that the state is tied to the plurality of sects seems to be non-existent. A threat to the internal security of the Ottoman state follows from a threat to its inhabitants, its subjects as a whole. Sectarian tensions, as a distinctive relationship among the various components of the populations tied to the state, is absent.

At any rate, in the cases that appear before the Lebanese judicial authorities, stoking sectarian tensions bears resemblance to other crimes, in which cases the facts must be shown to be features of stoking sectarian tensions and not some other crime in order to eventually decide which legal text applies.

THE SECTARIAN AS A CATEGORY OF SECULAR POWER   149

Thus, a set of facts may contain the apparent elements of a conspiracy or incitement to murder.² The former involves "the existence of an association or an agreement [...] between two or more persons" whose purpose is "to commit felonies against people or monies (*al-'amwāl*)" against "the authority of the state and its prestige (*al-haiba*)," or against the state's "institutions." A "criminal intent" must therefore exist, as well as "a mastermind (*ra's mudabbir*), plans[,] [...] roles assigned[,] [...] the unification of wills [...] and the making of definite decisions supported by a positive determination and backed by a fixed decisive will." A conspiracy possesses the features of rational action, which exceeds the mere "gathering" of "a few actors [...] revealing their thoughts to each other, or [...] communicat[ing] and exchang[ing] wishes and desires [of] transient interest, or fantasies [...] of [...] revolutions." It implies that "their decision [be] unified[,] [...] final and definitive" (Accusatory Authority in Beirut [henceforth AA] 2006, 449). According to a French legal textbook cited in one of the cases analyzed below, a "punishable agreement is that which is concretized or characterized by several material facts," such as "a vehicle containing weapons, hoods, surgical gloves, license plates and documents related to surveillance, the use of a stolen vehicle, weapons, wigs, arms purchases, or the testing of explosives" (AA 2006, 449).

Incitement to intentional murder is different, "requir[ing] [...] calm thinking and willing" and "sufficient time for "reflect[ion]," and implies organization and preparation by an inciter who "induces by any means another person to commit the crime." It is a crime in its own right, distinct from the criminal act that it leads to, identifiable by such acts as "temptation," "seduction" and "intimidation," all being "means to induce the actor to commit the crime." However, incitement also includes "an immaterial (*ma'nawi*) element," namely "the criminal consequence common between the criminal and the instigator [...] and the intention (*al-niyya*), which is the will (*al-'irāda*) to commit the crime as defined by law"(AA 2006, 450).

My point here is to examine some of the assumptions underlying the criteria by which stoking sectarian tensions is defined. Thus, whereas conspiracy is available to sense perception and incitement involves inter-subjectivity, stoking sectarian tensions is of a different order. It is accidental, contingent or the effect of an error of judgment, and the acts it involves are acts of signification; hence the place it occupies in the Lebanese Law of Publications: "[I]t is the public prosecutor's right to confiscate [...] and refer [...] to the competent judiciary" "publication[s] contain[ing] material denigrating any of the recognized religions (*al-diyānāt*) in the country, or what would (*min sha'nihi*) stoke sectarian tensions, disturb the public peace, expose to danger the state's security, sovereignty, unity, or borders, or Lebanon's external relations" (Law of Publications [henceforth LP] 1962, sec. 2, art. 25).³ Stoking sectarian tensions is a crime regardless of the means, "mechanical" or not, by which it is committed, insofar as it is public: actions and gestures, speaking and shouting, writings, drawings, pictures, photographs, films, signs and images. The public is broadly defined as a space "exposed to view" and occupied by "disinterested people" (PC 1943, art. 209).

The crime of stoking sectarian tensions is a crime of signification. It speaks to sentiments which, if "out in the open," charge with particular meaning a normatively neutral public space. This meaning and the sentiments that carry it accompany the putatively historical fact of religious difference. In other words, sectarian tensions are the affective dimension of the series of assumptions that "a population" is essentially composed of different religions or religious sects. The Penal Code takes sectarian tensions to be private; but, the code requires that they remain private, and punishes the acts that provoke them to be expressed in public. This articulation of the crime raises a few questions. First, given that the code distinguishes it from crimes against religion *and* ties it to religious difference, how is this distinction implemented, reasoned and justified in judicial practice? Moreover, the code assumes that a relationship exists between internal sentiments – sectarian tensions – and particular signs that externalize them. Which signs effectively stoke sectarian tensions? What is the relationship between signs and private sentiments? Do these sentiments and the signs that stoke them change over time? If these sentiments are private and must not be expressed, how is their existence confirmed? It is these questions that the judiciary attempts to answer, and in so doing disciplines language, affect and expression. The conclusion reached at the end of the judicial interpretive process, that a sign effectively stokes sectarian tensions, implies criminalizing particular kinds of speech or writing in terms of reasons of state. As the following cases illustrate, this involves specific articulations of history, politics and ethics relative to which both sectarian signs and sentiments are rendered legible.

Case No. 1, Year 1972: Religion, Colonialism and the Nation

Accusations of stoking sectarian tensions follow from a suspicion built into the assumptions that determine the way a word is read or heard, particularly about its associations with religion or religious sects and its relations with politics. It is with such assumptions about "proselytism" that the public prosecution approaches the Court of Publications (Mahkamat al Matbu'at) in 1972, at the request of the Lebanese Ministry of Information, with the claim that a pamphlet entitled *Proselytizing is an Instrument of Colonization: Its truth, its objectives, and our duty to resist it*, "stokes sectarian tensions (*'ithārat al-na'arāt tā'ifiyyah*)." The case involves two accusations: one issued by the pamphlet's authors, that proselytizing as an instrument of colonization stokes sectarian tensions, another – the prosecution's – that the pamphlet's claim about proselytism does so. While the court record does not explicitly mention it, the point of contestation is the confounding of a religious, specifically Christian, practice and a political enterprise. At any rate, the court dismisses the case on grounds that the evidence is insufficient, declaring it "necessary to examine the contents of the whole booklet" (Court of Publications [henceforth CP] 1972, 275).

Accusations of stoking sectarian tensions pit an accuser against an accused in a public forum, and thus entail processes of arbitration. Words and acts are perceived to stoke sectarian tensions by some touch and mobilize sentiments differently; the significance of sectarianism's discursive and practical vehicles mean different things to different people and are not self-evident. As the Lebanese Penal Code and Law of Publication suggest, they are of the order of signification and, therefore, the outcome of interpretation. However, interpretation is already framed, addressing a delimited set of questions that concern something already known as sectarian, a common ground for accusers and accused. It poses a particular set of problems: Does the act or speech stoke sectarian tensions? Is it sectarian or not and, if not, then what is it? Does it blur the boundaries between the religious, which includes sects, and the political? The outcome of this sectarian problematic and the interpretive effort it initiates is an authorized, yet always provisional, definition not only of the sectarian, but of religion and politics as well.

Three months after the first case was filed, the public prosecution presents the case again to the same court, and it is accepted. The claim is based on passages selected from a pamphlet that accused "Christian missionaries" of "stoking sectarian sensitivities (*al-hasāsiyyāt*)," and of "suspect [...] activities." The pamphlet "attacked the Papacy" which it associated with "the crusades," and argued that proselytizing "weakened the faith of Muslims" and that it did so "intention[ally]." It singled out "the machinations of the Company of Jesus under Papal patronage" and "the connection between the proselytizing movement and Zionism," and called for the "eradication of proselytism and the nationalization of its institutions." The public prosecution widens the scope of the evidence to include claims about the relationships between Christianity and Islam, religion and politics, and colonialism and missionaries (CP 1972, 280).[4]

The judicial process, starting from the prosecution's claim, is exclusively textual in the Court of Publications. It is a process in which a text's author is ironically excluded from the legal effort to interpret the meaning of the accused words. The interpretive and judicial process flows from a singular relationship between judge and text. In the current case, the court opens by asking whether "the defendant's intention (*ghāya*) – in other words, what he aimed at (*mā yarmi wa yahduf 'ilayh*) – was the stoking of sectarian tensions or not"; the court identifies this intention with "the spirit of the book [in its] totality." In this encounter between two authorities, judicial and textual, the author has no place and remains silent, his text standing for him in the judicial forum. Moreover, his intention is subsumed under the court's authoritative interpretation of his text and the meaning it ascribes to it. Thus, consistent with its first decision that "a few opinions [...] that may be wrong or extreme" are insufficient for judging, the court proceeds to consider the whole text (CP 1972, 280).

The accused text is not solitary, but is in turn placed in a wider context of an historical account the judiciary authorizes by excluding and silencing alternatives. The scripting of historical accounts is part of a judicial interpretive effort that involves the selection, emphasis and intensification of particular facts and not others. The scripted accounts are also normative commentaries on the present, authoritative pronouncements on what the present is, and the privileged place and status the authorizing voice occupies in it. Sectarianism, through the process of interpreting what stokes sectarian tensions, articulates more than just the relationships between religious sects, articulating notions, sensibilities and figures that constitute a whole historical domain.

In 1972, that domain was composed of two themes in counterpoint: the colonial struggle on the one hand and national/religious unity on the other, both together defining the dynamics and *raison d'être* of the postcolonial state, its enemies and the conduct expected of its citizens. Proselytism figures prominently in this account as a particularly insidious tactic of colonial power, and upon "reading the book," the court finds that "the plaintiff's intention was to point out to his compatriots (*muwātinīh*) [...] especially the Muslims, the dangers of religious and secular (*'almānī*) proselytizing, and their links with politics and Zionism." The court agrees with the authors that proselytism is particularly dangerous, but only after it interprets it as a site in which merge the religious and the secular, rendering both ambiguous. Proselytism is thus not a Christian activity *per se*, nor is it specifically aimed at Muslims. Rather, it is an activity employed for furthering worldly interests. What makes it particularly malicious is that distinguishing between its religious and secular aims depends on knowledge of the motives behind it. According to the court, the pamphlet seems to have discovered that, and intended to point out "how the political and economic interests of the countries to which the missionaries belonged [...] attempted to create two differing factions (*fi atain mutabāyinatain*) of citizens, widening the chasm between Muslims and their Christian brethren (*'ikhwānihum al-nasāra*)" (CP 1972, 280).

Religion plays an ambiguous role here: as the source of proselytism and as an aspect of colonialism, its role in politics is condemned; as resistance, however, and as a means of enlightenment about the "truth" of religion, politics and their distinctions, it is condoned. As proof of the author's intention to confirm that "Islam and Christianity are in origin brotherly religions," the court refers to the pamphlet's quotation of a Qur'anic verse and the tradition of the Prophet's flight to Christian Ethiopia. Finding support in a journal article entitled "Les conséquence du fait colonial en Amérique du Sud," it asserts that "the conclusion a reader would [draw from the pamphlet] is that Christianity and Islam are brotherly religions and remained so for a long time until politics in all its forms ruined the understanding between them, that is, the politics of the foreign and colonial state." Finally, the court rules that the pamphlet does not "stoke tensions between the Lebanese sects (*tawā'if*)" because the "intention behind publishing the book was to fight colonial politics dressed up *in the clothing of religion*, not to stoke tensions between the Lebanese sects (*tawā'if*)" (CP 1972, 280; emphasis added).

Questions about the truth of politics and religion, about the character and sense of their interconnections, belong to and emerge from the field of parameters that constitute the exigencies and priorities of the state. The very meaning of the religious – which includes sectarian diversity – is shaped by its twinning, as it were, with national unity. The religious is also political insofar as Muslims and Christians, as compatriots, together draw the "specific[ally] political distinction [...] between friend and enemy" (Schmitt 1996, 26), their compatriotism being, in turn, forged by that very distinction. Colonialism is the prime enemy, with its divide-and-rule tactics and its instrumental exploitation of religion – "dressed up in the clothing of religion" – to blur the distinction between religion and politics upon which rests Lebanese national/religious unity. The judiciary tackles the tension in its discourse on religion by shifting the emphasis to the question of religion serving as means and the kinds of ends its serves: to worldly utilitarian, or to spiritual national ends. Indeed, the judicial account tells of the spirituality of that desperately paradoxical defense of national/religious unity by keeping religion and politics apart. Yet, the question here is not whether the judiciary is consistent, but rather "how shifting grammar [of religion and politics] identifies" (Asad 2011, 673) what is legitimate and what is not at particular discursive conjunctures.

Case No. 2, Year 2005: Politics, Civil War and Sovereignty

The preceding case from 1972 stresses the moment when colonial strategy, which combined divide-and-rule tactics and the instrumental use of missionaries, aimed to drive a wedge between Islam and Christianity. The judiciary draws a particularly secular historical picture of the relationship between Muslims and Christians as brothers and compatriots under constant threat from external enemies. The common motive to preserve unity against foreign onslaught secures and supersedes – secures by superseding – religious diversity by attaching it to a republican ideal and orienting it towards an external enemy. The collapse of this ideal was lived a few years later in 1975, with the irruption of the 15-year long Lebanese Civil War. In 1972, sectarian tensions occur in and disrupt a progressive, teleological time of immemorial struggle to transcend them; in other words, sectarian tensions are here a transient point in the story of secularization. The year 2005, by contrast, is a time haunted by the past and finds a state possessed by an enemy within, which shifts the meaning of sectarian tensions, politics and religion, now characterized by different public sentiments, and places new demands on conduct.

In 2005, civil war replaces the progressive colonial struggle as a principle of interpretation of what stokes sectarian tensions. However, while the colonial struggle singularly affirmed the brotherhood of Muslims and Christians in their republican aspirations, the Civil War, as a substantive confirmation of sectarian tensions, is a defining feature of *and* must be excised from the present; civil war/sectarian tensions define the Lebanese population *and* must be suppressed. In the following two cases from 2005 and 2007, sectarian tensions, now hidden behind civil war which becomes the main motif, acquire Hobbesian proportions. As one lawyer describes it in a commentary on a ruling issued by the Criminal Court of Beirut in 1992, the war was a state of total moral and social collapse, a descent into a state of a war of all against all. "The events (*al-'ahdāth*) of Lebanon," he remarked, "took a sectarian (*tā'ifiyy*) turn, whereby brothers and neighbors turned against each other until the war [degenerated into] total destruction" and the "word 'innocent' [lost all] meaning." In this atmosphere, "merely belonging to another [political] party or sect (*tā'ifa*) implied that you are an enemy [...] and any incident occurring to a member of a sect, party, or family would elicit an arbitrary criminal reaction" (Jaber 1993, 312).

The second case effectively begins with the theme of a return from the past. Three men appear before the Accusatory Authority in Beirut after having convened a press conference to announce the comeback "to the Lebanese scene" of a certain political party they belonged to. The three, all members of the party's "executive committee," are accused of "stoking sectarian (*madhhabiyya* and *tā'ifiyya*) and racist (*'unsuriyya*) tensions." The Authority charges the three with the "misdemeanor (*al-jinha*) stipulated in article 317 of the Penal Code." The facts summed up in the case transcript are as follows:

> On Tuesday, September 13, 2005, the executive committee of a party called "Guardians of the Cedars" convened a press conference in which one of the defendants announced that the party "returns [...] after it

was banned by (*ghayyabahu 'anha*) [...] the Syrian occupation and its local instruments, [after] it and the rest of its leaders were unjustly accused, sentenced, and imprisoned." (AA 2006, 447)

So far so good, but then the Authority points out that the defendant "*digressed* ('*istarsala*) saying that the party remained, despite all that, committed to its principles, and called for a *return* to the Constitution of 1926, which he described as one of the best constitutions in the world" (AA 2006, 447; emphases added). By marking a digression, the Authority demarcates, in its very reiteration of facts, a historical domain of politics *and* a political history, the two being mutually constitutive. As the Authority makes perfectly clear in its ruling, the defendant's pronouncements signaled a return to the Civil War of 1975–90.

The defendant called for "the abrogation of article 95 of [the Constitution], and substituting for it the fourth of the Fourteen Truths declared by the party in 29/5/1975, and the adoption of the program the party put forth in 1977 entitled, *The New Lebanon as the Guardians of the Cedars See It*." After having read the above, the defendant offered "verbally" a definition of "the stranger (*al-gharīb*)" as "every non-Lebanese having carried a weapon or occupied Lebanon." "In this," he continued, "the Syrian, the Palestinian, and the Israeli are identical, or rather the Syrian is even worse than the Israeli, for whereas the latter occupied the land and left, the Syrian violated land, economy, judiciary, security [...]" In conclusion, he "reminded" his listeners of "the party's principles and its fixed doctrine ('*aqīda*)." The second defendant "demanded, during the same press conference, that Lebanon withdraw from the Arab League because [according to him] Lebanon is not part of the Arab world." The third defendant declared that "Arabism (*al-'urūba*) is one of our enemies, that we do not belong to it, that it caused us definite damage, and that Lebanon was the weakest link in the Arab-Zionist conflict, which induced the Arabs to conduct their wars in, and against, Lebanon." During the press conference a compact disc was distributed that included the party's "principles" and slogans, "most conspicuous among which being the one that says, 'there will be not a single Palestinian remaining on Lebanon's territory'." The disc also included a number of books. In addition to the founder's speeches "between 1977 and 1980," the books included articles stating the following: "history and fact have proven that Israel is a friend of Lebanon, and that since time immemorial cultural, political, military, social, and other diverse relations developed between the Lebanese and

Israeli states, and between the Lebanese and Israeli peoples"; "that the saying 'Lebanon's security is of Syria's security' must be modified to 'Lebanon's security is of Israel's security' 'for the stronger is Israel the stronger is Lebanon, and the weaker it is, the weaker is Lebanon'." The third book included an explanation of the party's two slogans regarding the Palestinians: one already mentioned above, another recommending that "every Lebanese must kill a Palestinian." The fourth and fifth books focused on "deporting the Palestinians away from the holy land of Lebanon" and "liberating Lebanese territory from the Palestinians that took refuge on it in and after 1948," respectively. (AA 2006, 447–8)

Effectively, the defendants were publicly reformulating the bases of the state – the very meaning of security, territory and population – and, by doing so, were impinging on sovereignty. While the linkage between sectarian tensions and sovereignty was already prefigured in the Penal Code in 1943, it becomes more explicit and takes on a new meaning in 2005 with the Civil War. In 1943, sectarian tensions bore on the state's internal security only; in the current case, they are involved in questions concerning the state itself, its existence, identity and orientation. The Authority asserts that these questions have been answered by the Lebanese people, against whose will the defendants are acting. Finally, the Authority charges the three defendants with the crime of "stoking sectarian (*madhhabiyya* and *tā'ifiyya*) and racist tensions"

> on grounds that they "proposed again the principles and program that [the party they belonged to] had publicly proposed and declared during the early Lebanese War in 1975, and considered them still valid today." Second, "by publicly disseminating their slogans [...] they have denied the identity of Lebanon and what the Lebanese have incontrovertibly agreed upon according to the [...] Lebanese Constitution and the agreements related to it." Third, "the compact disc [...] contains, in general and in spirit, regardless of the expressions and sentences enunciated, a call aimed to stoke sectarian tensions among the different sections (*sharā'ih*) of the Lebanese people, between [them] and their Arab surroundings, and [between them] and the people living on [Lebanese] territory [i.e., the Palestinians]." (AA 2006, 449)

The religious nationalism of the 1970s, which presupposed a unity among Muslims and Christians dating back to the Prophet's flight to Ethiopia, fades away in 2005 to be replaced by a return to an original and memorable social contract following the Civil War. Both the nation and religious sects are nowhere mentioned in the current case, which liberates the meaning of sectarian tensions from any necessary reference to them, and thus widens the scope of the crime of stoking sectarian tensions.

Case No. 3, Year 2007: Civility, Freedom and Culture

Sectarian tensions articulate religion and the nation, civil war and sovereignty, and politics and history in a web of interconnections that define the conditions under which individual acts are assessed, directed and interpreted. In the preceding case, the Accusatory Authority concludes that despite the fact that the defendants "expected" their views to provoke "tensions and conflicts [...] they nevertheless proceeded with their criminal project (*mashru'ihim al-jirmiyy*) careless about the consequences" and that "[t]heir ethics (*adabiyyāt*), slogans, and publications" attest to this conclusion. Therefore, "the defendants' act constitutes the felony stipulated in, and punishable according to, article 317 of the Penal Code [...] whether they purposely intended to provoke agitation, or if the provocation resulted from their acts, because the crime is considered intentional when the actors expect its criminal consequences yet still proceed to take the risk"(AA 2006, 450–51). Sectarian tensions are implicated in the constitution of an ethic distinct from religion and politics, whereby certain sensibilities and modes of conduct are encouraged and sanctioned, and the range of the state's punitive mechanisms is extended.

In the preceding cases, the judicial effort is directed at distinguishing – not unambiguously – the sectarian from the religious and the political. In the case from 1972, the common goal of fighting sectarian tensions is presented as a spiritual unity of religious differences; in the second case, the sectarian is a signifier of a past to be forgotten, a receptacle for an obsolete language that has no place in the present. In the following case, from 2007, the problem is drawing the line between one's right to exercise one's freedom of opinion, and the standards of conduct expected from individuals living in a civil society.

> In 2007, three men were accused before the Single Criminal Judge in Beirut of "stoking sectarian (*madhhabiyya*) and racist tensions through speeches they delivered in a gathering [...]" organized "in solidarity with" two other men prosecuted almost two decades earlier for assassinating the President of the Lebanese Republic. The court sentenced the men to "one year imprisonment" and "a fine," "in accordance with article 317 of the Penal Code." The gathering was organized by "the friends of Habib Chartouni and Nabil Alam," and "in solidarity with them to demand that they be granted amnesty [...] for [their sentencing in] the crime of assassinating the ex-President of the Republic, Bashir Gemayel [...]" (Single Criminal Judge in Beirut [henceforth CJ] 2008, 1365)

The judge noted that "the three defendants participated and delivered speeches [...] each [...] obviously surpass[ing] [...] the issue of solidarity [...] and exceeding the limit of demanding amnesty." If in the case analyzed in the previous section the judiciary points out a "digression" and a "return to the war," in the current case the culprits are a "surpassing" and an "excess" – a crossing of a boundary. The defendants cross beyond what is acceptable and permissible as citizens of a civil state, to "the point of glorifying the assassination that ended the President's life" (CJ 2008, 1365).

> Thus, [one of the defendants] described it as "a national and wonderfully heroic act in the face of the vicious Zionist offensive", while [another] considered "what the two struggling fighters (*al-munādilān*) [...] did was a national and patriotic act of struggle against the conspiracy of partition and the Israeli occupation [...]" [The third] described the crime of assassination [...] "as a blow [...] to Israel in the midst of its occupation of Lebanon, in the person of its greatest collaborators [...] and a death penalty against the Israeli spearhead [...] whom the occupation designated as President of the Republic despite the will of the Lebanese [people]." (CJ 2008, 1365)

The court states that "demanding amnesty on behalf of any person, whatever the crime he was sentenced for, or is accused of, is a legal act" and therefore "cannot be considered a violation of the freedom of opinion." Freedom of opinion is a constitutional right, and "the granting of a public or private amnesty is allowed by articles 150 to 152 of the Lebanese Penal Code." However, the defendants express more than solidarity with the two men to whom the gathering was dedicated. Their speeches are not limited to "demanding amnesty," but go as far as "glorifying the assassination that ended the President's life" (CJ 2008, 1365).

The court draws a tenuous distinction between acceptable political content and polemical form that involves an opposition between universal rights – a political concept – and cultural particularity. It asserts the latter as a premise for assessing "the legitimacy of the defendants' actions," which is "governed by what the Lebanese Constitution guarantees [...] in its Introduction and in Article '13' [namely] the respect of public freedoms, 'and above all the freedom of opinion and belief (*mu'taqad*)'" (CJ 2008, 1365). However, the court proceeds to explain that in Lebanon these rights are often abused because "the *culture* of the Lebanese [...] has been characterized, in general, by an inclination towards irascibility (*junūh ila al-hidda*) in the exercise of freedom of opinion" (CJ 2008, 1365; emphasis added). The legally constituted opposition between universal rights and cultural particularity rests on an epistemological opposition between reason and affect. The court, which embodies the former, lays claim over the latter, epitomized by "the culture of the Lebanese." The court presents itself as embarking on a civilizing mission aimed to temper the native's essentially emotional – read, irrational – character as a necessary condition of political rights. An important aspect of this mission is to suppress sectarian tensions as a distinctive articulation of affects, which the court *performs* by avoiding any reference to religious sects or religions whatever throughout the whole case.

Instead, the figures of a society "that has suffered intensely, and is still suffering, from the bitterness of political assassinations" and a population "constantly covered in the black of mourning" are emphasized by the court.[5] Moreover, the court outlines another strand of Lebanese history, the starting point of which is Lebanon's "independence" from the French in 1943, coded in terms of a series of assassinations that includes "two presidents, three prime ministers, and a large number of leaders, ministers, parliamentarians, and martyrs." Given this background, the court prescribes a termination of this bloody repetition by affirming a present in which "it is [no longer] possible in any way to consider glorifying the assassination of a president [...] a matter of opinion." Importantly, regulating speech, tempering sentiments and cultivating civility carry implications for the state itself. Thus, glorifying assassins not only offends "a significant section of the Lebanese citizenry that considered and still considers the [assassinated] President [...] a symbol (*ramz*)," it also "encourage[s] whomever does not recognize the state to attack it by way of political assassination if he feels that someone will glorify his crime and protect him from its consequences" (CJ 2008, 1365).

In conclusion, the judiciary in this last case specifies that celebrating the president's assassination "stokes racist and *sectarian (madhhabiyya*, not *tā'ifiyya*) tensions" because it "provo[kes] the sentiments of that section" of the population that "still considers [him] a symbol" (CJ 2008, 1365; emphasis added). As mentioned in the introduction to this essay, the Anglophone media often speaks of sectarian tensions with respect to any configuration of distinctive religious communities or sects, regardless of whether their members are Christians, Muslims, Hindus, Sunnis, Shi'is, Maronites, Copts, 'Alawis or otherwise. Lebanese judicial practice distinguishes between *tā'ifa* and *madhhab*, both of which are usually rendered as sect in Anglophone literature. However, the meanings of these two words are more complex, the former encompassing both the secular distinction between religion proper and religious confessions (see Kant 1991, 114 cited in Asad 1993, 42) and the generic Arabic sense of a wandering group of people (*Lisān al-'Arab*). In extrajudicial usage, *madhhab* refers to the schools of Islamic jurisprudence, namely the four Sunni *madhhab*s – *hanafi, hanbali, māliki* and *shāfi'i* – and the Shi'ī. Yet, the judiciary clearly and unproblematically distinguishes the two – indeed, fixes the meaning of each – by classifying Christians and Muslims under the category *tā'ifa* and the subgroups such as Maronite, say, or Sunni and Shi'i, under *madhhab*.

Conclusion

At the beginning of this essay, I pointed out that sectarian tensions are often singled out as a latent source of violence in situations where a plurality of religions or religious sects exist. I mentioned that sectarian tensions elicit concern regarding religious violence, sometimes expressed publicly in statements denouncing manifestations of such violence, occasionally followed by words of advice about domestic and foreign policies. However, along with the moral and political confidence in which it is deployed in discourse, the notion of sectarian tensions is often accompanied by a lingering ambiguity. The sectarian seems to group together under one sign a range of disparate groups, phenomena and events that have nothing in common, or whose cultural and historical specificity is ignored. I asked, besides the seemingly self-evident fact that sectarian tensions exist among sects, what it is we talk about when we talk about sectarian tensions. I noted that sectarian tensions belong to a wider domain designated as sectarian of which they are but an instance and that, more often than not, they are mentioned in contexts in which the character and quality of the governing power is at stake. In other words, sectarian tensions, and the sectarian more generally, figure in discourses of power that affirm particular modes of power. I analyzed the crime of stoking sectarian tensions in the Lebanese Penal Code and Law of Publications, and its determinations in three judicial cases, to argue that the meaning of the sectarian must be sought in its shifting grammar in different discursive contexts. In the judicial domain in Lebanon, the crime of stoking sectarian tensions enables the articulation of the lineaments of secular power through which politics, religion, history and ethics are defined. In the three judicial cases I analyzed, this articulation entails criminalizing or sanctioning a kind of speech and punishing or condoning its exponents. I conclude by proposing that sectarian tensions, and the sectarian more generally, be considered a concept of power that belongs to a genealogy of secularism, rather than an explanatory category of the social and cultural conditions that lead to the blurring of the boundaries between religion and politics in specific historical moments (Makdisi 2000; Masters 2001).

Notes

Translations in this chapter are my own unless otherwise attributed.

1 One need only glance at news reports on the Arab world since the US invasion of Iraq until the so-called Arab Spring for a sense of that pervasive fear sectarian tensions induce.

A search for "sectarian" in Google News yields around three thousand seven hundred results for November 2011 alone; the overwhelming majority of them are about the Middle East.
2 I use "conspiracy" for *jam'iyyat ashrār*, which is the translation of the French legal category association de malfaiteurs. The Lebanese Penal Code is based on the French Code Pénal.
3 See also article 48. The punishment of a publisher making illegal profits would be harsher if "the benefit were acquired in the aim of serving the interests of a state or association foreign or local in ways that conflict with the public interest or what threatens the political order or stokes sectarian tensions or incites disturbances and riots"(LP 1962, sec. 2, art. 48).
4 Note that cases 1 and 2 are based on the Law of Publications of 1962, not on the Penal Code.
5 These descriptions were written in 2007, two years after the assassination of a prime minister and the ensuing establishment of the United Nations Special Tribunal for Lebanon in 2005 with the presumed aim of putting an end to political assassinations. The prime minister's assassination triggered a popular movement against the Syrian military and security regime in Lebanon, which eventually ended by a Syrian withdrawal from Lebanese territory.

References

Accusatory Authority in Beirut. 2006. "Decision No. 794, 14/11/2005, Public Prosecution at the Court of Appeals vs. Naji Audi, Joseph Khoury, and Habib Younis." *Al-'Adl, Majallat Naqābat al-Muhāmīn, Bayrūt [Justice, the Journal of the Beirut Bar Association]* 40(1): 446–51.

Asad, Talal. 2011. "Thinking about the Secular Body, Pain, and Liberal Politics." *Cultural Anthropology* 26(4): 657–75.

———. 2003. *Formation of the Secular: Christianity, Islam, Modernity*. Stanford: Stanford University Press.

———. 1993. *Genealogies of Religion: Discipline and Reasons of Power in Christianity and Islam*. Baltimore: Johns Hopkins University Press.

Court of Publications. 1973. "Decision No. 73, 20 January 1972, Public Right vs. Naqqash." *Al-'Adl, Majallat Naqābat al-Muhāmīn, Bayrūt [Justice, the Journal of the Beirut Bar Association]* 7: 275.

———. 1973. "Decision No. 105, 9 March 1972, Public Right vs. Naqqash." *Al-'Adl, Majallat Naqābat al-Muhāmīn, Bayrūt [Justice, the Journal of the Beirut Bar Association]* 7: 280.

Daraghi, Borzou and Roula Hajjar. 2011. "Syrian Security Forces Accused of Killing 16 in Homs." *Los Angeles Times*. Online: http://articles.latimes.com/2011/jul/20/world/la-fg-syria-sectarian-20110720 (accessed 2 September 2011).

Gamble, Laura. 2011. "Will Saudi Arabia's Stimulus Calm Sectarian Tensions?" *CNBC*. Online: http://www.cnbc.com/id/42193439/Will_Saudi_Arabia_s_Stimulus_Calm_Sectarian_Tensions (accessed 2 September 2011).

Harb, Osama al-Ghazali. 2010. "The origins of sectarian tension in Egypt." Common Ground News Service. Online: http://www.commongroundnews.org/article.php?id=27341&lan=en&sp=0 (accessed 2 September 2011).

Ibn Mandhur. *Lissan al-'Arab*. Fourteenth-century Arabic lexicon.

Jaber, Hafez. 1993. "Commentary (*ta'līq*)." *Al-'Adl, Majallat Naqābat al-Muhāmīn, Bayrūt [Justice, the Journal of the Beirut Bar Association, Beirut]*, 312–13.

Kant, Immanuel and Hans Siegbert Reiss. 1991. *Kant: Political Writings*. Cambridge: Cambridge University Press.

Makdisi, Usama. 2000. *The Culture of Sectarianism: Community, History, and Violence in Nineteenth-Century Ottoman Lebanon*. Berkeley: University of California Press.

Master, Bruce A. 2001. *Christians and Jews in the Ottoman Arab World: The Roots of Sectarianism*. New York: Cambridge University Press.

Nasr, Vali. 2011. "The Danger Lurking in the Arab Spring." *Next*. Online: http://234next.com/csp/cms/sites/Next/Home/5740251-146/the_dangers_lurking_in_the_arab.csp (accessed 2 September 2011).

Schmitt, Carl. 1996. *The Concept of the Political*. Chicago and London: University of Chicago Press.

Sen, Amartya. 1999. "Democracy as a Universal Value." *Journal of Democracy* 10(3): 3–17.

Single Criminal Judge in Beirut. 2008. "Decision Issued on 25/6/2007, Public Right vs. Abdelhamid Safar and His Companions." *Al-'Adl, Majallat Naqābat al-Muhāmīn, Bayrūt* [*Justice, the Journal of the Beirut Bar Association*] 42(2): 1364–5.

Walpole, C. G. 1888. *The Ottoman Penal Code, 28 Zilhijeh 1274* (translated from the French text). London: William Clowes & Sons.

Chapter 8

THE COMMODIFICATION OF LOVE: GANDHI, KING AND 1960s COUNTERCULTURE

Alexander Bacha and Manu Bhagavan

Introduction

This essay explores why global revolutions ceased to utilize the politically transformative power of love after the activism of Gandhi and Martin Luther King by drawing connections between their religiously couched "ethic of love" and the secular capitalist commodification of 1960s hippie counterculture. Gandhi and King, utilizing their respective religious frameworks, practiced revolutionary techniques to make their opponents act in the interest of "selfless love," or *agape* in the Christian sense. By the association of hippie counterculture, however tangential, to this socially transformative power of love, corporate advertising during the 1960s effectively confused love of the agape and *eros* (erotic) varieties, hollowing out the term by the 1970s, and robbing love of its revolutionary potential. Our paper will be broken down into three parts: The first will discuss how Gandhi and King used the ethic of selfless love to revolutionary ends. The second will examine how the hippie counterculture of the 1960s was influenced and shaped by this ethic of love, and how, what Thomas Frank calls, "the rise of hip consumerism" (Frank 1997, iii) not only commodified hippie counterculture, but also commodified love as a political tool. Lastly, we will look at some political deployments of the ethic of love from the 1970s to the present, including the Chipko movement, or "treehuggers," an Indian environmentalist group that used Gandhian techniques to bring awareness to deforestation. Although successful in their activism, their "treehugger" moniker has become somewhat of a pejorative neologism for nature-loving environmentalists, and illuminates the ambiguity of contemporary activism based on an ethic of love.

Love and Revolutionary Power

In his famous tract *Hind Swaraj*, published in 1909, Mahatma Gandhi spelled out the principles of political action that would guide him, and the people of his region, for the decades to follow. While he would expand on these ideas over the years, modifying them in various ways, the ideas of *Hind Swaraj* remained largely intact, serving as the core of Gandhian philosophy and outlook. And this core, in turn, revolved around the key concept of love, which Gandhi asserts is the true, hidden hand guiding humanity's destiny.

Gandhi summed up his message with a four-point call to action: Indians must resist the English because it is their duty to do so, but not out of any animus towards English people; Indians must embrace "home-goods" (*swadeshi*) "in every sense"; and they must recognize that "real home-rule is self-rule or self-control." The way to exert this self-control is through "passive resistance," or "soul-force" or "love-force" (Gandhi 2003, 68–9).

Gandhi elaborates earlier in the work that while the force of arms represented one kind of force,

> [t]he second kind of force can thus be stated; [*sic*] 'If you do not concede our demand, we shall be no longer your petitioners; we shall no longer have any dealings with you'. The force implied in this may be described as love-force, soul-force, or, more popularly but less accurately, passive resistance. This force is indestructible [...] The force of arms is powerless when matched against the force of love or the soul. (Gandhi 2003, 53)

Gandhi illustrates his case with a discussion of a gang of robbers, who multiply in an increasing cycle of violence when they are forcibly resisted. He contrasts this with the possibilities opened by embracing the robber with pity, which Gandhi uses synonymously with love here. The result is that the robber might repent his/her actions. While this may or may not come to pass, this second option at the very least is best for the heart and mind of the actor. But this is not, and is not meant to be, some semantic point. What Gandhi describes here is the very essence of what he would call *satyagraha*, a term that had been coined to represent his campaigns of change. Writing several years later, Gandhi first clarified that the "force denoted by the term 'passive resistance'[...] is not very accurately described either by the original English phrase or by its Hindi rendering [...] Its correct description is satyagraha." He continued: "Satyagraha is pure soul-force [...] The soul is informed with knowledge. In it burns the flame of love. If someone gives us pain through ignorance, we shall win him through love [...] Non-violence is a dormant state. In the waking state, it is love. Ruled by love, the world goes on" (Gandhi 1917a, 9–10).

For Gandhi, famously, Love was Truth was God, so satyagraha was inherently a "religious" method. This did not mean that it was anchored to any one religion. Indeed, he always took pains to talk of the Truth and the *satyagrahis* in every religion, from Christ to Hussein at Karbala to various examples from Hindu traditions (Gandhi 1917a, 11–14; Gandhi 1917b, 6–9). Satyagraha was what might best be understood as pure, spiritual force. His early exposure to diverse religious traditions brought Gandhi into contact with the writings of Leo Tolstoy, whose *The Kingdom of God is Within You*, banned in Russia for its radical espousal of Christ's nonviolent resistance teachings as true gospel, so influenced young Gandhi that he named his South African community devoted to love, work and simple living Tolstoy Farm. Upon reading more of Tolstoy, Gandhi wrote, "I began to realize more and more the infinite possibilities of universal love" (Gandhi 1993, 160).

In *Hind Swaraj*, Gandhi broadens the argument to make the case that love is at the root of all that humans do. To underscore his point, Gandhi launches into a critique of Western notions of history, which, at that time, tended to focus solely on wars and the subsequent making and unmaking of rulers. Gandhi contends that "[h]istory [as an institutional inquiry as it was then understood in the West] is really a record of every interruption of the even working of the force of love or of the soul." Put another way, "[t]housands, indeed tens of thousands, depend for their existence on a very active working of this force [of love]. Little quarrels of millions of families in their daily lives disappear before the exercise of this force" (Gandhi 2003, 55).

Because all humans were bound together in love, Gandhi theorized that the political application of love involved those facing injustice enduring a form of suffering that made vivid the harm being caused by those perpetrating the injustice. The act of suffering would tug at the heartstrings of the perpetrators and turn them to better action. In the midst of the Civil Disobedience Movement and on the heels of his most famous campaign, the Salt Satyagraha, Gandhi wrote:

> I know that people, who voluntarily undergo a course of suffering raise themselves and the whole of humanity, but I also know that people who become brutalized in their desperate efforts to get victory over their opponents or to exploit weaker nations or weaker men, not only drag down themselves, but mankind also […] If we are all sons of the same God and partake of the same divine essence, we must partake of the sin of every person whether he belongs to us or to another race. You can understand how repugnant it must be to invoke the beast in any human being, how much more so in Englishmen, amongst whom I count numerous friends! (Gandhi 1931, 2–3)

Gandhi believed that all people had the potential for good, but many were caught up in systems and practices that were fundamentally unjust. Facing political injustice, groups of people practicing public disobedience would likely draw a fierce response. But in accepting that response willingly and making apparent the brutality inherent in such a relationship of inequality, Gandhi argued that the flame of love between the two opposing camps would be kindled, those doing harm regretting the acts they had committed.

Martin Luther King, Jr picked up on this philosophy and used what he called an "ethic of love" to achieve social change during the American civil rights movement. Much like his predecessor, who referred to hate as "the subtlest form of violence" (Gandhi 1934, 293), King realized that nonviolence proved inefficient and superficial if it did not stem from a deeper conviction in the power of love, writing that "[a]t the center of non-violence stands the principle of love [...] This can only be done by projecting the ethic of love to the center of our lives" (King 2010, 9). By identifying this subtle but troubling disconnect in the popular discourse of love and nonviolence, King continued Gandhi's legacy of not just using passive resistance, but going further to actively loving one's opponents. And much like the Mahatma, King drew centrally from the faith tradition most familiar and personal to him – in his case, Christianity – while still connecting his message to the basic underliers found in virtually all other traditions as well. In this way, King could address human difference while simultaneously preaching a sense of universalism, a combination with powerful politically motivating force. As King said himself, "Christ furnished the spirit and motivation while Gandhi furnished the method" (Carson 1998, 67).

King notes that in the early days of the movement, the rhetoric of passive resistance and nonviolence was unheard of, replaced instead by the phrase "Christian love," and he flatly states that "[i]t was Jesus of Nazareth that stirred the Negroes to protest with the creative weapon of love" (King 2010, 67). Christ's teachings from the Sermon on the Mount, most notably his insistence on "loving thy enemies" and his indelible connection of God and love (to which, upon reading Gandhi, he would add "truth" as an equal corollary) drove King from his earliest days as a young preacher delivering sermons on the subject of love's role in all aspects of society. Here, King ran into opposition, particularly from members of the church. As Richard Lischer notes, "King's more spiritualized opponents argued that such love doesn't belong in the midst of nasty confrontations and shouldn't be used as a tool for social policy [...] In bringing love into the fray, King rejected the old law-gospel method of interpreting the Bible (and the world) and reasserted the pervasive influence of Jesus in secular society" (Lischer 1995, 214–15).

Furthermore, King's interpretation of Christ's teachings on the ethic of love stressed the connection of "words and action." Distilling Christ's messages of love, passivism and forgiveness was nothing terribly novel, but King succeeded in actualizing this philosophy on a grand scale by bonding this ethic of love with unrelenting social activism. King revered Christ's "ability to match words with actions," and lamented the fact that "men seldom bridge the gap between practice and profession, between doing and saying" (King 1963, 40). Accordingly, and of particular pertinence to this paper, it should be said that King in turn realized the danger of love coming off as saccharine and superficial: the problem of love rhetoric without a living ethic of love. King warned that "[t]he meaning of love is not to be confused with some sentimental outpouring. Love is something much deeper than emotional bosh" (1963, 52).

King first seriously encountered the philosophies of Gandhi at a lecture delivered by Dr Mordecai Johnson, the president of Howard University, in 1950, a time when King admitted to seriously doubting love's possibility for true social transformation. Evidently, hearing about Gandhi stirred him to the point where he purchased a half dozen books by or about the nonviolent revolutionary after the lecture (Carson 1998, 23). King was truly a student of Gandhi, whom he referred to as "inevitable" and "inescapable [...] if humanity is to progress," the "first person in history to lift the love ethic of Jesus above mere interaction between individuals to a powerful and effective social force on a large scale" (King 1963, 67). In 1959, he visited India at the invitation of Prime Minister Nehru to, among other things, study nonviolence and civil disobedience. He even reputedly said to reporters at the airport, "[t]o other countries I may go as a tourist, but to India I come as a pilgrim" (Reddick 1959, 1). Later, in a speech he delivered on All India Radio, he added:

> If this age is to survive, it must follow the way of love and nonviolence that he so nobly illustrated in his life. And Mahatma Gandhi may well be God's appeal to this generation, for in a day when sputniks and explorers dash through outer space and guided ballistic missiles are carving highways of death through the stratosphere, no nation can win a war. Today, we no longer have a choice between violence and nonviolence; it is either nonviolence or nonexistence. (King 1959)

One of King's earliest experiences of using love as a weapon for social change came with the Montgomery Bus Boycott of 1955–56, one of the given nominal historic starting points of the American civil rights movement. In brief, the boycott took place in response to the egregious injustice extant in the Jim Crow laws of Alabama's city bus system, and was sparked by the defiance of black women such as Claudette Colvin and Rosa Parks. Days after Parks was arrested, King was elected to lead the Montgomery Improvement

Association and, along with other leaders of the boycott, asked African Americans in the city of Montgomery to peacefully stop using the bus system until the discriminatory policies changed. Over a year later, on 20 December 1956, a federal court ruled in *Browder v. Gayle* that Alabama laws requiring buses to be segregated were unconstitutional. Amid the boycott, black activists were constantly intimidated and physically assaulted; King, as well as fellow organizer Ralph Abernathy, had their houses firebombed in the violence. Many African Americans reacted by taking up arms with the intention of retaliating against King's assailants, to which King calmly pleaded, "[w]e want to love our enemies. I want you to love our enemies. Be good to them and let them know you love them" (Carson 1988, 80). He continued a few weeks later in the *New York Times*: "Let no man pull you low enough to hate him. We must use the weapon of love. We must have compassion and understanding for those who hate us [...]" (Phillips, 1956). King promised his most hateful opponents that he and his allies would use this "creative force" to "match your capacity to inflict suffering by our capacity to endure suffering" (King 1963, 56). Again, he continued:

> My personal trials have also taught me the value of unmerited suffering. As my sufferings mounted I soon realized that there were two ways that I could respond to my situation: either to react with bitterness or seek to transform the suffering into a creative force. I decided to follow the latter course. Recognizing the necessity for suffering I have tried to make of it a virtue [...] I have lived these last few years with the conviction that unearned suffering is redemptive. (1960, 1)

King gained much fame and notoriety with Montgomery, and further honed his philosophy and practice of reform through love with the formation and operation of the Southern Christian Leadership Conference (SCLC) in 1957. The SCLC organized individual black churches into a collective nonviolent protest aimed at using nonviolence to overcome segregation throughout the south. One of the group's first major campaigns began when they joined other civil rights groups, including the National Association for the Advancement of Colored People (NAACP) and the Student Nonviolent Coordinating Committee (SNCC) in an attempt to desegregate Albany, Georgia in 1961. King, along with many others, was arrested several times, and at one point called for a Day of Penance in the wake of reciprocated violence. After over a year of struggle, King left Albany, and the affair in and of itself is generally regarded as one of the least successful in the greater movement. The following year, King's involvement in the Birmingham Campaign fared much better, as he and fellow activists successfully brought national attention to the struggle that would play a huge role in the passage of the Civil Rights Act of 1964. Much of the effectiveness of the campaign came from the brutality of police under the leadership of Bull Connor, whose infamous use of dogs and fire hoses to assault peaceful black demonstrators shocked Americans when it was broadcast across the nation. When King was jailed in Alabama too, he penned the famous "Letter from Birmingham Jail," wherein he noted that while initially disappointed at being referred to as an extremist, he gladly accepted the role of acting as an "extremist for love" and encouraging as many people as possible to follow him in that extremism (King 1963, 1).

King continued to use love as a tool for social change throughout the 1960s, until his assassination in 1968. After leading the hugely famous March on Washington in 1963, and being awarded the Nobel Peace Prize in 1964, King saw the passage of both the Civil Rights Act and the Voting Rights Act in 1964 and 1965. The continued barbarism of southern whites during the Selma to Montgomery marches (the first of which came to be known as Bloody Sunday) further ossified King's goals and he appealed to the empathy of Americans in the same way he did in Birmingham. King remained equally committed to the ethic of love and nonviolent practice in Chicago, where he and protesters faced equal if not higher levels of resentment from civil rights opponents, King himself taking a brick to the face (Isserman and Kazin 2000, 200). Much of King's activism at the end of his life was also devoted to opposition to the Vietnam War, upon which issue he continued to espouse his relentless conviction in embracing an ethic of love. In his "Beyond Vietnam – Time to Break the Silence" speech in April of 1967, he remarked:

> This call for a worldwide fellowship that lifts neighborly concern beyond one's tribe, race, class, and nation is in reality a call for an all-embracing – embracing and unconditional love for all mankind [...] Love is somehow the key that unlocks the door which leads to ultimate reality. This Hindu-Muslim-Christian-Jewish-Buddhist belief about ultimate – ultimate reality is beautifully summed up in the first epistle of Saint John: "Let us love one another, for love is God. And every one that loveth is born of God and knoweth God. He that loveth not knoweth not God, for God is love." "If we love one another, God dwelleth in us and his love is perfected in us." Let us hope that this spirit will become the order of the day. (King 1967a)

Reinforcing how truly universal these principles were, he added: "When I speak of love I am not speaking of some sentimental and weak response. I am speaking of the force that which all the great religions have seen as the supreme unifying principle of life" (King 1967a). Months later, in his famous

"Where Do We Go From Here" speech, he not only reinforced the inefficacy of shallow love, but also dismissed what he perceived as the mutual exclusivity of love and power:

> One of the great problems of history is that the concepts of love and power have usually been contrasted as opposites – polar opposites, so that love is identified with a resignation of power, and power with a denial of love […] What is needed is a realization that power without love is reckless and abusive, and love without power is sentimental and anemic. Power at its best is love implementing the demands of justice, and justice at its best is power correcting everything that stands against love. (King 1967b)

Both Gandhi and King practiced agape, a type of love that can be defined as an uncompromising universal love, at once for both God and for one's fellow man. Agape assumes the solidarity of all of humanity through an active form of loving and, therefore, a responsibility to love even those that express extreme resistance towards this love. King was familiar with agape from its many associations with Christianity[1], as the term first found wide usage in Christian theology as a reference to self-sacrifice, for both God and humanity. Indeed, it was not until its application in Christian texts that the term took on such divinity and universality as in the passage, "He that loveth not knoweth not God; for God is love" (1 John 4:8 *KJV*). King would articulate this best in his musings on the Montgomery Bus Boycott, *Stride Toward Freedom*:

> Agape is not a weak, passive love. It is love in action. Agape is love seeking to preserve and create community. It is insistence on community even when one seeks to break it. Agape is a willingness to sacrifice in the interest of mutuality. Agape is a willingness to go to any length to restore community […] He who works against community is working against the whole of creation. Therefore, if I respond to hate with a reciprocal hate I do nothing but intensify the cleavage in broken community. I can only close the gap in broken community by meeting hate with love […] In the final analysis, agape means a recognition of the fact that all life is interrelated. All humanity is involved in a single process […] If you harm me, you harm yourself. (King 1958, 105–6)

Let's Buy the World a Coke

In simpatico with the message of King and Gandhi was the larger counterculture of the 1960s, a disparate and fragmented nebula of actors against the postwar status quo that included everyone from hippies to political activists like the New

Left and Black Panthers.[2] While different groups held different priorities and methods, ranging from expanding consciousness to dismantling capitalism, all these movements were scored by an unprecedented deluge of popular music that sought wider social transformation, a spectrum that included diverse artists from Peter, Paul and Mary to MC5. Bob Dylan (somewhat unwillingly) became the poet/speaker of his generation with songs reflecting on the changing social climate and scathing protest songs like "Masters of War." Jimi Hendrix, Jefferson Airplane and many others achieved massive success composing songs for young listeners that made music more social than ever; tens of thousands at a time gathered to festivals like Monterey Pop, Woodstock and a multitude of protests and "love-ins" where music played a key part. The revolutionary power of popular music peaked in the '60s in a way it had not before and has not since, as artists and songs mobilized listeners to shake the status quo, and no band got the word out more effectively than The Beatles. While the group never quite delivered the rich oeuvre of profound protest music that Bob Dylan produced, their devotion to motifs of peace and love, along with their staggering global omnipresence and popularity, hitched the socially transformative power of love to the vanguard of popular music.

An international cultural juggernaut the likes of which the world had never seen, the Fab Four launched American Beatlemania after their famous appearance on the Ed Sullivan Show in 1964. From this impossibly high pedestal of popularity, The Beatles only became more famous throughout the 1960s. For the duration of the decade, The Beatles had a number one single for a total of 59 weeks and the number one LP for a total of 116 weeks. Or, more strikingly, The Beatles had a chart-topping song one out of every six weeks from 1964 to 1970, and a chart-topping album for one out of every three (Schaffner 1977, 216). Furthermore, The Beatles matched their quantifiable popularity with a truly revolutionary breadth of scope, becoming arguably the first pop band to engage on a proper world tour, visiting European countries as well as Japan, Australia and the Philippines. Their popularity also grew through infamy, particularly after a backlash against John Lennon's "more popular than Jesus" comments in 1966 erupted throughout the American south and heartland, as well as in countries like Mexico and South Africa. Though their audience only grew larger, the controversy ignited a strong opposition that greatly affected the direction in which their music would head, and the band gave their last commercial concert, often considered a key turning point in their career, later that year.

In 1967, The Beatles released their seminal album *Sgt. Pepper's Lonely Hearts Club Band*, a veritable sea change in the echelon of popular music that even exceeded their previous game-changing effort, *Revolver*. The two albums marked a transformation in the ways The Beatles would discuss the concept of love and their involvement with late-60s counterculture. It goes without saying that love had always been truly ubiquitous subject matter for The Beatles, but not all of this love was created equal. The Beatles began their careers playing what can be called more "sentimental love songs," centered on pleasurable, individual-oriented love, but as they matured as artists, the type of love contained within their songs matured as well. Take for example the refrain from their 1962 song "Love Me Do":

> Love, love me do.
> You know I love you,
> I'll always be true,
> So please, love me do.
> Whoa, love me do.
>
> Someone to love,
> Somebody new.
> Someone to love,
> Someone like you.

Compare these lyrics to lyrics from Harrison's "Within You Without You" from *Sgt. Pepper's Lonely Hearts Club Band*:

> We were talking – about the love we all could share – when we find it
> To try our best to hold it there – with our love
> With our love – we could save the world – if they only knew
> Try to realize it's all within yourself
> No one else can make you change
> And to see you're really only very small
> And life flows on within you and without you

Sgt. Pepper's served as a paradigm shift for The Beatles' involvement as the musical stewards of counterculture. As Jonathon Gould writes, the album "dramatically enlarged the possibilities and raised the expectations of what the experience of listening to popular music on record could be" (2007, 418). With this, The Beatles would not only become "the major tastemakers of hippiedom" (Jones 1967, 2), but would "revolutionize both the aesthetics and the economics of the record business in ways that far outstripped the earlier pop explosions triggered by the Elvis phenomenon of 1956 and the [British] Beatlemania phenomenon" (Gould 2007, 418). In addition to their music, the group itself revolutionized the concept of music celebrity, inspiring and captivating countercultural types around the world with their mounting fragmentation and publicized trip to Rishikesh in 1968. Indeed, many listeners even saw The Beatles not only as musical stewards but also as a means through which to navigate the social landscape. Adds P. David Marshall, "[b]ecause of their popularity, the Beatles were seen – and used – as beacons from which to understand the contemporary [...] [T]heir work and their lives became a journey of self-discovery through which their dispersed and massive Western audience vicariously traveled towards some inner truth about the group and contemporary existence itself" (Marshall 2000, 173).

Unfortunately, as the decade progressed, corporations caught on to the influence of The Beatles and their peers, as well as the purchasing power of the expanding countercultural market, and realized that there was money to be made "selling love." The media's homogenization of 1960s "counterculture," which by the end of the decade essentially became "a term referring to all 1960s-era political, social, or cultural dissent, encompassing any action from smoking pot at a rock concert to offing a cop" (Braunstein and Doyle 2001, 5), greatly facilitated the sale. In his excellent book *What Happened to the 1960s: How Mass Media Culture Failed American Democracy*, Edward P. Morgan discusses how the mass media has vilified, marginalized and, perhaps most importantly, simplified our understanding of the decade and its vital endeavors for enhanced democracy. Morgan concludes that "much of what passes for history in conventional thinking is actually the public memory preserved for us by the mass media" (2011, 7), and indeed, much of our "public memory" of the '60s passes by in the haze of generic mob militancy and pot-addled nude drum circles. Jocular sayings like "If you remember the '60s, you weren't really there" reinforce the image of the decade as a time of hedonistic revelry, a wider public display of spoiled American youth refusing to grow up. Today, movies like *Forrest Gump* help provide this convenient spectacle by reinforcing the stereotypes of the '60s and stamping them as fact in public memory.

The media's power magnified missteps made by some musicians, hippies and other counterculturalists that blended various ideas and ideologies together in often contradictory or nonsensical ways. For instance, if The Beatles' music was seen as one body of work, the individualistic love of "Love Me Do" and the universalistic, selfless love of "Within You Without You" were easily equated.[3] Put another way, such confusion compromised the potential of political love by conjoining the agape and eros types, rendering both banal and apolitical, divorcing agape from a revolutionary history articulated by the likes of Mohandas Gandhi and Martin Luther King. As explained earlier in this chapter, agape is a universal love, a self-sacrificing love that, as Erich Fromm describes it, is more "faculty" than object. Eros, on the other hand, is the love of romantic passion and sexual desire, where the object of romantic love becomes the singular focus. In fact, the "quality" of the eros type of love is directly proportionate to its very exclusivity – the love's intensity is proven when "they do not love anybody except the 'loved' person" (Fromm 1956, 42–3). Hippie counterculture, from its love-ins to its insistence on "making (sexual) love and not war," greatly muddled the separate understandings of agape and eros, forming a well-meaning but vague amalgam that was at once antiwar and hedonistic, omnipresent yet selfishly egoistic. The schizophrenic nature of the message made it pliant, and the increasing cultural popularity of the hippies made this message extremely vulnerable to manipulation.

Accordingly, the media distilled counterculture as a whole into simplified and singular images surrounding the vague ideas of peace, love and general hippiedom. As a 1967 *Time Magazine* cover story pronounced in a somewhat patronizing tone, "[h]ippies preach altruism and mysticism, honesty, joy and nonviolence. They find an almost childish fascination in beads, blossoms and bells, blinding strobe lights and ear-shattering music, exotic clothing and erotic slogans. Their professed aim is nothing less than the subversion of Western society by 'flower power' and force of example" (Jones 1967, 3). Consequently, the corporate world began to envision and transform the hippie counterculture, replete with peace signs, flowers and doves, into what philosopher Guy Debord referred to as "spectacle." In 1967, Debord released *The Society of the Spectacle*, a Marxist tract that, among other agendas, attempted to expand Marx's reification theory by expanding the idea of autonomous commodities across society to include the images produced by the mass media, wherein the "spectacle is not a collection of images, but a social relation among people, mediated by images" (Debord 1995 [1967], 6). Hereby, individuals could buy into being participants in this counterculture through their consumption of anything from psychedelic pop songs to cosmetics to soft drinks.

As the media established a simplified, cohesive narrative of the counterculture, corporate interests could use these simplified images and ideas to employ entirely new tactics in the world of product marketing. Beginning in the 1960s, marketing strategies transformed from appealing to the consumer's desire to run with the status quo to engaging their desires to be nonconforming individuals. By capitalizing on the rebelliousness of the counterculture, as well as the "peace and love" images that were often associated with it, corporations and advertising companies changed alongside American youth. If one wanted to purchase a car, one could buy the Dodge Rebellion or the Pontiac Secession to reinforce one's commitment to running (or driving) against the grain. Love cosmetics, clad in psychedelic flowers, hearts and birds, appealed to women as the "anticosmetics," and used the image of young, free-spirited women to sell no-nonsense makeup that enhanced natural beauty. In both cases, the consequences came not so much from impressionable youth culture buying the products as it did from corporations using these images to establish a connection between counterculture (and one of their *raison d'etres*, love) and commodity. As Thomas Frank described the onslaught:

> Business dogged the counterculture with a fake counterculture, a commercial replica that seemed to ape its every move for the titillation of the TV-watching millions and the nation's corporate sponsors. Every rock band with a substantial following was immediately honored with a host of imitators; the 1967 "summer of love" was as much a product of lascivious television specials and *Life* magazine stories as it was an expression of youthful satisfaction [...]. (Frank 1997, 7)

Nowhere was this more apparent than in the "Cola Wars" of the 1960s. Taking advantage of Coca-Cola's established place as an all-American (and therefore "square" and outdated) soft drink, Pepsi crafted a means to increase their market share by appealing to youth counterculture, what they deemed the Pepsi Generation, though they skillfully labeled youth "an attitude toward living – and particularly consuming – rather than a specific age group" (Frank 1997, 171). As Coca-Cola refused to use rock 'n' roll music in their ads in the early 1960s, seemingly ossifying their "square" stance, Pepsi jumped onboard the countercultural wagon, first with Monkees-esque visuals in the mid-60s and then with more psychedelic tones after "1967". After the violence of 1968, Pepsi made it a point to stick predominantly to images of long hair and flowers as opposed to anything that would suggest more serious radicalism, and toned down their youthful intensity to reflect their championing of cultural dissent but not political dissent. Slowly creeping towards the center from its place on the cultural right, Coca-Cola responded by launching the "It's the Real Thing" campaign in 1969, stressing authenticity in a world replete with plastic images.

The commodification of love crescendoed when the "It's the Real Thing" campaign birthed the "I'd Like to Buy the World a Coke" ad in 1971. Coca-Cola's televised "Hilltop Ad" is a grandiose example of the marriage of consumer product allegiance and manufactured popular music used to sell the concept of an international ethic of love. The commercial, which was released in several iterations, shows a multicultural collection of "countercultural types" assembled on a bucolic hilltop, praising Coke as a means of achieving love and peace across the globe:

> I'd like to buy the world a home and furnish it with love,
> Grow apple trees and honey bees and snow white turtle doves.
> I'd like to teach the world to sing in perfect harmony,
> I'd like to buy the world a Coke and keep it company...
> It's the real thing, Coke is what the world wants today.[4]

Coca-Cola's campaign continued to praise the product's authenticity, but also sought to assuage the climate of dissent amid the Vietnam War protest by using a folk-rock jingle to portray "multicultural harmony [...] peace and love under the aegis of the universal product" (Frank 1997, 179). The commercial became a huge hit, the song itself being rerecorded by the band The New Seekers to enable it to climb the pop charts. Bill Backer, who devised the campaign, elaborated on the commercial's message of international harmony: "[I] began to see a bottle of Coca-Cola as more than a drink [...] [I] began to see the familiar words, 'Let's have a Coke,' as [...] actually a subtle way of saying, 'Let's keep each other company for a little while.' And [I] knew they were being said all over the world [...]" (Backer n.d., 1).

The End of *Imagine*-ation

The idea of love was central to social justice movements prior to the 1970s. As the 1970s unfolded, however, commodification transformed the 1960s and love itself into terms of naivety in the spheres of politics. Currents of thought in the '70s began to interpret the activism of the '60s as a series of mistakes, the exigencies of a spoiled and naïve generation. The *Los Angeles Times* expressed their disappointment in the inefficacy of the previous decade only two days into the new one, and prophesized a more pragmatic future: "Hardly anybody now shares the naïve faith in the glorious future that caused the last decade to be prebaptised the Soaring Sixties. The seventies, partially because of the misplaced confidence of what seems only yesterday, shape up as, at best, a decade of sorting out" (Kroft 1970, A7). As Todd Gitlin eloquently puts it, "it was time to go straight, from marijuana to white wine, from hip communes to summers on Cape Cod [...] Imperceptibly, the Sixties slid into the Seventies, and the zeitgeist settled down" (Gitlin 1987, 423).

Commodification pushed love out of the realm of politics and into the realm of consumption by driving a wedge between the public and private spheres. Or, as Habermas notes in his seminal work on the subject, "[i]n proportion to the increasing buying power of the broad masses, the public costs of private production were complemented by the public costs of private consumption" (Habermas 2001, 147). This certainly happened within the United States during the '70s and '80s, but that by no means limited the effect of this consumption on the rest of the world. By the '70s (though certainly earlier in many places), American military power was reinforced by the soft power of American cultural influence, extending American hegemony to the far corners of the globe, from Latin America to Europe, from the Middle East to India, giving birth to terms like "Coca-colonialism." American reach ensured that corporate messaging, commodifying the ideals of the '60s and emptying them of meaning and power, held sway in many parts of the world.

The success of such messaging is seen in a number of subsequent critiques that have observed the removal of love from the language of politics. Nick Southall notes that "[c]apitalist culture has purged political conceptions of love from language. Love has been corrupted by religious and romantic fantasies, it has been enclosed within the couple or the family, within narrow notions, as love of the same, love of those closest to you, love of a god, the race or the nation" (2010, 1). Michael Hardt and Antonio Negri echo this sentiment in *Multitude: War and Democracy in the Age of Empire*:

> People today seem to be unable to understand love as a political concept, but a concept of love is just what we need to grasp the constituent power of the multitude. The modern concept of love is almost exclusively limited to the bourgeois couple and the claustrophobic confines of the nuclear family. Love has become a strictly private affair. We need a more generous and more unrestrained conception of love. We need to recuperate the public and political conception of love common to premodern traditions [...] We need to recover today this material and political sense of love, a love as strong as death. This does not mean you cannot love your spouse, your mother, and your child. It only means that your love does not end there, that love serves as the basis for our political projects in common and the construction of a new society. Without this love, we are nothing. (Hardt and Negri 2004, 351–2)

The commodification of ideas like love was not accidental. In 1975 the Trilateral Commission, a nongovernmental political and economic group founded by David Rockerfeller that included members from the United States, Western Europe and Japan, released a report detailing what they called the "excesses of democracy" of the 1960s. The report, entitled "Crisis of Democracy," highlighted the failures and dangers of an abundance and plurality of activism in relation to the stability of individual Western governments and the stability of Western hegemony in the world. "The arenas where democratic procedures are appropriate, in short, are limited," the report concluded, noting that democracy in the '60s had spread to institutions where "it can, in the long run, only frustrate the purposes of those institutions." Consequently the report advocated that the authoritativeness of the federal government be restored through more "apathy and noninvolvement on the part of some individuals and groups" (Crozier, Huntington et al. 1975, 113–14).

John Lennon continued to fight for his ideals outside of the musical realm, but only bought further into the very processes of commodification that were undermining his goals. He commented in 1969 that he and Yoko Ono, in their "bed-in" at the Amsterdam Hilton, were "doing a commercial for peace on the front pages of newspapers around the world instead of a commercial for war [...] We're trying to sell peace, like a product, and sell it like people sell soap or soft drinks" (Gould 2007, 551).

By 1980, the hope and idealism of the '60s were all but dead. Weeks before his death on 8 December of that year, Lennon caught on to the jadedness and antagonism towards the movements of the '60s and futilely rallied against such cynicism:

> The media are saying that the 60's were stupid and naive [...] but look at how much of what was sniggered about in the 60's has become mainstream – health food, therapies and all the rest. And love and peace weren't invented in the 60's. What about Gandhi? What about Christ? The naivete is to buy the idea that the 60's were naive. (Palmer 1980)

Many of the obituaries for Lennon, while certainly mournful of the death of the legendary artist, exposed the degree to which the media, by 1980, viewed the aspirations of the 1960s as glib and immature. The *Anchorage Daily News* admitted that "the idealism of the period now seems naïve"; the *New York Times* added that "the nation is tired of Great Society rhetoric" (Campbell 1980, B4). The *Sarasota Herald-Tribune* concluded, fairly tastelessly, that "[w]e have been reaping the harvest sown from 1965 to 1975, and perhaps the violent death of a rock star who helped define that era [...] provides a particularly poignant and final epitaph" (Phillips 1981, 7A).

Like the Trilateral Commission, conservatives eschewed the "movement" (often brushed off with such quotation marks) as regretful and hopelessly ineffective, lamenting that even in the late '70s, 'people couldn't learn from their mistakes.' By 1980, they were publishing stories highlighting the impossibility of world peace, due to lack of a common framework of understanding (Kearns 1982). Meanwhile, The Beatles, the musical standard-bearers of the ethic of the '60s, experienced sluggish chart performance throughout the '80s and well into the '90s. Writing about Beatles-as-commodity, James M. Decker notes that the "Reaganite economic and social policies had been in place for nearly eleven years, and thousands of homeless poignantly reminded the nation that love is not all you need. In such a context, the Beatles' overt message of peace and love became positively naïve" (Decker 2006, 186). The polling of Americans during the 1980s also reflected more militant and "realistic" approaches to international policy and generally dismissed the love-based activism of the tumultuous era. A 1986 poll found that only 74 percent of Americans had a favorable opinion of Martin Luther King, which is lower than one would expect, considering it was the same year his birthday was made into a national holiday (People, The Press, and Politics Poll 1987). Similarly, a poll asking respondents if the antiwar protests of the 1960s influenced US foreign policy revealed that only 54 percent thought that the peace movements fomented change, and another poll found that in 1983 72 percent of Americans believed that they should support their country in wartime, even if they believed that its actions were wrong (New York Times Poll 1983). In this "culture and politics of consumption," David Burner notes the inchoate goals espoused by the Reagan-Bush administrations of, "ridiculing environmentalists [...] and supporting militarism [...]" fostered in the American public a self-satisfied detachment, one that occluded domestic sacrifice and accountability for violence abroad by persuading Americans to, "enjoy the fight, as spectators pretending to be participants" (Burner 1996, 222).

We find many examples of the marginalized efficacy of deployments of love in political movements in the 1970s and 1980s as well. One such example is the Gandhian Chipko movement, a group of activists who were using the power of love for social change, only for their nickname and mission statement to be marginalized after the fact by a society inundated with cheapened images of love. Starting in the Indian state of Uttarakhand, the Chipko movement, almost exclusively female, used a Gandhian "ethic of love" (that is, the selfless, universalistic agape variety) to bring attention to the rapid deforestation occurring in the region by staging a nonviolent protest and literally hugging the trees they sought to protect. Chipko was largely successful in their own time because, even up to 1980, there was no real omnipotent media saturation in India as a whole, and especially not much in their specific, nonurban region. Initially secluded from the media's commodifying messaging, Chipko was able to utilize the political power of love successfully. However, the increasingly pejorative slant to their moniker "tree hugger" tarnished their loving methodology and damaged the potential for future ecological groups to utilize their tactics and be taken seriously. From the early 1980s, "tree hugger" would begin appearing in Western media as a term for an individual who felt too much for the environment. In 1983 Anne Burford, chief of the Environmental Protection Agency, was asked to resign from her post, and later blamed her departure on her not being enough of a tree hugger. Burford commented, "I kept being asked, 'How do you feel about the environment?' I feel about my husband, I feel about my children, I try to think about the environment [...] The eastern press corps demands that you be emotive about the environment" (Darst 1985). Her attitude towards the environment, antithetical to that of the Chipko, demonstrated in the arena of environmentalism the extent to which the concept of love had been eradicated from political discourse in favor of a more "pragmatic" approach to successful reform.

Likewise, the increased popularity particularly in the West of Tenzin Gyatso, the fourteenth Dalai Lama, has led to his cultural consumption by millions of followers and also precipitated his inefficacy in the political arena. As the incarnation of the Buddha of Compassion, and as someone greatly influenced by Gandhi, there seem fewer people more qualified to promulgate an ethic of love than the current Dalai Lama. Establishing a Tibetan government in exile in India in 1959, the Dalai Lama's political philosophies greatly mirrored those of Gandhi, encapsulating such love ethic credos as "The enemy is the evil which men do [...] not the men themselves" (Puri 2002, 3501). Like Gandhi and King, the Dalai Lama established a universal appeal to his spiritual politics by engaging other religious leaders in interfaith dialogues about peace and religious harmony.

However, as Bharati Puri has noted, the stance of the Dalai Lama in regards to Tibet began to shift around 1978, his goals changing from independence to "compromise and negotiated settlement": "In this period, the Dalai Lama has been mobilizing western public opinion through the western media, while Tibetan popular opinion has taken the backseat" (Puri 2002, 3502). Throughout the 1980s and especially after he received the Nobel Peace Prize in 1989, the Dalai Lama's cultural popularity soared, and an acute lack of political traction followed. Worldwide celebrity through the auspices of Western culture led to bestselling books and, later, even an Apple ad challenging consumers to "Think Different." As Brendan O'Neill rebuked in the *Guardian*, "[d]espite the fact that he advertises Apple, guest-edits Vogue and drives a Land Rover, he is held up as evidence that living the simple eastern life is preferable to, in the words of Philip Rawson, Westerners' 'gradually more pointless pursuit of material satisfactions.' Just as earlier generations of disillusioned aristocrats fell in love with a fictional version of Tibet (Shangri-La), so contemporary un-progressives idolize a fictional image of the Dalai Lama" (O'Neill 2008).

Conclusion

While the idea of love was used in the early and mid-twentieth centuries to empower social justice campaigns and movements, exemplified by those led by Gandhi and King, it ceased to be politically effective in the 1960s. (Well-intentioned) countercultural forces in the United States confused selfless and individualistic love. Some of the leading proponents of love (here the kind is unspecified and vague) were themselves mega-brands like The Beatles and, even in advocating love, linked it to the selling of music or the furthering of their own brand. Campaigns to sell other products such as Coca-Cola latched on to '60s counterculture as a marketing tool, erasing the nuance of political intent from symbols now recast as hallmarks of particular products.

The commodification of love coincided with a concerted effort to push back against "'60s excess," and to reassert the old political order. American cultural influence helped to ensure that this message held a hegemonic position globally. While champions of selfless, political love continued to emerge in the '70s and on into the '80s, they found a landscape resistant to their message, bereft of the power of dreams, and cynical.

And yet the anomalous case of Nelson Mandela reveals that the ethic of a selfless, universalizing love remains able to touch human hearts and transform political scenarios. After his trial and subsequent 27-year imprisonment in 1964, idealization of Mandela became a global phenomenon. Mandela described the creation of a free and democratic society, "an ideal for which I am prepared to die" (Smith 2010, 354), and when he was released from prison in 1991, his weathered face illustrated the "suffering" of love that Gandhi and King similarly endured for their respective causes. After his release, people quickly and passionately embraced Mandela's methods for social change, which he would later describe in his autobiography *Long Walk to Freedom*: "No one is born hating another person because of the color of his skin, or his background, or his religion. People must learn to hate, and if they can learn to hate, they can be taught to love, for love comes more naturally to the human heart than its opposite" (Mandela 1994, 622).

Notes

1 King wrote his doctoral dissertation on Christian existentialist philosopher Paul Tillich, who called the love-force of agape, "the only sure guide to ethics in a changing world" (Rossinow 1998, 67).
2 Doug Rossinow links the ecclesiastical roots of love in both the civil rights movement and sixties counterculture, noting "Love was the most distinctively Christian theme of all [...] a crucial theme of both the civil rights movement and, later on, the new left and the counterculture" (Rossinow 1998, 83).
3 For a more in-depth look at the role of musicians and society in the sixties, see Gitlin, 195–221.
4 See "I'd Like to Buy the World a Coke Commercial – 1971," http://www.youtube.com/watch?v=2msbfN81Gm0; "Coca-Cola '70s Christmas Hilltop Commercial" http://www.youtube.com/watch?v=_zCsFvVg0UY (accessed 20 December 2012).

References

Backer, Bill. *Coke Lore: The Coca-Cola Company*. Online: http://www.thecoca-colacompany.com/heritage/cokelore_hilltop.html (accessed 12 August 2011).
Braunstein, P. and Michael William Doyle, eds. 2001. "Historicizing the American Counterculture of the 1960s and 1970s." In *Image Nation: The American Counterculture of the 1960s and 1970s*. London: Routledge.
Burner, David. 1996. *Making Peace With the Sixties*. Princeton: Princeton University Press.

Campbell, Mary. 1980. "The Culture of Two Decades Mirrored in One Man's Work." *The Anchorage Daily News*, 9 December.

Carson, Clayborne, ed. 1998. *The Autobiography of Martin Luther King Jr.* New York: Warner Books.

Crozier, Michael J., Samuel P. Huntington and Joji Watanuki. 1975. *The Crisis of Democracy.* New York: New York University Press.

Darst, Guy. 1985. "Former EPA Chief Blames Troubles On Incompetent Lawyers And Press." *New York Times*, 12 June.

Debord, Guy. 1995 [1967]. *Society of the Spectacle.* Cambridge, MA: Zone Books.

Decker, James M. 2006. "Baby You're a Rich Man." In *Reading the Beatles: Cultural Studies, Literary Criticism, and the Fab Four*, edited by K. Womack and T. F. Davis. Albany: State University of New York Press.

De Grazia, Victoria. 2005. *Irresistible Empire.* Cambridge, MA: Belknap Press.

Frank, Thomas. 1997. *The Conquest of Cool: Business Culture, Counterculture, and the Rise of Hip Consumerism.* Chicago: University of Chicago Press.

Fromm, Erich. 1956. *The Art of Loving.* New York: Continuum International.

Gandhi, Mohandas. 1917. "Satyagraha – Not Passive Resistance." In *The Collected Works of Mahatma Gandhi*, vol. 16. Online: http://www.gandhiserve.org/cwmg/VOL016.PDF (accessed 10 August 2011).

———. 1931. "Speech at Indian Students' Meeting." In *The Collected Works of Mahatma Gandhi*, vol. 54. Online: http://www.gandhiserve.org/cwmg/VOL054.PDF (accessed 10 August 2011).

———. 1934. *Harijans.* 17 August 1934.

———. 1993. *An Autobiography: The Story of My Experiments with Truth.* Boston: Beacon Press.

———. 2003 [1938]. *Indian Home Rule* or *Hind Swaraj.* Ahmedabad: Navajivan Publishing House. Online: http://www.arvindguptatoys.com/arvindgupta/hindswaraj.pdf (accessed 10 August 2011).

Gitlin, Todd. 1987. *The Sixties: Years of Hope, Days of Rage.* New York: Bantam.

Gould, Jonathan. 2007. *Can't Buy Me Love.* New York: Three Rivers Press.

Habermas, Jürgen. 2001 [1991]. *The Structural Transformation of the Public Sphere.* Cambridge, MA: MIT Press.

Hardt, Michael and Antonio Negri. 2004. *Multitude: War and Democracy in the Age of Empire.* New York: Penguin.

Isserman, Maurice and Michael Kazin. 2000. *America Divided: The Civil War of the 1960s.* New York: Oxford University Press.

Jones, Robert. 1967. "The Hippies: Philosophy of a Subculture." *Time Magazine*, 17 July. Online: http://www.time.com/time/magazine/article/0,9171,899555,00.html (accessed 9 August 2011).

Kearns, Burt. 1982. "End of Illusions." *The National Review*, 11 December.

King Jr, Martin Luther. 1958. *Stride Toward Freedom: The Montgomery Story.* Boston: Beacon Press.

———. 1959. *India Speech: February 1959.* Online: Audio available at http://www.npr.org/templates/story/story.php?storyId=99480326 (accessed 12 February 2011).

———. 1960. *Suffering and Faith. The Papers of Martin Luther King Jr.*, vol. 5. Online: http://mlkkpp01.stanford.edu/index.php/encyclopedia/ documentsentry/suffering_and_faith (accessed 1 August 2011).

——. 1963. *Letter from Birmingham Jail*. Online: http://mlk-kpp01.stanford.edu/index.php/resources/article/annotated_letter_from_birmingham/ (accessed 29 July 2011).

——. 1967a. "Beyond Vietnam: A Time to Break Silence." Speech delivered at Riverside Church, New York, NY. 4 April. Online: http://www.americanrhetoric.com/speeches/mlkatimetobreaksilence.htm (accessed 1 August 2011).

——. 1967b. "Where Do We Go From Here?" Speech delivered at the 11th Annual SCLC Convention, Atlanta, GA. 16 August. Online: http://mlk-kpp01.stanford.edu/index.php/kingpapers/article/where_do_we_go_from_here/ (accessed 1 August 2011).

——. 2010 [1963]. *Strength to Love*. Minneapolis: Fortress Press.

Kroft, Joseph. 1970. "The Function of the Seventies: Getting Our Bearing Again." *Los Angeles Times*, 2 January.

Lischer, Richard. 1995. *The Preacher King: Martin Luther King and the Word that Moved America*. Oxford: Oxford University Press.

Mandela, Nelson. 1994. *Long Walk to Freedom: The Autobiography of Nelson Mandela*. Boston: Little Brown.

Marshall, P. David. 2000. "The Celebrity Legacy of the Beatles." In *The Beatles, Popular Music, and Society: A Thousand Voices*, edited by Ian Inglis. New York: Macmillan.

Morgan, Edward P. 2011. *What Really Happened to the 1960s: How Mass Media Culture Failed American Democracy*. Lawrence: University of Kansas Press.

New York Times Poll. 1983. iPOLL Databank, The Roper Center for Public Opinion Research, University of Connecticut. November. Online: http://www.ropercenter.uconn.edu.proxy.wexler.hunter.cuny.edu/data_access/ipoll/ipoll.html (accessed 27 August 2011).

O'Neill, Brendan. 2008. "Down with the Dalai Lama." *Guardian*, 29 May.

Palmer, Robert. 1980. "Lennon Known Both as Author and Composer." *New York Times*, 8 December.

People, The Press, and Politics Poll. 1987. iPOLL Databank, The Roper Center for Public Opinion Research, University of Connecticut. April. Online: http://www.ropercenter.uconn.edu.proxy.wexler.hunter.cuny.edu/data_access/ipoll/ipoll.html (accessed 27 August 2011).

Phillips, Kevin P. 1981. "Lennon Era Reconsidered." *Sarasota Herald-Tribune*, 1 January.

Phillips, Wayne. 1956. "Negroes Pledge to Keep Boycott." *New York Times*, 24 February.

Puri, Bharati. 2002. "Deconstructing the Dalai Lama on Tibet." *Economic and Political Weekly* 37(34): 3500–3503.

Reddick, Lawrence Dunbar. 1959. Press Conference in New Delhi. February. Online: http://mlkkpp01.stanford.edu/primarydocuments/Vol5/10Feb1959 (accessed 31 July 2011).

Rossinow, Doug. 1998. *The Politics of Authenticity: Liberalism, Christianity, and the New Left in America*. New York: Columbia University Press.

Schaffner, Nicholas. 1977. *The Beatles Forever*. Harrisburg: Cameron House.

Smith, David James. 2010. *Young Mandela: The Revolutionary Years*. New York: Little Brown.

Southall, Nick. 2010. "Love and Revolution." *Links International Journal of Socialist Renewal*, 30. Online: http://links.org.au/node/1674 (accessed 20 April 2011).

Chapter 9

THE RELIGION OF BROTHERLY LOVE: LEO TOLSTOY AND MAX WEBER

Bryan S. Turner

Introduction: Axial-Age Religions

The world religions have, through much of human history, embraced radical criticisms of earthly violence and, at the same time, have been deeply implicated in the conduct of violence. In this chapter I look at war and peace through the lens of Max Weber's sociology of religion, and explore his relationship to the radical pacifism of Leo Tolstoy. Weber's contrast between an ethic of absolute ends and an ethic of responsibility offers a powerful insight into the contradictions that attend religion's response to the world. However, before turning to Weber, we need a framework within which to understand the idea of a "world religion" and in order to get that initial perspective I turn to the philosophy of Karl Jaspers. In his controversial *The Origin and Goal of History* (1953), originally published in 1949, Jaspers proposed that an "axial age" (*Achsenzeit*) occurred between 800 and 200 BC, and that the critical turning point was around 500 BC. For Jaspers, this period was the great age of the prophets and religious leaders, such as Confucius and Lao-Tse in China, the Buddha in India, Zoroaster in Iran, the prophets of ancient Israel and finally the poets and philosophers of ancient Greece. Through apocalyptic revelation, the prophets offered humanity a notion of an alternative world beyond and different from the mundane world of the here and now. On the basis of a vision of transcendence, they developed ethical codes of conduct that established norms of virtuous behavior for individuals and political constitutions to guide communities. These early religio-ethical ideas established a fundamental division between a spiritual sphere and the world, and hence they offered an alternative to the empirical world of violence, greed and self-interest. According to Arnaldo Momigliano (1975, 9) "everywhere one notices attempts to introduce greater purity, greater justice, greater perfection and more universal explanations of things […]

we are in the age of criticism." For example, Plato looked towards Socrates the philosopher as the kingly personality and not to war heroes such as Achilles. In China, it was Mencius who championed Confucius as the wise official whose political and ethical vision offered guidelines towards peace and stability. In South Asia, it was the Buddha who created an alternative to the legacy of caste, challenged the inherited status of the Brahmins and preached the supreme doctrine of noninvolvement through a spiritual pathway. Finally, the prophets of ancient Israel condemned the corruption of the monarchy and the temple priests in the name of a single transcendent God who demanded the loyalty of the Jewish tribes as a confederation of chosen people. In summary, these religious leaders separated the spiritual world of self-discipline and development from the mundane callings of kings and warriors through critical worldviews that were revolutionary. In so doing, they set up a lasting tension between the secular and the religious.

These axial-age movements erupted on the basis of important social and economic changes. In particular, these critical worldviews came into existence against a background of literacy, complex political organizations, early urbanization and advances in mental technology. There was a transition from bronze to iron with concomitant technological developments and, importantly, the emergence of coinage, facilitating an enhancement of international exchange, brought in widespread economic developments. The axial age was, as a result, defined by rising prosperity and constant warfare between small states and occasionally by the rise of powerful empires. While these factors in the rise of the axial age have been questioned by historians, Jaspers' work has been important in shaping both history and sociology. The historians included Eric Voegelin and Arnaldo Momigliano, and the sociologists S. N. Eisenstadt and Robert Bellah. In this chapter, I am primarily concerned with Weber's comparative sociology of religion, which examined the tensions in various religious traditions between the secular world and the religious quest for salvation, whether individual or collective. However, it is difficult to discover overt or explicit references in Weber's sociology to an axial age, though there is a reference to the "prophetic age" (Weber 1978, 441–2). Jaspers and Weber had a close personal and intellectual relationship, but Jaspers' development of the theory of the axial age came long after Weber's death. Jaspers gave the eulogy at the ceremony at the University of Heidelberg to commemorate Weber's death (Henrich 1987) in which he defined Weber as a philosopher and not as a historical sociologist of comparative religion.

Jaspers' evaluation of Weber as a philosopher was correct in one respect, namely to identify Weber's response to religion as somewhat parallel to perspectives of Kierkegaard and Nietzsche. Weber also had "a nose" for hypocrisy and humbug, and hence admired the seriousness of Tolstoy's project even though he ultimately thought it was unrealistic. Weber's notion that the vitality of religious or charismatic movements depends on their conflict with secular reality informs the entire body of his work on religion. The idea of "religious orientations" to the world, conflicting with dominant economic and political realms, was pivotal to his analysis of the significance of "world religions." In the Jewish prophets and the sermons of Jesus, Weber found the roots of an ethic of brotherly love in opposition to this-worldly greed, self-interest and violence. In Weber's analysis of world religions, Islam was in origin a "political religion" in which the Prophet had, through the Constitution of Medina, established a political community of tribes that quickly evolved after the Prophet's death into an imperial system (Weber 1965). Weber's view of the Prophet is clearly controversial, but I shall not return here to an assessment of his analysis, having already discussed the idea of *jihad* in the Introduction. However, his sociological vision of an ethical realm standing over and against politics was tragic rather than triumphal in the sense that, for Weber, selfless love is always compromised in this world. In a secular age, the best that honest men can achieve is a calling in science or politics wherein the ethically minded might exercise some vestige of virtue. Before turning to Weber's sociology of brotherly love, we need to consider some obvious objections to Jaspers' general thesis.

I shall only consider two obvious objections to the idea of an axial age. The first is the question of chronology. It is significant that Jaspers and Momigliano identified the end of the axial age before the birth of Christianity and well before the emergence of Islam. One obvious objection is that the Sermon on the Mount, to take one example from the New Testament, is the encapsulation of the prophetic message of peace and forgiveness that was anticipated by the Israelite prophets, or one might argue that the universal vision of justice that is basic to the Qur'an is also consistent with axial-age principles. The implication of Jaspers' argument is indeed that the Judaism of the Exile, New Testament Christianity and the message of the Prophet of Islam were simply variations on a theme of transcendence that emerged long before the Christian Era. These later prophetic religions did not contribute anything that was new to the stock of ideas that had already appeared in the axial age. The second issue, which is important in the work of Weber, concerns the problem of defining what religion is. This problem arises critically in the idea of the "religions of China," such as Confucianism, but is equally problematic in judging the status of the "religions of India," namely the Vedic and Brahminical movements of spirituality. How can we locate what later was to be known as "Hinduism" in Jaspers' historical scheme? The implication of Weber's comparative sociology of religion is that "religion" implies some systematic and enduring tension with the empirical reality of "the world" and therefore religions that compromise their values and practices under pressure from economic and political institutions begin to lose their status as religions, becoming instead useful ideologies that legitimize hegemonic systems of power from kings to modern presidents. Weber regarded both Hinduism and Confucianism as questionable examples of "religion" because they did not develop any sustained ethical criticism of secular powers; they were too immersed in the secular world to offer radical alternatives. To overstate Weber's position, Hinduism was an ideology of pollution that justified the caste system and Confucianism was a theory of social order based on loyalty to the state and filial respect for authority in the household.

Religion and the Calling of the Warrior

Contemporary scholarship has underlined the fact that Hinduism, as a late product of the colonial period, is not a unified or singular religion and attempts therefore to capture the diversity of an evolving tradition by noting that "it is a cumulative collection of communities, faiths, beliefs, and practices that have come together over the centuries, although its ancient roots are traditionally seen in the cultures of the Indus Valley, Saraswati River civilization, and Indo-European people" (Narayanan 2005, 15). Weber was obviously aware of these conceptual difficulties observing "it may well be concluded that Hinduism is simply not a 'religion' in our sense of the word [...] What the Occidental conceives as 'religion' is closer to the Hindu concept of *sampradaya*. By this the Hindu understands communities into which one is not born [...] but to which one belongs by virtue of a common religious aspiration and common sacred paths" (Weber 1958, 23). For Weber, these communities (or *theophratries*) include, among others, both Jainism and Buddhism. In the study of China, he noted similar difficulties with the idea of Confucianism as a religion. He declared that "Confucianism exclusively represented an inner-worldly morality of laymen. Confucianism meant adjustment to the world, to its orders and conventions" (Weber 1951, 152). As we have noted, in Weber's sociology, religion has to be distinct from and in some degree of tension with "the world" of politics, sexuality and economics. This tension gave rise to two principal orientations to the world – asceticism on the one hand and mysticism on the other. This dichotomy meant either active engagement with or against the world through ascetic discipline or adjustment to or flight from the world in terms of a mystical retreat. This model of religious orientations was the basis of the famous essay "Religious Rejections of the World and Their Directions" (Weber 2009a).

We must deal with yet one more preliminary issue, namely Weber's definition of Hinduism in terms of its relationship to the caste system.

He correctly saw the rise of Buddhism in South Asia against the background of a diffuse spiritual tradition known subsequently as Hinduism, which he described as a religion associated with notions of ritual pollution and castes. We cannot fully understand Buddhism without a prior grasp of the history of the religious traditions in ancient India that were organized around the values of the Brahmins. Furthermore, we cannot understand this early Vedic tradition without coming to terms with the idea of caste, which in turn is associated with controversial interpretations of the origins of the Brahmins. There are two radically opposed interpretations of the early history of ancient India. The first regards Vedic spirituality as an indigenous product of South Asia and not dependent on any external Aryan additions. The second approach, which Weber followed, argues that the cultures of South Asia were produced by numerous migrations, involving a long history of conquest and assimilation. This procession of "Aryan conquests" over many centuries gave rise to a large number of petty kingdoms and ruling princes. In this hierarchical system, incoming workers were eventually consigned to a lowly caste or pariah group that undertook menial tasks, often considered to be polluting. These diverse religious ideas and institutions operated at a village level, and Weber argued that India was a system of villages in which membership was defined by birth.

It is not surprising therefore that *The Religion of India* starts with an account of caste in relation to Hinduism. Weber boldly asserted that caste is "the ritual rights and duties it imposes, and the position of the Brahmans, is the fundamental institution of Hinduism. Before everything else, without caste, there is no Hindu" (Weber 1958, 29). Indian caste hierarchy was based on the four *varnas* – the Brahmin, the warrior (Kshatriya), the people and the servants (Shudra). This hierarchical division of society by basic functions cut across the differentiation of the society into tribes and lineages. Caste was an inherited position and therefore the most prestigious members of the Brahmin caste were defined by several generations of ritual purity. Brahmins had control of major rituals and were guardians of the written tradition. While the Brahmins were ritually separate, they also encompassed or completed the social system, whereas lower castes were seen to be, as it were, ontologically incomplete. One important feature of this system was that ritual authority (the Brahmins) was separate from the system of economic and political power (the Ksatriya caste). In Weber's terms, the symbolic power of the Brahminical caste did not necessarily translate into political power, but it was nevertheless in his vocabulary a form of symbolic violence.

Generally speaking, contemporary anthropologists of South Asia have been skeptical about the value of the notion of a caste system that had so dominated early scholarly writing about India (Srinivas 1989). In short, recent anthropological research claims that the caste system was more fluid than conventional views allowed. It was a good deal more porous, fluid and fragmented, and that the real core of the system was the *jati*, namely the hereditary endogamous group often associated with occupational specialization. These concepts and their implications remain a contested field, but what cannot be disputed is that, in South Asia before the teaching of the Buddha, social inequality existed in terms of a system of hereditary and hierarchical distinctions in which the Brahmins were at the pinnacle of rules defining and controlling pollution. The varna system, to use Émile Durkheim's terminology, was a form of primitive classification that was both cosmological and sociological in providing legitimacy for the secular distribution of power (Smith 1994).

Max Weber and Early Buddhism

Rather than concentrating on the factors that inhibited capitalism, Weber claimed, with reference to Hinduism, that "legitimation by a recognized religion has always been decisive for an alliance between politically and socially dominant classes and the priesthood" (Weber 1958, 16). But did the same apply to Buddhism? Before attempting to evaluate Weber's sociology of Buddhism in the light of contemporary research, we need to consider his argument in *The Religion of India* (Weber 1958). The decisive feature of early Buddhism was that it developed a system of spirituality for monks to the partial exclusion of the laity. What he referred to as "Ancient Buddhism" is a "specifically unpolitical and anti-political status religion, more precisely, a religious 'technology' of wandering and intellectually-schooled mendicant monks. Like all Indian philosophy and theology, it is a 'salvation religion', if one is to use the name 'religion' for an ethical movement without a deity and without a cult" (Weber 1958, 206). More precisely, he argued that early Buddhist philosophy is indifferent to questions about divinity because it is a spiritual technology that aims to release the individual from suffering in order to eventually achieve a state of nothingness or nirvana. The crucial issue here is the exclusion of the laity from complete fulfillment of Buddhist disciplinary demands simply because lay engagement in the everyday world of production and reproduction meant that they could never undertake, let alone complete, the comprehensive requirements of the Eightfold Path. He argued in *The Religion of China* that, in the historical development of Buddhism and its eventual spread to Japan, Buddhism had become a "folk religion" with distinctively magical elements. Thus, "Buddhism in its imported form was no longer the redemptory religion of early Indian Buddhism, but had become the magical and mystagogical practice of a monastic organization" (Weber 1951, 225). One consequence of these developments was that there were no religious communities for the laity and individual laypeople went to the monks for magical services to restore their health or to bring them comfort. Buddhism did not develop a strong congregational structure that was characteristic, for example, of Christianity. Hence, Buddhism was, in Weber's eyes, an essentially spiritual technology and a technology that was remote from politics and hence from the power structures that are necessary for the exercise of power.

Whereas Islam is often seen by Western critics as deeply involved with the political (as in the expression "political Islam"), Buddhism is by contrast seen to be associated with pacifism or at least seen as fundamentally an apolitical spirituality. Buddhist doctrines of suffering, mindfulness and release from this world through self-discipline appear to be far removed from the history of Christian Crusades and the Islamic jihad. Among academic sociologists, this understanding of Buddhism as an apolitical and pacifist movement may well have been fostered by the legacy of Weber's sociology of religion. This contrast, in Weber's terms, between a political religion like Islam and Buddhism as the practice of solitary monks was associated with his notion of the social carriers of the world religions. He claimed that the carrier of Islam was a warrior class, that Confucianism was the ethical system of cultured prebendaries with a literary education based on secular rationalism and that the social carriers of the primitive church in early Christianity were artisans. In terms of early Buddhism, the carrier of mindfulness was the forest-dwelling mendicant monk. These early carriers of religion had a long-term historical impact on their values and institutions. In *Weber and Islam* (Turner 1974), I criticized his account of Islam, pointing out, among other issues, that the carriers of Islam from the Arabian Peninsula and the African coast to the city-ports of Southeast Asia were Sufi traders, who were members of brotherhoods with international connections. It was trade rather than the sword that brought the message of the Prophet to Southeast Asia, but I need to dwell at some length on Weber's interpretation of Buddhism and Hinduism as apolitical because, in that regard, it has been interpreted as pacifist rather than war-like in the case of Islam or egalitarian in relation to Hinduism.

Against my "materialistic interpretation" of the interaction between the Buddhist monastic elites and the laity, Ilana Silber (1995) proposed that the exchange relationship between them can more accurately be understood as a gift relationship within the conceptual framework of Marcel Mauss's anthropology of the gift. First published in 1924, he argued that gift exchange had to be understood as a total social phenomenon with multiple legal, social and economic aspects (Mauss 1976). Applying this idea to Buddhism, Silber claimed that there was always a complex combination of interest and disinterest in the relationships between monks and laypeople in terms of gift giving through lay donations. To been seen as valid, the gift has to deny any selfish interest or motive on the part of the person who gives the gift and at the same time has to create solidarity between monks and laity. Lay donations were an important foundation of Buddhist monasticism, but they cannot be fully understood as simply an economic payment for soteriological services of monks. From the perspective of the laity, to emphasize the social services of the monks to the laity would compromise their spiritual vocations. Thus, she proposed that a more adequate interpretation of these donations "is that they contribute to mediating between two otherwise polarized and even antagonistic sectors, between a religious elite exemplifying certain ideals, and lay believers willing to acknowledge the same ideals but unable or unwilling to commit themselves to their fullest enactment" (Silber 1995, 213). The donation mediates between the selfless commitment of the monk and the unavoidable worldly involvement of the laity, and the religious gift in this context is a materialization of trust rather than the expression of any competition between elite and laity. In Asian societies, before the development of either markets or banking institutions, the Buddhist monasteries "came to constitute the most reliable channels for the conservation, fructification, and display of wealth" (Silber 1995, 215), and their very continuity over time was the foundation of the social solidarity binding elites and laity together.

Silber's analysis provides a valuable understanding of the complex interaction between ideological and economic aspects of the gift in supporting monastic institutions and the ascetic lifestyle of monks. While her study contributes to a more subtle and complex analysis of lay donations in the reciprocity between monks and laypeople than my emphasis on simple economic exchange in *Religion and Social Theory*, she may have nevertheless underestimated the political role of Buddhism and its historical connections to monarchy. Contemporary scholarship has explored the necessary connections between Buddhism and politics as a correction to Weber's analysis of monks as forest-dwelling ascetics with no connection to political institutions. Thus, while the aim of followers of the Buddha was to seek ultimate overcoming of the world through meditation and related techniques, the Path had to take place within the world, and hence Buddhists are forced to engage with political institutions rather than simply to avoid any engagement with secular politics. In the teachings of the Buddha, there was, in fact, a theory of politics in which there appears a clear distinction between "the wheel of law" which is the teaching of the *sangha* and "the wheel of command" which is the work of the state. In this interpretive framework, the state is necessary for maintaining the social order and for defending Buddhist institutions.

These early Buddhist principles, in which the evils of war were criticized but the state was accepted as a necessary institution, are often illustrated by the history of King Ashoka (268–239 BCE) whose empire extended over much of

India. From his capital in modern day Patna, Ashoka made a public conversion to the Buddhist way and through the idea of "righteous conquest" he extended Buddhist values in his kingdom and beyond. After repenting the violence of his early conquests, he promulgated a version of the *dharma* consisting of moral virtues and his reign is celebrated in various legends that are known as the *Ashokavandana*. In these narratives, Ashoka became the symbol of authoritative Buddhist rulership, combining compassion and power in order to establish a stable, peaceful and enduring society.

Under pressure from the spread of Islam and as a consequence of the growth and reform of the religion of the Brahmans, Buddhism had all but disappeared from India by the twelfth century CE. By that time, Buddhism had spread to Tibet, China and Japan. During Buddhist expansion outside India, the Asokan model of kingly power remained significant as a normative framework for the intersection of religion and politics, and was adopted in Sri Lanka and Southeast Asia. As Buddhism developed outside India, Theravada Buddhism became a popular religion of the peasantry in spreading through the countryside and Buddhist teaching was translated into vernacular literature. Despite these developments at the local level, the principles of Asokan rulership remained influential in the sense that the Theravada kings were not given legitimacy on the basis of royal descent but on the basis that they represented the dharma and were hence *dharmarajas*. Their charisma came from behavior in their past lives, and their political legitimacy was based on their patronage of the sangha. The early Buddhist kingdoms have been described as "galactic polities" in which the cosmic order was reflected in the social order (Tambiah 1976). A powerful centre under the control of a dharma king was surrounded by dependent principalities, and the authority of the king guaranteed the expansion of his rule and the defense of Buddhist institutions. The stability and harmony of a Buddhist kingdom was thought to reflect the harmony and coherence of the cosmic order.

These religio-political structures were remarkably resilient and enduring, but they were eventually disrupted by the arrival of French and British colonialism from 1815 to the end of French Indochina in 1954. In Burma, the British East India Company sent agents as early as 1612, but they were resisted. British colonial governments were not seen as legitimate, mainly because they were foreign and they did not support Buddhism. By contrast, French colonialism allowed for the appearance of continuity with the old order by maintaining monarchies and support for the sangha, but French colonialists were clearly not Buddhists. Siam was not colonized by European powers and remained a Buddhist monarchy, but its absolutist rulers undermined or abolished autonomous centers such as Chiang Mai and Na. The Siam government centralized authority in Buddhism, by placing all monks under a single institution. In addition, the state ideology was nationalist rather than Buddhist, especially after King Vajiravudh (1881–1925) came to the throne in 1910. His principal objective was to use nationalism to buttress the monarchy in a period when there was agitation against royal absolutism. He undertook a number of major works including building a railway system, but the national debt eventually forced the government to take out a large loan from Britain. His taxation system also produced discontent, such as the insurgency in Pattani in 1922. By 1925 when Prince Prajathipok came to the throne, the monarchy was at its lowest point, and was seen to be corrupted by favoritism and by a royal family that was bastion of the elite whose Western education and life style cut them off from the people. Throughout the region, there was Buddhist opposition to colonial rule often in terms of millenarian movements and charismatic monks (Keyes 1976). By the 1920s, these millenarian protests had failed and they were replaced by Buddhist-inspired nationalist movements, for example in Burma. The movements laid the foundation for opposition to colonial and postcolonial governments. In Vietnam, the self-immolation of Thich Quang Duc in June 1963 was a major turning point in opposition to the Republic of Vietnam and its American ally. Through these anticolonial struggles, historians have shown that it is not possible to argue that Buddhism has remained separate and aloof from worldly politics.

In the modern period, Buddhism came under severe and frequently violent control by Communist governments after the unification of Vietnam in 1976. In China, the Cultural Revolution (1965–75) and the Khmer Rouge regime of Pol Pot (1975–79) resulted in the systematic destruction of Buddhist culture; and in Thailand, social unrest and military regimes had fragmented the Buddhist sangha, but the state was largely successful in controlling Buddhism to its own ends (Keyes 1971). Furthermore, the conflict with Muslims in the southern provinces has underlined the nationalist identification of Thailand with Buddhism, virtually making it a state religion. The Chinese invasion of Tibet has also caused a significant dislocation of Buddhism, especially with the exile of the Dalai Lama. While some Tibetan monks have actively resisted Chinese control, His Holiness has so far been opposed to violent opposition. The Tibetan situation raises in an acute form the traditional question of the legitimacy of Buddhist involvement in politics, and thus in violence. From this brief historical sketch, it is obvious that the integrity and influence of Buddhism were severely shaken by various colonial interventions, civil conflict and colonial wars.

Krishna, Arjuna and the Buddha

In a lecture given in 1997 and later reprinted in *The Robert Bellah Reader* (2006), Robert Bellah offered an analysis of Weber's notion of *Liebesakosmismus*, which is often translated as simply "acosmistic love." Bellah suggested that it is better translated as "world-denying love" and connected the concept with Weber's ideas about an ethic of brotherly love that Weber saw as the fundamental ethic of the great prophetic religions. In some respects, these ideas about world-denying love anticipated the analysis of the religions of the axial age in Jaspers' *The Origin and Goal of History* (1953) and later in Eisenstadt's *The Origins and Diversity of Axial Age Civilizations* (1986). The basic idea of a world-denying religion found its expression in the so-called *Zwischenbetrachtung* or "Intermediate Reflections" that came in Weber's *Collected Essays* between *The Religion of China* and *The Religion of India*.

These prophetic or axial religions constructed a universal message, thereby breaking with the loyalties of locality, kith and kin. They are salvational religions, because they offered a solution or resolution of this generic tension between spirituality and violence, and in his ideal typical model they were either ascetic or mystical and inner-worldly or other-worldly. These religions are contrasted with magic which offers material benefits by magical practices, and which are thus fully accommodated to worldly society. The literature on Weber's sociology has concentrated largely on the inner-worldly asceticism of the Protestant sects, but Bellah, in drawing attention to the idea of world-denying love, offered an alternative version of Weber's sociology of religion, namely the rationalization and routinization of acosmistic love and its eventual transformation into a "social organic ethic" that is compromised with the dominant institutions of secular society. While asceticism was treated by Weber and his followers, such as Talcott Parsons in his introduction to Weber's *The Sociology of Religion* as the most radical and challenging of religious orientations, acosmistic love appears to be closer to mysticism than to asceticism and thus closer to saviors than to prophets.

Bellah opened this account of world-denying brotherly love with ancient India, and in particular with the idea of Buddhism as the religion of a renouncer. He argued that the core meaning of religious renunciation in the Indian context was to leave the household, typically becoming a mendicant. To give up the role of the householder was to free oneself from the necessary round of work and reproduction. The Brahaminical system incorporated the idea of leaving home into a concept of the lifecycle that is divided into four stages: studentship; householder; forest-dweller; and finally the renouncer. Bellah claimed that in Vedic ideology only a married householder could undertake the two crucial activities sustaining society as a whole, namely offering sacrifices and procreating children. There remained, therefore, an unresolved tension or contradiction between these two roles of the householder and the renouncer. While he believed that Weber's virtuoso-mass distinction is extreme, the conclusion was that "without householders there would be no one to feed the renouncers" (Bellah 2011, 529).

In Bellah's attempt to develop an evolutionary theory of religion, one can propose that, through his analysis of the axial religions, he wanted to establish the historical conditions that gave rise to ethical universalism, namely ethical and religious systems that broke out of the concentration of kinship loyalties to proclaim that all humans are brothers. The crucial point about Buddhism is that it launched the axial age in South Asia by an "ethicization of the world" (Gombrich 1996). Buddhism declares an ethical system of radical nonviolence, and undermines the tradition of the Brahmins by rejecting their hereditary status, along with the four varnas. Only a person following the Eightfold Path can aspire to attain enlightenment and consequently be regarded as a true Brahmin. The end of the path of renunciation and adherence to the dharma is nirvana or the ultimate extinction of earthly desire. The dharma – the teaching of the Buddha – is available to everybody regardless of any inherited social status if they can cling to the full rigor of Buddhist practice. While I have been making this contrast between Hinduism and Buddhism, we must, in fact, be careful to avoid thinking that these two traditions have enjoyed separate and independent histories in South Asia. For one thing, Brahmanism (and later what we now call Hinduism) reacted to the rise of Buddhism and in many ways absorbed Buddhist teaching. Buddhists had, in any case, to make public use of Sanskrit to compete with Brahmins to defend their interests at court. By the middle of the first millennium, the Brahminical vision of society and politics had become dominant, and Buddhism created a version of this vision by developing the notion of the king as a *bodhisattva*.

The political dilemma of violence in the religious traditions of South Asia can be illustrated through the story of Krishna and Arjuna in the famous epic of the *Mahabharata*. The *Mahabharata*, an epic poem of some 90,000 stanzas, was composed between the second century BCE and the first century of the Common Era. Originally a martial ballad, the poem was preserved and transmitted by the Brahman caste, and came to describe the ethical duties of different sections of Indian society. Although the *Bhagavad Gita* contains a message of supreme spiritual insight, it is also the case that Krishna, the avatar of Vishnu, instructs Arjuna in the duties that are appropriate to his varna as a warrior (Kshatriya). The pivotal episode is known as the *Bhagavad Gita* or "The Song of the Lord," and for many disciples of Vedic spirituality the epic spells out the essence of Hinduism as offering various but valid and universal pathways to personal salvation. This narrative of war describes struggle between the descendants of King Bharata, whose name can reasonably be interpreted as "India," resulting in contestation between two families – the Pandavas and the Kauravas – in which the Kauravas attempt to cheat the Pandavas in order to gain control of the kingdom. Before the battle of Kurukshetta begins, a discussion takes place between Krishna, the incarnation of Vishnu and Arjuna, one of the Pandava brothers, regarding the necessity and inevitability of violence and the obligations of Arjuna as a warrior. Resting in their chariot, Arjuna is depressed by the inevitability of human suffering and by the realization that he may be forced to slaughter his own kin. In response to his spiritual malaise, Krishna describes the three paths to salvation. The root of this model is the dharma, or the "Word," defining the obligations and responsibilities associated with his particular status as a warrior. Obviously, unless people fulfill these obligations, the social order would fail. In Arjuna's case, his role as a warrior compels him to engage in violent conflict. Dharma, signifying more than a collection of earthly duties, spells out the way to perfection and these duties must be carried out in a spirit of nonattachment in which the virtuous warrior follows his calling without any sense of personal gain or glory. The virtuous warrior is committed selflessly to a calling, and thus the poem spells out the three modes of being – devotion, selfless action and knowledge. In accepting the logic of righteous service, Arjuna is granted a vision of divinity at the conclusion of the poem.

This famous epic, regardless of its evolution and transformation over time, is quite clearly not a radical pacifist doctrine. On the contrary, Arjuna fulfills his spiritual quest by accepting his responsibilities as a warrior. Therefore Buddhism, which teaches absolute nonviolence, challenged the idea that Brahminical piety could be guaranteed by birth and inheritance. As we have seen, Buddhism could not escape the conundrum presented by the need for a political order to protect the monastery, or sangha, and periodically to cleanse it of corruption. The monastic Buddhist tradition required a righteous king who would guard the dharma from decay – by force, if necessary. In this way, the religious and the political were always woven into the journey to salvation. However, the early Buddhist version of discipline does not offer a clear legitimation of the role of the warrior over the monk. In the Hindu scriptures, Arjuna was forced to recognize that no being lives in this world without killing such that even the isolated ascetics living deep within the forest cannot fully escape from this world of violence. The *Mahabharata* is a tragic tale of the inevitability of human violence, because righteousness exists in the same world with power. However, when Arjuna, in following the requirements of his caste, kills his enemies in defense of the community, he will incur no sin.

I have suggested that when students think of religious violence, they are inclined to look towards the Christian Crusades or to "political Islam" and jihadism for examples. By contrast, Buddhist movements are seen to be the ultimate negation of violence, greed and human passion. However, even Buddhism could not entirely escape the compromise that is forever presented by the necessity of power in human institutions. In Japan, for example, Buddhism became deeply integrated into the samurai culture and within the court. Sons of the imperial family were regularly assigned to selected temple establishments and Zen statesmen-monks were important in the diplomatic service of the court. For the samurai, "the stern intellectual and physical discipline of Zen influenced many men" (Jansen 2000, 216). The dilemma of Buddhism in relation to secular power and hence to the means of violence perfectly illustrates the core theme of Weber's sociology of religion, namely the endless historical dance that has taken place between the political and the religious.

Tolstoy and Weber on Love

Weber's metatheoretical views on war and peace were matched by his contrast between brotherly love and sexual passion (Weber 2009a). Both dichotomies were connected to his understanding of the conflict between the secular and the sacred as manifest in the endless struggle between religion and the world. As we have seen, this struggle was, for Weber, beautifully described in the epic story of the *Bhagavad Gita*. It is not surprising that Weber was drawn to Leo Tolstoy's teachings about love, war and religion. Weber was fascinated by Russia as a land of endless opportunity just as much as the land of endless steppes. It was, for him, the land of imagination. He was especially interested in the peasant commune in the Russian social structure and in the prospects of radical social change. By 1904, Weber was reading Russian newspapers and talking to Russian émigrés in Heidelberg about the prospects of radical change in Russia. Weber produced various articles for the *Archiv für Sozialwissenschaft* Russian society and politics in 1905–06 on the prospects of liberalism and "bourgeois democracy," and there were additional articles in 1917 on the "Pseudo-democracy" and the Russian Revolution. These have been published as *The Russian Revolutions* (Weber 1995). Joachim Radkau (2009, 237), in his biography, points out that Weber's interest in the revolutionary situation in Russia was not directed at the intellectuals and the political parties that were driving it, but on the agrarian situation, and in particular the role of the *obshchina* as "the natural community rooted in social instincts." Because land ownership and usage were grounded in the family and not in individuals, there was an incentive to have large families. The result was overpopulation and overexploitation of the land. This system of land usage was the basis of peasant autarky, and hence Weber's sociological investigation of Russia was another aspect of his connection to Tolstoy, who was committed the agrarian reform and to the improvement of the lives of the peasantry. In his novels, and especially in *Anna Karenina* (2008), Tolstoy paid considerable attention to issues about land-holding and peasant agriculture, and Vladimir Nabokov (1982, 143), in his famous *Lectures on Russian Literature*, was forced to complain that the discussion of these agrarian problems in the story of Lyovin's farming was "extremely tedious" and an aesthetic "mistake."

Weber was deeply influenced by Tolstoy's life as much as Tolstoy's philosophy. Among the German intelligentsia, Tolstoy's last novel *Resurrection* (2009) was highly popular and, for Weber, expressed the depth and complexity of the soul of Russia. When Tolstoy finally died of pneumonia at the Astapovo railway station in 1910, Weber decided to write a book about Tolstoy as the charismatic prophet of the spirit of Russia. His reflections on Tolstoy were the occasion of a new direction in Weber's thought, away from the study of asceticism and the Protestant sects, and towards the idea of love, especially mystical love, though not as individual passion but rather as the basis of communal energy and solidarity. For Weber, this "a-cosmistic love" was a religious driving force in the political struggles of Russia. It was Tolstoy's celebration of peasant labor and the commune that came to influence Weber's recognition of the organic cycle of life as meaningful as opposed to the abstract and ultimately artificial life of the intellectual. Weber was apparently influenced by Tolstoy's *Resurrection* in coming to this interpretation, in which Tolstoy presents his philosophy that progress towards equality can only be achieved by love rather than by political action. We can find a related theme in *Anna Karenina* (2008) when Lyovin, having failed to win the hand of Princess Kitty Shcherbatski, returns to his estate to participate in the harvest with his peasants. Lyovin is based on Tolstoy's own personality as a man of conscience and his evolution in the novel towards religious maturity is also the story of Tolstoy's own spiritual maturation. In addition to the central love story, the novel offers an analysis of the dilemmas of the Russian agrarian economy that is consistent with Weber's own analysis. Unlike the passionate but tragic figures of Anna Karenina and Vronski, Lyovin eventually finds a simple life close to the land and family as deeply meaningful and satisfying. Therefore, passionate sexual desire is dangerous and destructive but, more importantly, ultimately meaningless. By contrast, the quiet but secure love between Lyovin and Kitty describes a religious relationship that is meaningful. The attraction of Tolstoy for Weber, according to Joachim Radkau's comprehensive biography, is that Weber's own life was also a tortuous struggle between unattainable sexual satisfaction and the ascetic and disciplined life of the scholar, especially before the recovery that began during the visit to the United States in 1904. According to Radkau, Weber also yearned for a communal life based on simple agrarian production in contrast to the rational and bureaucratic life of urban society that had emerged alongside modern capitalism. The attraction of Tolstoy's philosophy, therefore, rested on two contradictions: first, sexual passion versus "brotherly love" and, second, simply war and peace.

To understand these two sets of contradiction, we need to turn to a fundamental contrast in Weber's political sociology between an ethic of ultimate ends and an ethic of responsibility. Weber's language for describing these contrasted forms of commitment varied. He spoke of an ethic of conviction (*Gesinnungsethik*) or "ethic of the Sermon on the Mount" and by contrast the ethic of responsibility (*Verantwortungsethik*). As we have seen, Weber deeply admired Tolstoy, who epitomized the radical religious and pacifist ethic of complete conviction. In practice, this stark contrast was always more complicated in Weber's unfolding commentaries on politics and religion, especially towards the end of his life. Faced with the complexity of Germany's engagement in war, Weber wrote that these two ethics are complementary rather than opposed. Indeed the two ethics are most fully tested by the horror of modern warfare. In the 1880s, when he was influenced by the theological writing of William E. Channing, a committed pacifist, Weber complained that Channing had no actual experience of warfare. Channing's moral views were somehow disconnected from the practicalities of politics and war.

These issues were most fully explored in the two lectures that Weber gave at the end of his life on science and politics. In "Science as a Vocation," Weber (2009b) returned to Tolstoy's ethic of conviction, arguing that the core of Tolstoy's work is the belief that, in modern times, death can have no meaning. The theme, although continuous in Tolstoy's work, was most completely expressed in the short story *The Death of Ivan Illyich*, which Tolstoy published in 1886. Weber identified death as the major theme of Tolstoy's work and commented that "Death can have no meaning for civilized man placed into an infinite 'progress,' according to its own imminent meaning should never come to an end; for there is always a further step ahead of one stands in the march of progress" (Weber 2009b, 139–40).

Let us look more closely, therefore, at "politics as a vocation." Dieter Conrad (1986) has suggested that Weber, in his study of Indian dharma, outlined an ethical position that resembled his own view of modernity in which the various spheres of life are separate and autonomous. The caste system endorsed a form of ethical relativism, because the righteousness of one caste had no necessary consequences for some other caste. In the modern world the differentiation of spheres has also, for Weber, created a form of ethical polytheism, namely a world of competing "gods" without any ultimate source of authority. Tolstoy appears to be an even more dominant presence in "Politics as a Vocation," where the relationship between conviction and responsibility finds its ultimate Weberian treatment. In this lecture, he describes the "evangelistic commandment" in the ethic of ultimate ends or conviction as "unconditional and unambiguous" (Weber 2009c, 119).

There is much debate in the literature about which of these ethics Weber supports or accepts (Webster 1987), but in the politics lecture he makes his position very clear: the ethic of conviction is not realistic and it is not an adequate response to the practical necessity of politics. The ethic of absolute commitment, such as the injunction to turn the other cheek, makes no sense unless you are already a saint like Tolstoy. Weber, who had grown up in a student culture that championed dueling and masculine aggression, believed that an ethic of turning the other cheek could only lead to indignity and humiliation. Whereas the Sermon on the Mount commands us to resist force, the politician must use force to achieve desirable ends. Whereas the ethic of conviction does not ask about consequences, the ethic of responsibility has a duty to take consequences seriously. Whereas the saint must adhere to truthfulness, the politician is required to use subterfuge. Why are these two realms so diametrically different? Before considering Weber's answer we must keep in mind that this lecture was delivered to students in Munich in 1918, after the destruction of a generation of young Germans. Let us also return to the *Bhagavad Gita* and Arjuna before battle, deciding not on conviction but on his military duties in full knowledge of the consequences. Weber's answer to these ethical dilemmas was brutally simple: "The decisive means for politics is violence" (Weber, 2009c, 121).

The result is a world of moral compromise. While "the Sermon on the Mount, an acosmic ethic of ultimate ends, implied a natural law of absolute imperatives based upon religion" (Weber 2009c, 124), the church recognized that force was necessary to suppress heretical views. Luther safeguarded the righteous from acts of violence by accepting the role of secular authorities in the conduct of war, and Calvinism also accepted the necessity of violence in defense of the faith. The inescapable feature of political life is violence (Weber, 2009c, 121) and, hence, anybody who becomes involved in politics must recognize these "ethical paradoxes" (Weber, 2009, 125). The ethical dilemma for people of conviction, in concentrating on their motives and ideals, is that they do not consider carefully the consequences of their actions. The actual day-to-day exercise of politics requires both passion and perspective, but ethical compromise is inescapable for those people who take responsibility for their actions.

Max Weber's sociology of religion is also, in one sense, a tragic account of the rationalization of religious pathways to salvation. But the salvation offered by either saviors or prophets is no longer available to us. The secular world is dominated by the economic market and the bureaucratic state, and these are not institutional arenas within which the ethic of brotherly love has any place. The various spheres of life in the modern world function independently of religion, and, at best, some of these spheres, such as the aesthetic and the erotic, might offer some compensation for the loss of a meaningful world.

References

Bellah, Robert N. 2011. *Religion in Human Evolution: From the Paleolithic to the Axial Age.* Cambridge, MA: Belknap Press of Harvard University Press.

Bellah, Robert N. and Steven M. Tipton, eds. 2006. *The Robert Bellah Reader.* Durham, NC and London: Duke University Press.

Eisenstadt, Shmuel N., ed. 1986. *The Origins and Diversity of Axial Age Civilizations.* Albany: State University of New York Press.

Gombrich, Richard 1996. *How Buddhism Began: The Conditioned Genesis of the Early Teachings.* London: Athlone.

Henrich, Dieter. 1987. "Karl Jaspers: Thinking with Max Weber in Mind in Wolfgang," in *Max Weber and his Contemporaries,* edited by J. Mommsen and Jürgen Osterhammel, 528–44. London: Allen & Unwin.

Jansen, Marius B. 2000. *The Making of Modern Japan.* Cambridge, MA: Belknap Press of Harvard University Press.

Jaspers, Karl. 1953. *The Origin and Goal of History.* London: Routledge & Kegan Paul.

Keyes, Charles F. 1971. "Buddhism and National Integration in Thailand." *Journal of Asian Studies* 30: 551–68.

Mauss, Marcel. 1976. *The Gift.* New York: Norton.

Momigliani, Arnaldo D. 1975. *Alien Wisdom: The Limits of Hellenization.* Cambridge: Cambridge University Press.

Nabokov, Vladimir. 1982. *Lectures on Russian Literature.,* London: George Weidenfeld & Nicolson.

Narayanan, Vasudha. 2005. "Hinduism," in *Eastern Religions,* edited by Michael D. Coogan, 10–109. London: Duncan Baird Publishers.

Parsons, Talcott. 1965. "Introduction" to Max Weber, *The Sociology of Religion,* xix–lxvii. London: Methuen.

Radkau, Joachim. 2009. *Max Weber: A Biography.* Cambridge: Polity Press.

Robinson, C. 2009. Review article: "The Ideological Uses of Early Islam." *Past and Present* 203 (May): 205–28.

Silber, Ilana Friedrich. 1995. *Virtuosity, Charisma and Social Order: A Comparative Sociological Study of Monasticism in Theravada Buddhism and Medieval Catholicism.* Cambridge: Cambridge University Press.

Smith, Brian K. 1994. *Classifying the Universe: The Ancient Indian Varna System and the Origins of Caste.* New York: Oxford University Press.

Srinivas, Mysore Narasimhachar. 1989. *The Cohesive Role of Sanskritization.* Delhi: Oxford University Press.

Tambiah, Stanley J. 1976. *World Conqueror and World Renouncer: A Study of Buddhism and Polity in Thailand against a Historical Background.* Cambridge: Cambridge University Press.

Toltsoy, Leo.1999. *Anna Karenina.* New York: Oxford World Classics.

_____.2009. *Resurrection.* New York: Oxford World Classics.

_____.2010. *War and Peace.* New York: Oxford University Press.

_____.1981. *The Death of Ivan Illyich.* New York: Bantam Books.

Turner, Bryan S. 1974. *Weber and Islam: A Critical Study.* London: Routledge & Kegan Paul.

_____.2012. *Religion and Modern Society: Citizenship, Secularisation and Society.* Cambridge: Cambridge University Press.

Weber, Max. 1951. *The Religion of China: Confucianism and Taoism.* New York: The Free Press.

———.1958. *The Religion of India: The Sociology of Hinduism and Buddhism*. New York: The Free Press.
———.1965. *The Sociology of Religion*. London: Methuen.
———.1978. *Economy and Society: An Outline of Interpretive Sociology*. 2 vols. Berkeley: University of California Press.
———.1995. *The Russian Revolutions*. Cambridge: Polity Press.
———.2009a. "Religious Rejections of the World and Their Directions," in *From Max Weber: Essays in Sociology*, edited by Hans Gerth and C. Wright Mills, 323–59. London: Routledge.
Weber, Max. 2009b. "Science as a Vocation," in *From Max Weber: Essays in Sociology*, edited by Hans Gerth and C. Wright Mills, 129–56 . London: Routledge.
Weber, Max. 2009c. "Politics as a Vocation" in *From Max Weber: Essays in Sociology*, edited by Hans Gerth and C. Wright Mills, 77–128. London: Routledge.
Webster, David. 1987. "Max Weber, Oswald Spengler and a Biographical Surmise" in *Max Weber and his Contemporaries*, edited by Wolfgang J. Mommsen and Jürgen Osterhammel, 515–27. London: Allen & Unwin.

Chapter 10

CONCLUSION: WAR AND PEACE

Bryan S. Turner

Introduction

Leo Tolstoy, a veteran of the Crimean War, wrote *War and Peace* as a serialized novel in the journal *Russian Messenger* between 1865 and 1867. Published in its entirety in 1869, the novel records the traumatic effects on a number of aristocratic families of Napoleon's invasion of Russia in 1812 and the eventual occupation and burning of Moscow. Like any great novel, it can be read from a variety of perspectives, but at least two major themes stand out. Firstly there is the futility of war and its destructive consequences on the lives of the rich and the poor alike. Secondly there is Pierre Bezukhov's search for a satisfactory meaning for life via debauchery, married life, the Masonic League, and public service. Nothing satisfies Pierre until he finds comfort and eventually meaning in the simple lives of peasants and in the ordinariness of everyday life. Only after suffering and deprivation can he realize that life itself is the paradoxical meaning of life. The novel intertwines the destructive nature of pride and ambition with the peaceful reassurance that comes from engagement with life on its own terms. It has remained a compelling and damning statement about the horrors of war and an inspiration for radical pacifism throughout the twentieth century. It offers a suitable framework for the various chapters in this book which has explored both war and peace as companions of the religions of the world.

One obvious but important conclusion to be derived from the present volume is that religious violence in the modern world appears to arise when different religious claims to Truth overlap in the same space, and when the secular framework of the rule of law and citizenship fails to produce a "level playing field" between minorities and the majority. The state is typically implicated in such conflicts in civil society, and in these circumstances religious conflicts or tensions are magnified when religion becomes deeply embedded in ethnicity or nationalism. With globalization, these tensions are exaggerated by conflicts over resources (both symbolic and material) in societies where, through global migration, minorities compete in a context of economic scarcity. The nation-state is deeply involved in such conflicts insofar as it attempts to impose a religio-cultural homogeneity on its citizen-subjects in defense of its own sovereignty. Generally speaking, states do not abide by the idea of the freedom of religion; they prosecute cults, regulate school curricula regarding religious instruction, proscribe certain dress codes, prohibit certain forms of marriage, suppress blasphemy where possible, and limit the application of religious law. This hegemonic role of the state over religion is the logical outcome of the system of confessional states created in the seventeenth century in the West by the Treaty of Westphalia.

Social conflict is often magnified when a majority feels it is threatened by a minority; much of the Islamophobia in Europe has assumed this character. We can take Norway as a case study of such a conflict with a religious minority. Muslims, arriving first in Norway as labor migrants in the 1960s, are a heterogeneous community as are Christians. With Norway's military involvement in overseas conflicts, there has been a flow of refugees from Iraq, Afghanistan and Bosnia-Herzegovina to the country. The Muslim population in 2009 was 160,000, representing only 3 percent of the total population of 4.8 million. Many of these Muslims do not attend the mosque; they are not actively practicing their faith; and the majority of them can be regarded as "secular" citizens of Norway. Nevertheless Anders Breivik, who attacked a group of Norwegian youth in 2011, killing 68 people, claimed in his manifesto that he was defending Europe against the spread of Islam and the dominance of the Shari'a. For right-wing groups such as the Norwegian Defence League, Muslims have a definite and separate identity which means they cannot be assimilated into Norway's Christian civilization. In modern Britain, similar tensions have arisen between the host society and its many Muslim communities from South Asia, especially after the London underground bombings that are now referred to as 7/7. The English Defence League, which often recruits its followers from alienated and unemployed young men who are associated with the fan clubs of English football teams, has also sought to portray English identity as under threat. In South Asia itself, conflicts between religions – primarily between Hindu and Muslim communities – are closely connected to economic and political conflicts at the local community level, and Hindu nationalism often arose because Hinduism provided a language whereby intellectuals and political leaders could talk to the masses (Gould 2012). In a globalized environment, "identity politics" is invariably a conflict over religious identity.

War and Peace explored the destructive impact of mass armies confronted by artillery, against which the heroic charges of aristocratic cavalry had little effect. The bloodiest confrontation in the Napoleonic Wars was the Battle of Borodino in which there were 70,000 casualties and, by the end of the retreat from Moscow, the French army had lost 380,000 men and 100,000 were captured. As Jonathan Keller reminds us in Chapter 3, there were 620,000 casualties in the American Civil War (1861–65), a war that can be regarded as the first mechanized war of modern history. Killing is the main purpose and instrument of battle in an age of technological sophistication, and raw recruits, while willing to die as Christian soldiers, had to overcome religious barriers to killing. Drew Giplin Faust in *This Republic of Suffering* (2008, 32) quotes Tolstoy as being more concerned with the reality of killing than the maneuvers and strategies of war at the battles of Austerlitz and Borodino.

Against this historical background of military conflict in nineteenth-century America and Europe, the technological capacity of modern warfare has greatly increased the scale of destruction, especially the destruction of civilians. In the First World War there were some 15 million deaths and 20 million wounded, and in the Second World War it is estimated that 60 million were killed. Although these figures are approximations, it is assumed that 6 million Jews died in the Holocaust, and the estimates for those killed at Hiroshima and Nagasaki are 135,000 and 64,000 respectively. As the scale of human killing has increased with the industrialization of warfare, the need for mutual respect, care and responsibility has also increased. The manifestations of the need to recognize the suffering of civilians in modern warfare are the growth of recognition ethics, the global progress of human rights, and the demand for cosmopolitanism in response to human vulnerability in the face of the destructive power of modern military technology (Turner 1993). We can regard the development of human rights as one significant factor in the decline of human violence which can be quantified in terms of interracial violence, lynching, hate crimes, rape and domestic violence.

Perhaps the tragic lesson of these military conflicts is that warfare has been the midwife of modernity. This bitter interpretation of modernization may well be the real message of Max Weber's sociology. It is difficult to know where to start this chronology of violence. In the Introduction I suggested plausibly that modern history starts in the West with Cromwell's massacre of the inhabitants of Drogheda and Wexford in the name of religious truth. His New Model Army certainly had the characteristics of modernity – they were trained, disciplined, efficient and organized. Perhaps more importantly Cromwell's troops "were well and regularly paid; pressing was no longer required to fill the ranks; and for both officers and men the army had become a regular professional career" (Tanner 1928, 163). The forces they opposed in Scotland and Ireland proved no match for a modernized army. To what extent has the spread of human rights placed some legislative restraint on mass killing?

The Declaration of Human Rights

Human rights may be defined as the entitlements of individuals *qua* human beings to life, security and well-being. These rights are regarded as universal, incontrovertible and subjective, that is individuals possess them because of their capacity for rationality, agency and self-autonomy. Human rights conventions assume that individuals have fundamental powers or inalienable rights that no political order can legally expunge. These rights are the juridical means by which governments (or more frequently their despotic leaders) can be held criminally responsible in international law and prosecuted for the ways in which they have mistreated their own citizens. Their implementation was a twentieth-century legal response to atrocities committed against civilian populations in wartime. Where contemporary atrocities have been witnessed by a world audience, owing to the spread of worldwide communication systems, people begin to think and act as global citizens (Brysk 2002).

Three stages have been identified in the development of human rights (Robertson 2002). In the last quarter of the eighteenth century, the American War of Independence from the British monarchy and the French Revolution's overthrow of another absolute monarchy established the liberty of the individual as a constraint on the powers of the Crown. These individual rights were entitlements of persons rather than rights of national citizens. Such rights were associated with the growth of individualism. Immanuel Kant (1724–1804) defined "enlightenment" as freedom from tutelage to think and act as an autonomous individual and these Enlightenment ideas had a significant impact on the French Revolution (1789–99) which famously proclaimed the ideas of liberty, equality and fraternity. Although these revolutionary events had different causes and outcomes, the essential principle behind the English Civil War, the American Constitution and the French Revolution was that human beings should not be subject to arbitrary and tyrannical powers. The law had to be blind to social divisions because it was to apply to all without distinction.

The second stage was marked by the Nuremberg trials in which Nazi crimes against the Jews were defined as "crimes against humanity", and article 6 (c) of the Nuremberg Charter established the legal grounds by which those responsible for torture and genocide would be prosecuted in an international court of justice. These laws recognized individuals as victims of state crimes, and made special provisions for political refugees. During the Cold War, human rights became part of the rhetorical struggle of the West against the Soviet Union. Thus in the postwar struggle between communism and Western capitalism, international protection of refugees became an important aspect of Cold War international relations. With the fall of the Soviet Union between

1989 and 1992, Western nations, supported by neo-liberal economic strategies, were more inclined to regard refugees as threats to security, national culture and economic growth. As American foreign policy attempted to come to terms with the economic growth of China, human rights problems in China after the reforms of Deng Xiaoping became a constant theme of American diplomacy. With a new emphasis on border security after 9/11, there was also greater concentration on asylum abuse, people trafficking, repatriation, burden sharing and short-term protection. While national governments have shown increasing reluctance to accept the burden of providing protection to refugees, there has been a corresponding growth in voluntary-sector responses from both non-governmental organizations (NGOs) and international non-governmental organizations (INGOs), especially as regards the protection of women and children who constitute the overwhelming majority of refugees. These organizations can be reasonably regarded as an emerging global civil society.

The development of a global civil society has concerned the protection, security, development and representation of local communities. There are many thousands of civil society organizations that are recognized by the UN. There was a proliferation of human rights groups such as Charter 77 after the signing of the Helsinki Accords in 1975. There was a similar expansion of local activist groups after the 1992 Global Forum and Earth Summit in Rio de Janeiro, after the population conferences in Beijing and Cairo, and after the Vienna Conference on Human Rights in 1993. Many of these organizations have direct links with the United Nations, but others have only an indirect connection with formal human rights institutions. For example, article 71 of the Charter from the UN Economic and Social Council contributed to the formation of the World Health Organization and the UN Educational, Scientific and Cultural Organization (UNESCO). Formal organizations such as UNESCO have been important in fostering local activism among environmental lobby groups. States can work as partners of both NGOs and INGOs, but they are also frequently in an antagonistic relationship to anti-government organizations (AGOs). Other organizations such as Médecins Sans Frontières, Oxfam and Greenpeace function with a mixture of self-reliance, opposition to and dependency on governments and international organizations. Although the heterogeneity of values and organizational structures prevent a unified political program, global civil society can now act as a constraint on the aggressive activities of national governments. Nevertheless the implementation of human rights still rests primarily, and some would say wholly, on the support of nation-states (Donnelly 2002). The future problem for human rights activism is that, if globalization weakens nation-states, then the enforcement of human rights may become more rather than less difficult.

In short, a vigorous assembly of voluntary associations in civil society cannot replace the role of the state.

In the third stage, human rights began to emerge fully on the global political agenda in the 1970s when deep dissatisfaction with the conventional role of states in the international order and critical recognition of the failures of organized communism opened up innovative opportunities for rethinking the place of rights in international relations. Human rights emerged eventually as a plausible and appropriate ideology for social movements such as women's internationalism, for political dissidents in Poland and Hungary, and as the basis of global NGO activity. Further recognition of human rights in international affairs came with the presidency of Jimmy Carter, who in his campaign had criticized President Gerald Ford for his lack of attention to human rights. At his inauguration in 1977, Carter declared an absolute commitment to human rights in American foreign policy.

However, the crucial development occurred when academic lawyers began to recognize human rights as the normative foundation of international law. Without international law and international legal institutions, especially international courts, human rights could not play a significant role in modern politics (Moyn 2010). In the field of international law, scholarly attention has been drawn to the growth of a network of legal arrangements that bind nation-states to agreements that enforce behavior with regard to key issues of mutual interests such as slavery, serfdom, genocide and above all scarce resources such as water. International human rights laws can be said to rest on three recognized sources: treaties, customary law and the "general principles of law" (Lepard 2010). These sources have been recognized by the Statute of the International Court of Justice, but the most significant features of this juridical framework are *erga omnes* obligations, which are of concern to all sovereign states. These shared obligations are created by a common recognition of a set of fundamental human rights relating in particular to war, genocide and slavery. As a result, international lawyers now recognize that the autonomy of states is often limited by multilateral treaties that address issues of common interest. For example, the United Nations Convention on the Law of the Sea in 1982 was significant in this regard (Charney 2002). Yet another illustration is the Treaty Establishing the European Coal and Steel Community which in 1951 made provision for an independent court, the Court of Justice, to enforce the treaty's provisions. These international legal relations have multiplied with globalization in clear recognition of the need to create a set of universal norms to address global concerns relating to major issues, especially the environment.

There now exists an international legal system, however imperfect, that constrains and regulates the behavior of nation-states through consensual multilateral forums. Where there is recognition that a common good is threatened, there are compelling reasons for legally enforced co-operation between states (Charney 1993). In this emerging system, *jus cogens* or "compelling law" is a pre-emptory legal principle that is regarded as binding on states, irrespective of their actual consent. Where there is an obvious need for common action over a shared problem, it is claimed that there is a "community necessity" about which there should be binding agreements. These ideas, especially around "customary law," have been much disputed, but there is some agreement that, where a majority of states supports a legal norm, there is a threshold in which a customary norm is regarded as binding on states, including those that actively oppose the norm. The implication of these legal developments that recognize "community necessity" is that, in the absence of legitimate global governance, there is a legal framework for the enforcement of human rights.

Consequently, the late twentieth century has been an age of rights enforcement, enabling the use of truth commissions in post-Apartheid South Africa, and illustrated by the extradition of General Pinochet, the occupation of East Timor by UN troops, the Lockerbie verdict, the Japanese apology for wartime treatment of "comfort women" and the trial of Slobadan Milosevic. These legal and political efforts to enforce human rights conventions are seen by some to counteract the criticism that human rights are not justiciable without a world government to enforce them. However, the international failure to act effectively over the Darfur crisis in western Sudan in 2003–2004 supports the argument of critics that the United Nations is reluctant to intervene in situations where the interests of the major powers are not at stake, and that the UN is ineffectual without the backing of US military force. The crisis in Syria in 2011–12 was further evidence of the limitations on the human rights framework when the state interests of China and Russia undermined the more general humanitarian concerns for the victims of the conflict.

Nevertheless, recognition of civilian populations rather than states as victims of war has been a major achievement of human rights legislation. One can argue plausibly that the human rights movement in the late twentieth century has accompanied the erosion of the strong Westphalian doctrine of state sovereignty. There has been growing recognition of the need to protect the individual as the victim of war between and within states. In the aftermath of the First World War, the Allies had remained committed to the traditional legal view that only states were legitimate subjects of international law. A new emphasis on the status of victims has been the foundation of the modern doctrine of reparations – of making good again (*Wiedergutmachung*). For example, rape was historically regarded as an inevitable outcome of war, but in 2001 the International Tribunal for the former Yugoslavia found (in the "rape camp case") Serbian soldiers guilty of rape as a crime against humanity. These developments in international law in which there has been recognition of mutual responsibility or "community necessity" contrast sharply with the treatment of civilian populations during the Napoleonic Wars, the context for Tolstoy's investigation of military killing and the attendant destruction of civilian life.

From this brief sketch, we can see that the growth of human rights is often seen as a secular history involving a "civilizing process" (Elias 2000), in which human aggressiveness is increasingly regulated, not just by coercive institutions, but by self-control. This notion has been taken up recently by Stephen Pinker in *The Better Angels of Our Nature* (2011) to argue that human beings have acquired a greater capacity for self-control and consequently have become less inclined to respond aggressively to each other. His study of self-control depends overtly on the historical sociology of Norbert Elias. In *The Civilizing Process*, Elias developed a theory of self-control and self-discipline against the background of the historical emergence of the modern state in Europe. Describing this transition of the man-on-horseback in warrior societies through feudalism to the rise of court society and finally to the bourgeoisie household, Elias argued that norms of self-control meant that society depended less on external force, or the threat of it, to achieve social order. He examined etiquette books, manuals describing correct knightly conduct, guides to courtesy and refined manners at table in order to demonstrate the decline of interpersonal violence. The control over bodily functions is a clear marker of the spread of civilized manners and respect for the comfort of others.

Elias's theory of the history of manners has to be understood alongside the evolution of the modern state. Personal forms of violence – such as the duel – declined because the state, to use Max Weber's terminology, acquired a monopoly of violence. English aristocrats abandoned their swords and shields in public, and carried walking sticks, umbrellas and handkerchiefs on their way to the office; they exchanged the battlefield for the city and acquired norms of fair play on the cricket fields of Eton and Harrow. Elias's work, its scope and consistency, is widely respected, but it has also been heavily criticized. His parents died in German concentration camps and, against the background of the destruction of the Jews of Europe, his critics have asked how he could ever believe that Europeans had become more civilized. One possible answer is to contrast the Viking sagas with tales of modern combat. If you read the Norse epics in the Prose Edda, you encounter the narrative of warriors who killed with enthusiastic gusto. This type of killing contrasts with modern wars of the twentieth century in which men kill at a distance with little emotional engagement when destruction by drones occurs through computers. Rampage is the exception, not the rule.

This debate around Elias's legacy raises a question that also runs through Pinker's book – are we talking about the nature of men or the social relationships and the normative structure of interaction that deliver less violence? Have social conditions improved (for example through laws and policing that protect women from rape in and out of marriage) or has there been an actual change in human nature, in our human ontology? Is it the better angels of our nature that provide the answer or more civilized societies or both? While the title of Pinker's book obviously points to psychological change, most of his explanations of change are sociological and political. The principal cause of the reduction in violence appears to be the Matthew Effect. He suggests for instance that the decline of violence against women is connected with a set of "wholesome factors" – "democracy, prosperity, economic freedom, education, technology, decent government" (Pinker 2011, 413). However, these causes cannot be the whole story, because developed societies like South Korea and Japan have relatively high rates of domestic violence. The difference may be explained by societies in which women have greater empowerment and hence more representation in government and the professions, and by individualistic cultures that promote women's rights to enable women to function equally alongside men in the public domain. In short, the Matthew Effect is not so much causation as correlation. The decline of violence against women in the West is "pushed along by a humanist mindset that elevates the rights of individual people over the traditions of the community" (Pinker 2011, 414). This claim suggests that the legacy of filial piety in Asia treats women as inferior to men, daughters as inferior to sons and the ruled as inferior to the ruler. In Asia, Confucianism elevated rule of virtue over rule of law.

Elias's sociology of civilizational processes is a valuable sociological paradigm for understanding historical change and yet it is interesting that he typically neglected the important role of Christianity in controlling human aggression. Pinker does not ignore religion, but he is critical of the Abrahamic religions, because he claims that their commitment to notions of divine revelation has made it difficult to accept alternative interpretations of reality. However, these psychological theories of individual constraint overlook the contributions of such figures as Jacques Maritain, a major Roman Catholic philosopher in the Thomist tradition, who played a significant role in the drafting of the Declaration of Human Rights. Warning against the dangers of a democracy based merely on the opinions of the majority, he promoted the idea of an "organic democracy" grounded ultimately on natural law (Maritain 1958). Enthusiastic about Franklin D. Roosevelt's ambition that freedom should be a basic right of all nations, he proposed that freedom of belief is very different from the relativistic claim that every individual opinion is valid and valuable. Rather the principle of freedom of religion meant freedom to participate in rational debate and dialogue, and hence the state should never simply coerce belief in the interests of social order. His argument thereby anticipated the critical theory of communication, namely that a post-secular society requires both religious and secular citizens to engage in a process of public reasoning in order to achieve a general consensus of values (Habermas 1990, 2006).

Deeply influenced by both Aristotle and Aquinas, Maritain sustained a belief in the capacity of human reason to direct action without recourse to violence and this belief was the basis of what he called "integral humanism" which, while rejecting secularism as barren and empty, sought to construct some reconciliation between the Christian tradition and secular politics (Maritain 1968). In opposition to secular political theory, he claimed that, without a strong religious and moral foundation, democratic institutions and individual freedoms could never flourish. The overtly secular tradition of human rights ultimately required a robust Christian underpinning. We may legitimately regard the twentieth-century spread of human rights as the result of many causes, but one of them has been the impact of Christian ideas on the secular civilizing process.

The Cosmopolitan Imagination

Against the Huntington thesis, there have been many attempts in the past to create a social philosophy that energetically engaged with and then recognized the value of other cultures. As I argued in Chapter 9, of particular importance in this regard is the work of Karl Jaspers in *The Origin and Goal of History* (1968) in which he promoted the idea of an "Axial Age" by which to examine the origins and value of different world civilizations. In sociology, these ideas were further developed by Shmuel N. Eisenstadt whose analysis of the interdependencies between civilizational complexes gave rise to the key notion of "multiple modernities" (Eisenstadt 2000). This notion avoids the trap of regarding Western modernity as the only pathway to economic prosperity, democratic freedoms and human enhancement. Similarly, in modern philosophy, the issue of recognition of the Other has been a dominant theme, producing powerful defenses of so-called recognition ethics. Concentrating on the legacy of Hegel's analysis of the master-slave relationship as the foundation for the study of individual freedom and respect for others, the tradition of recognition ethics as a basis for modern cosmopolitanism can be found in R. R. Williams's *Hegel's Ethics of Recognition* (1997) and Charles Taylor's *Multiculturalism and the Politics of Recognition* (1992). Because the modern individual resides in a global world of "Other" subjectivities, there is a mode of existence that is referred to as "being-for-others." In the work of Emmanuel Levinas (1998), the Other is seen to play a positive role in questioning the confidence and assurance of the subject. The face of the Other challenges us to take responsibility for the well-being of other persons, and hence otherness creates the conditions that make ethics possible. Another source of such ideas is the work of Jacques Derrida (2000) who wrote creatively about the significance of hospitality to ethical understanding. There are other approaches most notably that of Kwami Appiah (2006) who has connected the need for cosmopolitanism with the advent of a world of strangers and the problems that confront postcolonial societies especially in Africa.

Unfortunately much philosophical and theological debate about recognition ethics and cosmopolitanism has not engaged seriously with anthropological and sociological research findings on actual or vernacular cosmopolitanism. It is important to distinguish between normative arguments in favor of "cosmopolitan virtue" and the empirical constraints and limitations on such a world vision of care for the Other (Turner 2002). It is partly for this reason that the recent upsurge in sociological investigation of cosmopolitanism is timely and important. Ulrich Beck (2000; 2006) has been at the forefront of attempts to develop a post-national cosmopolitan sociology. His comparative and historical investigations have also served to show that cosmopolitanism is not a single topic, but a network or field of research issues including ideas as diverse as the second modernity, multiple modernities, human rights and globalism. However, the integrating theme of these empirical investigations is how local cultures interact with global processes to shape individual identities, and the empirical results suggest that modern identities are not determined wholly or simply by "civilizations," but by the interaction between identity, location and culture. It appears that religion, far from disappearing in the nexus of modern forces shaping identities, has become more significant, especially for the so-called nomadic subjects of global migration pathways.

Conclusion: From Augsburg to The Hague

In the introduction to this book, I began with a commentary on the Peace of Augsburg and the Treaty of Westphalia, because these treaties ushered in the age of nation-states and our system of international state relations. They also began to map out a system of secularization in which the Christian churches became clearly subordinated to the secular power of princes. These two treaties were crafted in the context of religious conflict and war, but they were directed towards the creation of a social peace in which there would be a truce between Catholicism and Protestantism. Our world in the West, while shaped by those treaties, is now a very different social and political environment. We are confronted by major technological changes in the conduct of war that now threaten to bring about a catastrophic destruction of human life.

Given this prospect of human extinction, several chapters in this collection have raised questions about the humanity of humans in relation to each other. The calculated destruction of the European Jews in the Holocaust, which was explored by reference to Poland in Chapter 1 by Alisse Waterston, raised inescapable questions about the dignity and humanity of our species. The destructive force of the nuclear bombs dropped on Japan marked a dividing line in human history, and Ran Zwigenberg's chapter offered a haunting picture of the struggle over the interpretation of history and conflicts about memorialization that have emerged in the nuclear age. Religion can both justify our inhumanity – for example the biblical justification of slavery in colonial America – and provide a massive criticism of violence, for instance via the social movements inspired by the principle of love in the lives of Martin Luther King and Mahatma Gandhi. The quest for hope in the face of adversity is not, however, an exclusive response of the West, as Eben Kirksey showed in his chapter based on field work from West Papua. Kirksey's chapter underlines the fact that in modernity we are now obsessed by the prospect of catastrophe and apocalypse. The struggle over sovereignty and the sacred can be said to constitute both politics and religion. Consequently, while we are engulfed by the apocalyptic threat of our own destruction, religion remains an essential dimension of the study of war and peace.

References

Appiah, Kawmi A. 2006. *Cosmopolitanism: Ethics in a World of Strangers*. New York: W. W. Norton.
Beck, Ulrich. 2000. "The Cosmopolitan Perspective: Sociology in the Second Age of Modernity." *British Journal of Sociology* 51(1): 79–105.
_____. 2006. *Cosmopolitan Vision*. Cambridge: Polity Press.
Brysk, Alison, ed. 2002. *Globalization and Human Rights*. Berkeley: University of California Press.
Charney, Jonathan. 1993. "Universal International Law." *American Journal of International Law* 87(4): 529–51.
_____, ed. 2002. *International Maritime Boundaries*. 2 vols. Dordrecht: Springer.
Derrida, Jacques. 2000. *On Hospitality*. Stanford: Stanford University Press.
Donnelly, Jack. 2002. *Universal Human Rights in Theory and Practice*. Ithaca, NY: Cornell University Press.
Eisenstadt, Smuel N. 2000. "The Reconstruction of Religious Arenas in the Framework of Multiple Modernities." *Millennium: Journal of International Studies* 29(3): 591–611.
Elias, Norbert. 2000. *The Civilizing Process: Sociogenetic and Psychogenetic Investigations*. Oxford: Blackwell.
Faust, Drew Giplin. 2008. *This Republic of Suffering: Death and the American Civil War*. New York: Vintage Books.
Gould, William. 2012. *Religion and Conflict in Modern South Asia*. Cambridge: Cambridge University Press.

Habermas, Jürgen. 1990. *Moral Consciousness and Communicative Action.* Cambridge, MA: Polity Press.
_____. 2006. "Religion in the Public Sphere." *European Journal of Philosophy* 14(1): 1–25.
Jaspers, Karl. 1968. *The Origin and Goal of History.* New Haven: Yale University Press.
Lepard, Brian D. 2010. *Customary International Law: A New Theory with Practical Applications.* Cambridge: Cambridge University Press.
Levinas, Emmanuel. 1998. *Entre Nous: On Thinking-of-the-Other.* London: The Athlone Press.
Maritain, Jacques. 1958. *Reflections on America.* New York: Charles Scribner's Sons.
Maritain, Jacques. 1968. *Integral Humanism: Temporal and Spiritual Problems of a New Christiandom.* New York: Charles Scribner's Sons.
Moyn, Samuel. 2010. *The Last Utopia: Human Rights in History.* Cambridge, MA and London: Belknap Press of Harvard University Press.
Pinker, Stephen. 2011. *The Better Angels of Our Nature: Why Violence has Declined.* New York: Viking.
Robertson, Geoffrey. 2002. *Crimes Against Humanity: The Struggle for Global Justice.* New York: The New Press.
Tanner, J. R. 1928. *English Constitutional Conflicts of the Seventeenth Century.* Cambridge: Cambridge University Press.
Taylor, Charles. 1992. *Multiculturalism and the Politics of Recognition.* Princeton: Princeton University Press.
Turner, Bryan S. 1993. "Outline of a General Theory of Human Rights." *Sociology* 27(3): 489–512.
_____. 2002. "Cosmopolitan Virtue, Globalization and Patriotism." *Theory, Culture & Society* 19(1–2): 45–64.
_____. 2006. *Vulnerability and Human Rights.* University Park: Pennsylvania State University Press.
Weber, Max. 1978. *Economy and Society.* 2 vols. Berkeley: University of California Press.
Williams, R. R. 1997. *Hegel's Ethics of Recognition.* Berkeley: University of California Press.

www.ingramcontent.com/pod-product-compliance
Lightning Source LLC
Chambersburg PA
CBHW020911020526
44114CB00039B/340